Ethical Issues
in Archaeology

Edited by
Larry J. Zimmerman
Karen D. Vitelli
Julie Hollowell-Zimmer

ALTAMIRA
PRESS
A Division of
ROWMAN & LITTLEFIELD PUBLISHERS, INC.
Lanham • Boulder • New York • Toronto • Plymouth, UK

Published in cooperation with the
SOCIETY FOR AMERICAN ARCHAEOLOGY

ALTAMIRA PRESS
A division of Rowman & Littlefield Publishers, Inc.
4501 Forbes Boulevard, Suite 200
Lanham, MD 20706

Estover Road
Plymouth PL6 7PY
United Kingdon

British Library Cataloguing in Publication Information Available

Library of Congress Cataloging-in-Publication Data
Ethical issues in archaeology / edited by Larry J. Zimmerman, Karen D. Vitelli,
and Julie Hollowell-Zimmer.
    p.   cm.
  Includes bibliographical references and index.
  ISBN 0-7591-0270-8 (alk. paper) — ISBN 0-7591-0271-6 (pbk. : alk. paper)
    1. Archaeology—Moral and ethical aspects. 2. Archaeology—Philosophy. 3.
Archaeologists—Professional ethics. 4. Antiquities—Collection and preservation—
Moral and ethical aspects. I. Zimmerman, Larry J., 1947– II. Vitelli, Karen D. III.
Hollowell-Zimmer, Julie, 1952–
  CC175 .E825 2003
  174'.993—dc21   2002151888

Printed in the United States of America

♾™ The paper used in this publication meets the minimum requirements of American
National Standard for Information Sciences—Permanence of Paper for Printed Library
Materials, ANSI/NISO Z39.48–1992.

Contents

Foreword

Ethics used to be simple in archaeology, or at least it seemed so when I took my first archaeology course in 1970. Ethical questions were all about things: Did the person use up-to-date scientific methods to dig things up and adequately document the process? Did the researcher analyze the things to learn about the past? Did the things end up in a museum and not for sale at Sotheby's? Did museums obtain their things from archaeologists and not from looters? Did the archaeologist publish what he learned from digging up and analyzing the things? If the answers to all of these questions were "yes," then a person was an ethical archaeologist. If the answer to any of them was "no," then an archaeologist's ethics were suspect, and if the answers to *many* of them were "no," then that person was not an archaeologist at all; he or she was a looter or pothunter. As the chapters in *Ethical Issues in Archaeology* show, however, at the dawn of the twenty-first century ethics in archaeology are not simple. They are very complex, conflicted, and confusing. Today, ethical questions and dilemmas are more about relations among people than about things.

My first archaeology course explicitly assumed that archaeologists studied things to learn about people who were dead and implicitly assumed that archaeologists shared a common cultural identity or social persona. Archaeologists were well-educated, Euro-American males. The chapters in this book confront a far more complex social and cultural field than my first course prepared me for.

Some of them very appropriately continue to grapple with the ethical dilemmas that spring from the nature of the material culture that we study. Most archaeologists study ancient or at least old material culture. As the conservation ethic in archaeology points out, archaeological sites are a nonrenewable resource. The process of archaeological research destroys these sites. The data can only be preserved in documentation and in the curation of museum collections. Professional archaeologists are not the only ones with an interest in things from the past. Hobbyists and casual collectors, for example, pick up arrowheads and brightly painted potsherds for their mantels and coffee tables. More problematic, many of the things that we study have considerable economic value, and thus entice looters and pothunters to engage in large-scale and destructive excavations. Private collectors, and sometimes art museums, purchase these items on an international, multimillion-dollar antiquities market. Yet, even this destruction pales in comparison to the destruction of archaeological sites due to economic development. My introductory course in 1970 taught me that archaeologists are the stewards of something that is priceless, irreplaceable, and threatened. This concept is still true.

In 1970, ethics served primarily to define archaeologists as professionals who had privileged access to the archaeological record. The argument went, and for some still goes, like this: The archaeological record is priceless, irreplaceable, and threatened and should be the property of all people. Archaeologists, because of their training and certification, have the ability to learn things from that record that others cannot. Thus, we should be the stewards of the archaeological record so that knowledge can be derived from it and so that that knowledge will be made publicly available.

What my introduction to archaeology did not teach me is that archaeology is a human endeavor. Many of the chapters here address the ethical dilemmas that arise from this fact. Archaeology studies the pasts of living peoples who also have a present and a future. These peoples have interests in their pasts that may or may not coincide with the interests of archaeologists. Native Americans very forcibly made this point in the 1970s and 1980s, and their efforts led to state and federal legislation to protect their burials and religious artifacts from looters and archaeologists. Historical archaeologists and archaeologists who work in foreign countries study the pasts of other descendent communities. Archaeologists enter into social relationships among themselves to conduct their research. Social relationships entail social differences; they involve power and the possibility of exploitation. Ethical dilemmas arise in the relationships of teachers and students and in the gendered relationships between individuals in positions of differential power.

How have ethics in archaeology gotten so complicated? Is it because the field has so profoundly changed in the last thirty years, or were they really this complicated in 1970 too? The answer to both of these questions is yes.

Perhaps, the most profound change in archaeology over the last thirty years has been the development of contract archaeology or cultural resource management. Congress passed the key federal laws that mandated contract archaeology in the late 1960s, and they began to have a significant impact on the field in the 1970s. Archaeology became a business, something which it had not really been before. Currently, most of the archaeology done in the United States and the majority of the archaeologists employed in the United States are involved with contract archaeology. This growth in contract archaeology has raised or accentuated ethical issues pertaining to the relationship of research to legal compliance, the relationship of academic archaeology to business, the training of students, publication, and public outreach.

Another profound change in archaeology over the last thirty years has been a massive increase in the number of female archaeologists. Archaeology has included female practitioners since the beginnings of the profession in the late nineteenth century. A female professor taught my introduction to archaeology course in the 1970s, but it is only since the 1970s that women have come to make up a sizable part or even majority of the profession. This does not, however, mean that ethical issues related to sexual harassment and gender discrimination arose with this massive increase. To the contrary, it could be argued that sexual harassment and gender discrimination are at the heart of why there were so few professional female archaeologists prior to 1970.

More recently, since the 1990s the passage of the Native American Graves Protection and Repatriation Act has notably altered the practice of archaeology in the United States. Archaeologists now must share control of the archaeological record with Native Americans, and Native Americans have the right to request the return of their ancestors' bodies and religious artifacts. The ethical questions that surround the relationship of archaeologists and descendent communities did not, however, begin with this act. Rather, this act resulted from a struggle by Native Americans to bring these ethical concerns to the attention of archaeologists, concerns that originated with the genesis of archaeology in North America. The vast majority of North American archaeology has been a form of colonial practice—the study of the conquered by the conquerors. Archaeologists have come to face the ethical dilemmas of such a practice only with great reluctance.

The examples of gender and Native Americans point to the fact that archaeological ethics were as complicated in 1970 as they are today. Archaeologists simply did not recognize this fact. *Ethical Issues in Archaeology* recognizes that archaeology is a human endeavor and that archaeological ethics involve a trinity of obligations: 1) as I was taught in 1970, that we have an obligation to the archaeological record itself, 2) that we have obligations to a variety of publics, most notably descendent communities, and 3) that we have obligations to each other as professionals. This book provides a starting point for students and professionals to consider ethics in archaeology. It is only a starting point because the complexity of human endeavors and the contradictions that can arise in the trinity of obligations mean that ethics must be dynamic. They require an ongoing discussion of professional accountability and a continuing process of debating and learning ethical practices.

Randall H. McGuire

Introduction

This book continues a discussion begun more than a decade ago when several archaeological organizations began seeking approaches to archaeological ethics that were more appropriate for today's discipline. To date, the discussion has resulted in new codes of ethics for most of our professional organizations (see the appendix) and, on the part of most professionals, a growing awareness of the ethical implications of our work. In 1996, AltaMira Press published a collection of essays on topics involving ethical choices—reprints of papers that had appeared in *Archaeology* magazine—to help bring the discussion of the new sense of ethics into our classrooms (Vitelli 1996b).

No sooner had that volume appeared than Mitch Allen, the publisher, began urging a number of us to "write the textbook on archaeological ethics." Each of us responded, "Good idea. Maybe when I finish *x, y*, and *z*." The years passed. Some of us began avoiding Allen, knowing he'd bring the subject up again—and *x, y*, and *z* were either still in the works or had been replaced by at least *a* through *m*. Finally, Larry Zimmerman, the acting chair of the Society for American Archaeology (SAA) Ethics Committee, devised a feasible solution. He produced a list of chapter titles for the ethics textbook AltaMira wanted. Each chapter, he suggested, would be authored by a member of the Ethics Committee, with additional colleagues for the chapters we couldn't cover, and the committee's chair and acting chair would serve as the book's editors. The project would be an appropriate way for the committee to fulfill its charge to "keep ethical issues at the forefront for the membership" and to satisfy the need for a teaching tool with minimal effort.

Zimmerman's plan made the project look doable and got us started. The SAA, still in the initial stages of organizing its own monograph series, agreed that while the project had originated in the Ethics Committee, its initial impetus had come long ago from Allen and therefore it could and should be published by AltaMira in cooperation with the SAA.[1] We canvassed the chairs of other SAA committees for suggestions of additional topics and potential contributors, revised the outline, and began inviting colleagues to contribute chapters. It was very gratifying—for Zimmerman and Vitelli who remember when it wasn't so—to discover how many (often difficult) choices there were for potential contributors, and how many colleagues were qualified and willing to take this assignment on such short notice, putting aside other obligations because they believed the volume was important and urgently needed.

A lucky accident added Julie Hollowell-Zimmer to the editorial team. Hollowell-Zimmer was working as a graduate assistant for Karen D. Vitelli, who put her to work organizing some of the early correspondence for this volume. Hollowell-Zimmer, who is currently writing her dissertation on the legal trade in ancient ivories from St. Lawrence Island, provided so many fresh ideas and suggestions, such excellent organizational skills, and such commitment to the project that it would have been unethical not to give her full credit for them. So Zimmerman and Vitelli made her a coeditor, as well as a contributor (chapter 4). She also helped achieve a balance of contributors from a wide range of stages in their careers, in- and outside academe, male and female, all of whom have addressed in earlier works the issues about which they write here.

One editor at least (Vitelli) had not initially shared Allen's sense of the need for a textbook on ethics. The 1996 collection of articles worked well in her archaeological ethics classes, and, based on feedback she had received, apparently in similar classes taught by some of her colleagues. Students, even some with majors outside of archaeology and anthropology, found that the challenging and compelling real-world issues presented by a course in archaeological ethics made the discipline quite exciting and appealing. So why produce another book on the same topic now?

In the preface to the 1996 book, Vitelli wrote that many students in her first seminars on ethics arrived with little background and only a vague sense of what such a class would address. Just a few years later, this is no longer the case. Students show up knowing that archaeological ethics means discussions of looting and the antiquities market, the Native American Graves Protection and Repatriation Act, and the "Kennewick Man." Most arrive already condemning not only looters, but also collectors, including museums. They are strongly supportive of Native American rights—and less willing or able to, for example, make a case for scientific "rights" or the contributions of collectors. They assume archaeological organizations have codes of ethics; some have even read them. The codes seem to them to provide fairly obvious rules for appropriate professional behavior.

Ironically, the existence of our professional codes may actually serve in part to stifle discussion in the classroom. Those codes seem to imply "right answers" to whatever questions or hypothetical scenarios their professor, an archaeologist, might pose. There is less spontaneous exploration of alternative responses to specific situations, less eagerness to appreciate the perspectives of all parties—responses that the present volume makes clear are more essential than ever. Today's students represent a generation that has never known the profession without its codes of ethics. At least until they find themselves in positions of responsibility, they run the risk of assuming that those codes are absolute rules of appropriate behavior that professionals simply learn and live with, without questioning.

The present volume aims to change that perception, to persuade and demonstrate that to be useful and effective, ethics cannot be a set of static rules, but must be an ongoing discussion and debate of what Randall H. McGuire refers to as a "trinity" of responsibilities: our accountability to the archaeological record, to our publics, and to each other as professionals. We need to engage directly in an ongoing process of learning and debating ethical practice. We cannot assume that ethics are learned by osmosis, and cannot afford to learn ethical behavior by trial and error. This book provides a resource with which to study and debate ethics and to simulate ethical dilemmas. It moves the discussion beyond the important, but basic question of "who owns the past?" to a deeper investigation, critique, and understanding of the relationships of archaeology and archaeologists to other, often quite different approaches to the past, to other groups' ethics, and to the many contexts in which these occur. The contributors of the following chapters pursue the kind of critical reflection on the implications and ethics of archaeological practice that is a necessary part of the continual reevaluation of ethical codes and principles that ensure the health and growth of the discipline.

The book begins with two chapters that provide some needed context to the discussions that follow. First is Alison Wylie's explanation of what professional ethics are, how they differ from laws and personal ethics or morals, and some considerations of ethics unique to archaeology. Mark Lynott's history of archaeological ethics helps us understand where we have been and how we've arrived at our present understanding of archaeological ethics. He reminds us of our early link to antiquarianism that has produced a legacy of fascination with the spectacular object that we are still fighting, even as the discipline, the social context in which it operates, and our professional ethics have gone through radical changes.

Responsibilities to the Archaeological Record

Lynott's history of archaeological ethics explains why stewardship and conservation are currently seen (in the SAA principles) as the first of our trinity of obligations. Looting and the associated commercial market in antiquities remain a serious problem, raising multiple ethical concerns. Looting is destructive, regardless of when, where, and by whom it is done. Still, we thought there might be advantages to subdividing the huge topic. We asked for separate chapters, one by Neil Brodie and David Gill, on looting for the "high end" of the international art market; they look at the impact of the art market on the archaeological record. The other, by Hollowell-Zimmer, discusses looting geared to the "low-end" market; she explores what we might need to consider if we truly want to limit undocumented excavation and human destruction of the archaeological record. The contributors certainly came up with very different discussions; whether this is a useful way to subdivide this monster remains to be seen. George F. Bass, in exploring some of the unique legal, ethical, and safety challenges presented by shipwreck archaeology, brings in yet another face of looting—that of underwater treasure salvors. Alex W. Barker, exploring the intersection between archaeological and museum ethics, poses many challenges, not least of which is a sobering question about the quality of archaeological field practices, with the implication that some professional archaeology may not be as far removed from looting as we would like to think.

Chris A. Bergman and John F. Doershuk talk about the concerns and practice of cultural resource management archaeology, of working within government mandates and balancing responsibility to the archaeological record with the concerns (and different ethics) of clients and developers. Michael K. Trimble and Eugene A. Marino tackle the overwhelming task of conservation and curation, reminding us that this encompasses not just objects, but the complete documentation of and by the entire field project. Their discussion, together with Barker's, should make each of us reexamine our priorities and question whether we are truly meeting our full responsibilities to the archaeological record.

Responsibilities to Diverse Publics

Our second responsibility, demanding increasing attention as social concerns around us develop, is to the diverse publics of archaeology, from the taxpayer who directly or indirectly funds most of our work to descendent communities whose experience and use of and claims on the past are often at odds with traditional archaeological interests and practices. We are finally acknowledging that there are other legitimate stewards of the past, whose voices we can no longer ignore.

When it comes to amateur collectors, Jason M. LaBelle disagrees with the guidelines of our current codes and suggests that by lumping together all collectors we may be doing our cause more harm than good. Joe Watkins shows how consideration of the claims of American Indians has changed a great deal about the practice of American archaeology and will continue to do so. Using examples from their own work with descendant communities, Theresa A. Singleton and Charles E. Orser Jr. offer practical advice on how to gain access to the community, how to address conflicting site interpretations between archaeologists and the community, and how to handle community disinterest.

John H. Jameson Jr. reviews the huge and multifaceted task the National Park Service and other government agencies in the United States have undertaken to interpret archaeology and inform the general public about our discipline. Brian Fagan's extensive experience makes him a reliable commentator on the opportunities—and the potential pitfalls—of taking archaeology to the public through the media of television, radio, and the Web. Mark Rose adds the ethical concerns that editors of a popular archaeology magazine must consider, including the effects of overstating the significance of our discoveries. Claire Smith and Heather Burke evaluate the priorities reflected in ethical codes of a number of archaeological organizations from around the world, noting a tendency for most to privilege the goals of the discipline and archaeological stewardship over the concerns of living people. How should we expect diverse publics to respond to such priorities?

Responsibilities to Colleagues, Employees, and Students

Archaeologists have special responsibilities to those with whom they work most closely, especially students under their direction. A fundamental responsibility that has tended to receive only passing mention at best is that of basic safety in the field. Donald L. Hardesty's chapter on the subject should make every director of a field project, as well as the staff and volunteers, think twice about their own practices. Directing attention to the increasingly common training ground for students, the field school, K. Anne Pyburn examines what students learn about ethics and archaeology from our actions and behavior in the field. She and, in a separate chapter, Rita P. Wright raise the ethical dimensions of gender bias in our discipline. Wright specifically looks at how the discipline of archaeology has handled—or avoided—matters of gender, providing the basics of what we need to know about the legal and ethical approaches to differential treatment based on gender. Christopher Chippindale, writing about the ethics of research knowledge, argues, among other things, that "there are large benefits for the individual and the community if archaeological knowledge is seen, primarily, as a public good." In the final chapter, Hester A. Davis provides guidance through a grievance procedure and explains why it is important to have one, and to use it.

Rather than simple answers, our contributors provide food for thought and critical evaluation, not just of the ethical codes and principles, but also of the situations archaeologists encounter and the decisions they must make on a daily basis as they interact with the archaeological record, with nonarchaeologists, and with their colleagues. The editors hope these chapters will encourage archaeologists to think about the intentions and consequences of their actions, and perhaps, as Wylie (see chapter 1) suggests, even undertake the systematic research necessary to evaluate the consequences of the ethical positions in our codes, to document whether they are being effective in accomplishing their objectives, and to explore where and why they conflict with daily practice. Can we now, for example, document the relationship between publishing nonprovenienced artifacts and site destruction?

The editors also asked the contributors to pose a series of questions for archaeologists, be they practicing professionals or students, to get them thinking about what ethical practice might be. They were also asked to provide, in addition to the usual citations, recommended readings for further research and other approaches to their topics. Both the discussion questions and recommended readings can be found at the end of each chapter. Since codes of ethics are necessarily amended periodically, a list of websites has been included in the appendix where the most current version of the code for each of the various professional organizations can be found.

When Zimmerman, Vitelli, and Hollowell-Zimmer began work on this volume, they tried to cover everything that might legitimately be considered to fall under the rubric of archaeological ethics. Now that the manuscript is complete, the editors realize they have failed to mention a number of issues, for example, the ethics of sponsorship and funding, archaeotourism and the commodification of archaeological sites, multicultural curation standards and techniques, the intersection of intellectual property rights and archaeology, teaching archaeology to young children in our public schools, the ethics of preservation, and the responsibilities of archaeologists in times of war and social unrest—among others. These, and surely others that reviewers and readers will point out to us, are already on the list for the next edition.

Until reading the manuscripts for this volume, Vitelli began her ethics seminar by telling the students that they needed to have a class like this because, if they stayed in the field, sooner or later they *would* encounter one or more situations in which they would have to make an important ethical choice. They needed to have thought about and talked about ethical problems, to have practiced listening to and understanding other perspectives, and to have worked through hypothetical situations and their consequences if they were to avoid the mistakes of the past—which are what form the basis of our current codes. After reading the chapters that follow, it should be clear that, while valid in some respects, advice to students represents what Barker (see chapter 6) calls "passive ethics," that is, ethics that respond to specific situations. This collection of chapters makes clear that today's archaeology calls for "active ethics"; the awareness that essentially everything we do as professionals has ethical implications. For all those contradictions that inevitably arise from what we ought to do and what we actually do, whether specifically addressed in this volume or not, ethical practice today needs to be based more on discussion and critical reflection on our practice and on open processes for reaching resolution than on aiming for specific outcomes.

Note

1. All the contributors agreed to sign over any royalties from the sale of this volume to the SAA.

PART I

Where Archaeological Ethics Come From

ALISON WYLIE ⚱

Chapter One

On Ethics

Definition by Contrast

The domain of ethics—ethical claims and decisions, principles and theories—is generally defined in terms of a series of contrasts. In common usage, an ethic is a set of standards that guides action, social norms that prescribe or prohibit certain kinds of behavior, or a code of conduct (Resnik 1998:14). Ethics is the study of these standards, an expansive field of inquiry within philosophy with many subfields of its own. But our action is guided by all kinds of standards; what distinguishes those constitutive of an ethic from legal statutes, or from religious norms or social conventions? Is there a difference between ethics and morality?

However else the domain of ethics is defined, an overarching distinction is typically drawn between normative and factual claims. An ethic falls on the normative side of this divide. That is to say, an ethic consists of statements about what you *should* do, what makes an action right or a situation just, in contrast with factual claims that describe what you actually do, or what members of a community or people in general typically do. If all the archaeologists you know are involved in the antiquities trade—in buying and selling artifacts, to use the language of an early Society for American Archaeology (SAA) statement on ethics (Champe et al. 1961)—this fact about local conventions does not establish anything about whether or not the practice is justified ethically. By extension, if ethnographers or historians were to study a community of archaeologists at a particular time in a particular context, they might well conclude that their subjects conform to a complex set of rules in their interactions with one another and with various external communities, in the ways they handle their data, their publishing practices, and so on. Many of these rules will simply be shorthand descriptions of behavioral regularities, but others will have normative force; if a subset of these rules is understood within the community to specify not just what members typically do but what they must do to be considered archaeologists in good standing, they may constitute a community ethic. The study itself will be a descriptive ethnography (or, descriptive ethics) if it reports these findings but does not engage questions about whether the rules and practices in question are justified (either internally or comparatively); to take this further step is what characterizes normative ethics. The distinctive content of ethical claims is captured by the well-worn maxim that you can't get an *ought* from an *is:* as important as it is to know the facts of a situation when assessing it normatively, the facts themselves will not tell you what's right or wrong about it in an ethical sense.

So, an ethic is intended to articulate a set of ideals that can give us leverage in judging existing practices as well as in making decisions about how to go on when conflicts arise or conventions are problematic. But not all normative principles constitute an ethic; further distinctions are drawn between ethics and the norms embodied in legal statutes or in conventions of politeness. Where laws often set outer limits on acceptable action, ethical standards typically define more narrowly how we should conduct our lives. Conversely, ethical considerations can provide grounds for calling the law into question when it legitimates practices that are immoral or unjust. Debates about the commercial salvage of underwater wrecks often turn on disagreements about the relationship between legal and ethical commitments (see George F. Bass, chapter 5). Those who defend the decision to collaborate with commercial salvors routinely point out that, in some jurisdictions at least, such salvage operations are perfectly legal, while those who condemn them object that archaeologists have an ethical responsibility to protect underwater sites that goes well beyond anything currently specified in the law. At the very least, they argue, archaeologists should refuse to participate in commercial salvage even if it is legal; their choices should be subject to tighter constraints than set out in the law. But in addition, many urge that archaeologists should do all they can to change such laws. If their protests were to include one or another form of civil disobedience, they would be engaged in illegal action that might nonetheless be ethically justified.

By contrast, norms of politeness or social convention often delimit the scope of acceptable action much more narrowly than can be justified ethically, sometimes enforcing a code of conduct that violates widely accepted moral principles. For example, conventions of loyalty within close-knit research teams may dictate that insiders never share information with outsiders as a matter of long-established disciplinary practice—to invoke the terminology of the 1961 SAA statement on ethics again, insiders may hoard their data, treating it as a private preserve and refusing access to professional rivals, the wider discipline, interested publics, and anyone who was not involved in its original recovery—even though this violates a commitment to open communication and public accountability that many (perhaps even these same practitioners, on reflection) would consider to be central to the ethics of scientific practice.

Although the terms "moral" and "ethical" are often used interchangeably (e.g., moral and ethical theory, moral and ethical judgment), a distinction is sometimes drawn between standards of morality and ethical standards that is especially salient here. An ethic consists of standards that apply to members of a particular sub-group—for example, to lawyers and doctors, engineers and scientists, parents and teachers, coaches and judges, or those who hold public office—by virtue of the special expertise, authority, powers, and responsibilities that characterize their status or role in society. By contrast, a moral code "consists of a society's most general standards . . . standards [that] apply to all people in society regardless of their professional or institutional roles" (Resnik 1998:15). Archaeologists have all the moral obligations and entitlements of other citizens; lists of moral standards typically include such things as honesty and fidelity (telling the truth and keeping promises), beneficence and nonmaleficence (a responsibility to do well by and to avoid harming others), and respect for the autonomy of others (a right to self-direction—to make informed choices—and to freedom from interference). But in addition, by virtue of their training, their membership in societies like the SAA, and often their employment, archaeologists have special responsibilities defined by the goals of their discipline and the professional roles they play as archaeologists.

For example, an *archaeological* ethic might stipulate particular requirements of truth telling and fidelity given the goals of archaeology as a research discipline and the authority, the public trust, invested in archaeology as a profession. The scope of requirements of beneficence and nonmaleficence will also be specified more broadly and the bar set higher in any area on which archaeological expertise has a bearing. In this spirit, archaeologists are often said to have responsibilities to benefit, and not harm, not only other (living) peoples who have an interest in archaeological sites and materials, but also those cultures and communities who produced the record, and on some accounts, the archaeological record itself and human cultural heritage in general. Where truth telling is concerned, archaeological codes of conduct typically require archaeologists not just to be honest in reporting what they believe (i.e., not just to avoid dissimulation or deception), but also to do everything they can to ensure the accuracy and reliability of what they report; an archaeologist qua archaeologist has a special responsibility to ensure that others can depend on the credibility of what he or she claims about archaeological matters. Most codes also include a requirement that you publish or in other ways communicate the results of research in a timely way. It is not enough that you be honest whenever you have occasion to discuss archaeology with others; you have a positive responsibility to ensure that you communicate widely and effectively about the work you do as an archaeologist. In addition, professional codes of conduct, like that endorsed by the Society of Professional Archaeologists (SOPA) and now the Register of Professional Archaeologists (RPA), require not just that archaeologists avoid lying, but that they "avoid *and discourage* exaggerated, misleading, or unwarranted statements about archaeological matters *that might induce others to engage in unethical or illegal activity"* (Society of Professional Archaeologists 1991:1.1[d], emphasis added). As professionals, RPA/SOPA members have a particular responsibility to set a standard of integrity, and as archaeologists, they must avoid compromises in truth telling that might, for example, put the archaeological record at risk. In short, what an archeological ethic acknowledges and codifies is the principle that archaeologists have a special responsibility to ensure that they use their expertise wisely, and that they do not cause harm to those who depend on them or are affected by the work they do as archaeologists.

Finally, it is crucial to distinguish moral and ethical judgments from assertions of personal preference or taste (Rachels 1998:16–17). If you claim that you love doing archaeology, or that you find Moche ceramics or Cycladic figurines incomparably beautiful, or that you dislike the taste of beer, your statements may each be a true description of your tastes (if they are honest and accurate reports on how you feel), but they do not have normative content; they do not, on their own, imply that others should feel as you do, and typically they do not require justification by appeal to reasons. By contrast, if you claim that an action or convention of practice is wrong—for example, that archaeologists have an obligation to meet the highest standards of practice possible in all aspects of their work (whether they love their work or not), that the commercial trade in Moche ceramics and Cycladic figurines is immoral, that no serious, upstanding archaeologist should ever drink beer(!)—then you are making claims about what you and others should do (or not do). In this case, you have an obligation to justify your claims; you must be prepared to provide an argument in the philosophical, not the pugilistic, sense. That is, you must be prepared to give an account of the underlying assumptions—the premises—that justify your conclusion, both factual and normative. Ethics as a field of study and a practice is, then, a matter of working out the reasons for prescriptive judgments at various levels of generality and practicality. There may be no final court of appeals, no buck-stopping set of first principles that are themselves beyond question and that anchor moral deliberation, providing definitive answers to the moral questions that arise in practice. Nonetheless, there is a great deal of useful work to be done clarifying the principles that inform our moral/ethical judgments and the arguments by which we deploy these principles to criticize or justify our actions.

Strategies of Moral Reasoning

Often, moral or ethical issues arise when taken-for-granted conventions of practice are disrupted, when a "rupture" occurs, as sociologists sometimes describe it, that makes it impossible to go on as you've been used to doing, or when you confront a situation where it just is not clear what you should do. Archaeology is rife with such situations, especially given fundamental changes in the kinds of employment available to archaeologists, the widespread destruction that threatens archaeological sites both as a consequence of land development and of looting and commercial trade, and the challenges to conventional goals and standards of archaeology that have been raised by descendant communities worldwide.

When a rupture first takes shape, the initial response of those grappling with it is often to invoke the conventional wisdom embodied in well-established moral maxims. To take a standard philosophical example, if you find yourself in a situation where a lie would save a friend from harm, you might begin by appealing to the principles of beneficence and nonmaleficence; even though one well-worn rule of practice is "never tell a lie," you also have a responsibility to help others and to protect them from harm if you can. If the rules themselves offer no clear answer, you may step back from the immediate situation and the close-to-the-ground maxims that seem applicable to it. You might ask why you should never tell a lie; what is the justification for this moral directive? If you know the justification, perhaps this will help determine how the rule should be applied and how it should be weighed against other rules. At this point, you move to the level of general moral principles and moral theory. Far from being disconnected from practice, I would argue, with D. Jamieson, that "moral theorizing is part of moral practice" (1991:479); practical moral deliberation is always already richly theoretical.

There are any number of moral theories that have taken shape in, and that inform, rupture-generated debate about moral issues. Overviews of philosophical ethics now routinely include discussion not only of the history and diversity of theories that make up the tradition of ethics in Western philosophy, but also of moral theories developed as part of Indian, Chinese, Native American, and African among other cultural and philosophical traditions.[1] For present purposes, consider just two broad families of moral theory that have been dominant in Western philosophical ethics and that often figure (implicitly) in debate about ethical issues in archaeology: consequentialist/ utilitarian and deontological theories. Put most simply, on the first approach, that of consequentialism, what makes an action right or wrong is what effect it has in the world, its consequences assessed in terms of happiness or well-being. By contrast, on the second, deontological approach, it is the intrinsic quality of an action that makes it right or wrong, regardless of its consequences.

For a utilitarian, lying is not categorically wrong; it should be avoided insofar as it has negative consequences. The key question is, then, how positive and negative consequences should be weighed. Utilitarians have long argued that a focus on consequences does not necessarily justify a self-serving, shortsighted hedonism.[2] Typically, they insist that the well-being of everyone affected by an action or a practice should be considered, not just that of an individual or of a narrowly defined community. And "rule utilitarians" argue that positive and negative effects should be assessed, not for individual actions and their immediate consequences, but in terms of the wider impact of categories or classes of action, practices like that of lying or truth telling. On this kind of consequentialism, it is certainly legitimate to consider trade-offs and qualifications of conventional moral maxims, but the justification for lying to save a friend from harm carries a heavy burden of proof. A rule utilitarian will object that, even if a particular lie is trivial and promises a positive outcome, the practice of lying compromises the integrity of the individual in all kinds of insidious ways, and widespread acceptance of lying will undermine the conditions of trust necessary for society to function at all; in this case, everyone's well-being is compromised.[3] In colloquial terms, the principle at work in utilitarian thinking of this kind is something like "what goes around comes around"; there may be some circumstances in which you are justified in breaking a general proscription against lying (or other such moral principles), but the well-worked tradition of consequentialist theorizing suggests that such decisions should be weighed very carefully against indirect and down-the-line consequences.

Even given these elaborations and refinements, the perennial problem with which utilitarians grapple is the prospect that, if consequences (broadly or narrowly construed) are all that distinguish right from wrong, it is difficult to see how, in terms consistent with utilitarianism, you can block counterexamples in which the harm done to a small number of people is justified by appeal to an outcome that improves conditions of life for a sufficiently large majority of people over the long term. The motivation for an influential alternative tradition of moral theorizing, the deontological theory associated with Immanuel Kant, is an appreciation that we do often judge actions to be wrong even if they have good consequences and no negative repercussions; what makes an action right or wrong cannot be its consequences alone. To make sense of these judgments, Kant argues that moral theory must give central place to the ideal of "the good will" that is manifest, not in good effects, but in a commitment to do one's duty—to do what one should—for its own sake. On this account, duty is characterized in terms of what Kant refers to as a "categorical imperative": doing one's duty is a matter of acting in accord with moral principles that can be universalized (i.e., extended to everyone or, for Kant, to all rational beings). In a sense, the central intuition here is a variant of the Golden Rule (under some formulations): You should follow only those principles of action in your dealings with others that you could consistently endorse as principles that they should follow in their dealings with you and with others.

The more specific formulation Kant gives the categorical imperative is a principle for which he is famous: that we should treat others as having intrinsic value, as "ends in themselves," never as a means only. However worthy our ends may be, if you use others as instruments (only), you follow a maxim that you could not consistently extend to yourself. On this moral theory, lying is intrinsically wrong because (or, insofar as) you violate a duty to treat others with the kind of respect they deserve as "ends in themselves." Indeed, Kant and other deontologists argue that you could not consistently follow a maxim that allowed everyone to endorse claims they know are false or to make promises they do not intend to keep. In this case, promise making and truth telling would become conceptually impossible, in principle, not just as a consequence of a contingent loss of trust. Deontological theory thus sets (absolute) limits on the kinds of action that are acceptable where others are concerned; it establishes that all human beings (for Kant, all rational beings) have certain basic rights to respect and to freedom from harm. For this reason, although deontological and utilitarian theories have been developed as opposing traditions in ethics, they can be seen as complementary in some important respects. While a utilitarian approach to moral problems has a powerful pragmatic appeal in sorting out competing moral claims, its shortcomings lead some to suggest that the calculus of positive and negative consequences should only operate within parameters set by the kind of categorical principles that deontologists have defended. In fact, utilitarian and deontological considerations do often coexist in practical moral deliberation in just this way.

Ethics Issues in Archaeology

Consider how these strategies of moral argument play out in terms of the principles that constitute an emerging, evolving archaeological ethic. I have already indicated how a general moral principle like the requirement of truth telling may take on particular significance in an archaeological context. But often, archaeologists confront situations in which closely specified requirements of honesty and publicity come into conflict with an equally strong commitment to conservation principles,[4] and in these cases they must carefully weigh the consequences of following competing directives. For example, in some contexts details about the location and layout of archaeological sites are rarely published, despite a commitment to make archaeological results as widely available as possible, because they would provide looters with a blueprint for exploiting these sites (Halsey 1991).

More controversial cases have to do with the publication of material that has already been looted and is held in private collections.[5] Those who defend the publication of looted data argue that archaeologists have a primary responsibility to document and preserve whatever information survives of the archaeological record that will make a difference to our understanding of the cultural past.[6] Sometimes, this commitment to the evidential value of archaeological data is presented in categorical terms. Serving the interests of inquiry—making full use of archaeological data as evidence—defines what it is to be an archaeologist; it is an intrinsic good that must be upheld whatever the consequences. More often, this principle is formulated in consequentialist terms, but with such weight given to the research goals of archaeology that they trump all other interests or responsibilities; they are effectively (if contingently) nondefeasible.[7] Those who criticize such arguments for analyzing and publishing looted data typically object that whatever understanding may be

gained by such a practice is outweighed by direct and indirect negative consequences that threaten to undermine the enterprise as a whole, for example, by stimulating the commercial trade in antiquities that fuels the destruction of the
archaeological record and by compromising the credibility of archaeologists who
otherwise oppose the commercial exploitation of archaeological resources. Sometimes, these critics appeal to a broad conception of archaeological responsibility according to which research goals cannot be granted absolute or unique priority; they
must be balanced against other professional obligations, such as a commitment to
protect archaeological resources. This represents a shift in emphasis that reflects, in
turn, fundamental changes in the roles archaeologists play professionally; a growing
majority of archaeologists are now employed in industry and by regulatory agencies
where they are charged with mitigating the destructive effects of land development
that many regard as inevitable.

Despite some sharp conflicts, for the most part everyone engaged in debate
about the relationship between archaeology and commercial interests subscribes to
both research and conservationist goals and sees them as interdependent. What they
disagree on are factual claims about whether, or to what extent, looted data have archaeological value given a loss of provenience;[8] whether archaeological publication
actually plays a role in stimulating the market for antiquities or in legitimating the
commercial trade in antiquities; to what extent archaeologists are effective in coun-
teracting the destruction of the archaeological record (e.g., through public education
and outreach); and whether these strategies are compromised if they publish looted
data. The consequentialist structure of the debate throws these questions into sharp
relief and suggests that an adequate response to conflicts over the propriety of ever
using looted data will require a systematic evaluation of the empirical claims about
negative and positive consequences that underpin normative directives.

Another context in which consequentialist reasoning is explicit is in William
D. Lipe's influential argument for a conservation ethic. He urges archaeologists to
take responsibility "for the whole resource base" (1974:214)—to make it their primary goal to identify, protect, and conserve archaeological resources "for maximum
longevity" (223)—and he draws out a number of implications for archaeological
practice, including the controversial recommendation that archaeologists should
forego the excavation of sites that are not threatened if there is any possibility of
meeting "the data needs of a problem . . . from the available pool of sites requiring
salvage" (231). In this context and in a later discussion, "In Defense of Digging"
(1996), Lipe makes it clear that conservation is desirable, not as an end in itself, but
as a means of ensuring that future archaeologists, who may be able to make more effective use of the archaeological record, will have a database with which to work.
The trade-off he envisions is between long- and short-term consequences; archaeologists should forego some gains in understanding that they might make now for
greater potential gains in the future. In his later discussion, he qualifies this principle, arguing that a broader range of short-term consequences should be considered:

It would be counterproductive to prohibit all "consumptive uses" of the archaeological record in the short term inasmuch as "an archaeology without excavation is one that cannot fully achieve its potential social contributions" (1996:24). Here, archaeologists negotiate many of the issues that have been central to the philosophical debate about utilitarian principles: whose interests (or well-being) should be considered, how should different kinds of consequences be weighed, and what range of indirect and down-the-line effects should bear on moral judgments about a particular class of actions or action-guiding rules.

It is in debate about the accountability of archaeologists to descendant communities that appeals to intrinsic value are most prominent. When Native Americans insist that archaeological sites and materials have value as part of their cultural heritage and that they have an interest in this heritage that is not necessarily served by archaeological research, sometimes they argue that the calculus of consequences should be expanded again, but in a new direction.[9] A commitment to learn more about the cultural past in the ways made possible by archaeological research should be balanced against interests in cultural integrity and heritage; this may require archaeologists to avoid studying some types of material or sites, or to practice in particular ways and publish in different venues than they have been used to doing. Often, Native Americans reject consequentialist arguments out of hand on the ground that these are fundamentally at odds with their cultural values. They may accord an intrinsic value to material remains that archaeologists value chiefly as evidence—as a means to the end of understanding the cultural past—and, given this, they may insist that, like living members of the community, sacred sites and ancestral remains should never be treated instrumentally.

On many formulations, these arguments presuppose Native American worldviews that cannot be articulated in terms of Western moral theory without obscuring their most distinctive features, risking just the kind of cultural imperialism that Native Americans protest more generally.[10] Nonetheless, there are sometimes points of convergence or strategic translations that put the challenge to archaeological interests in terms of an appeal to categorical principles of civil rights or human rights that are familiar from debate about the limitations of consequentialist theories. Whatever insights archaeological uses of the record might afford, the dignity of ancestral graves should not be disturbed; those whose material remains make up the archaeological record and, indeed, the surviving remains themselves, deserve to be treated as intrinsically valuable ends, not as a means (only). In addition, where the cultural identity and heritage of a living descendant community is constituted in part by archaeological sites and materials, members of this community may claim rights of autonomy and of self-determination with respect to the disposition of these sites and materials that must be respected.

One way that the force of these claims is conveyed is by a form of table-turning comparative analysis that brings to bear a justificatory principle along the lines of Kant's categorical imperative. Native Americans have a long history of challenging practices of grave digging and the collection of skeletal material that would never have been tolerated (indeed, that were often legally prohibited) where Euro-American graves and cemeteries were concerned.[11] Surely, the predominantly Euro-American community of archaeologists cannot consistently endorse a maxim that would allow for the desecration of their own forebears' graves. But even if they do not especially value their own ancestors' graves and skeletal remains, surely they cannot endorse a maxim that would allow others to desecrate the sites they do consider intrinsically significant just because, in the tradition of these others, such sites are not especially important. The categorical imperative may thus require that you recognize and respect what it means to treat others with dignity—as an end in themselves—in their own terms. This is just one example of how lines of argument well established within Western traditions of ethical thinking may reach beyond themselves, providing support for the principle that we should respect the integrity and autonomy of cultures very different from those that have given rise to the utilitarian and deontological theories I describe here.

Conclusion

The process of moving from ethical conflicts and uncertainties encountered in practice through various levels of ethical theorizing cannot be counted on to settle the issues archaeologists confront once and for all. The principles and strategies of argument that are uncovered in this process—that underpin normative claims—are always themselves open to question. While the dream lives on of establishing a bedrock of fundamental principles that require no further justification—that cannot be questioned, that everyone must accept as true, and that are self-vindicating—most ethicists consider this to be a very distant prospect. This is the dream that fuels religious and moral absolutism and if anything is to be learned from living in a pluralistic and increasingly global society, it is that convictions of this kind are the cause of considerable harm.

Recognizing that any moral claim is open to question does not imply, however, that anything goes or that there is nothing more to ethical argument than dogmatic assertion. In the process of clarifying close-to-the-ground moral and ethical intuitions ("considered moral judgments," in the language of ethicists) and then working back from them to the principles they presuppose, both intuitions and orienting principles are likely to be reframed. Sometimes, you will want to rethink practical judgments that you have held with great confidence once you have clarified the principles on which they depend. Often, the intuitions generated by grappling with new situations (with ruptures) will put pressure on principles you have long taken for granted, drawing attention to limitations and implications of these principles that you had not considered. There may be no final stopping place, although you may tentatively achieve a balance between principles and practice that philosophers sometimes describe as a point of "reflective equilibrium."[12] Even so, the process of systematically assessing the ethical commitments embodied in practice will certainly eliminate some options as incoherent, unjustifiable, or impractical, and clarify the limits of those we embrace.

It is in the spirit of ensuring just this kind of ongoing dialectic of critical reflection that the SAA Committee for Ethics in Archaeology has argued that ethics principles and codes of conduct should be treated as a work in progress; they are never final, never written in stone. If they are to be effective in helping practitioners negotiate the complex and rapidly evolving ethics issues that are now endemic to archaeology, formalized statements of ethical commitment must be subject to continuous assessment and fine tuning. It is only through such a process of active, reflective debate that archaeologists can be accountable for their practice.

Discussion Questions

1. You find yourself in a situation where sharing information about "looted" material with a collector might help save the collection from being broken up and sold. How would you think through your decision? What ethical principles would you use to justify the action you decide to take?
2. Discuss reburial in light of both consequentialist and deontological approaches.
3. What are some of the competing interests in archaeology? How are the ethics of these stakeholders alike or different? Who are some of the other groups that claim a stake in archaeology? How are their ethics similar to or different from those of archaeologists?
4. Describe some of the "ruptures" that have emerged recently in archaeology. What approach(es) might you advise to address them?
5. How do the ethics of descendant communities and of government differ from those of archaeologists? What approaches might help to balance these various interests?
6. As a member of an art museum board, you have to discuss and vote on whether to purchase a collection of looted artifacts said to come from a single, very rich, ancient Persian grave. The dealer has said that if the museum doesn't purchase the group, he will attempt to sell the pieces individually. What ethical arguments do you use to persuade the other members of the board to follow your position?
7. Use the forms of reasoning illustrated in this chapter to decide what your ethical approach would be in the following scenarios:
   a. Last summer, your field project's living quarters were visited several times by black bears, in one instance, causing considerable damage and

a rather close call for one of the volunteers. Weather conditions this year promise to be better and further such visits by the bears seem unlikely. Should you warn and prepare this year's volunteers to deal with black bears, or skip the whole subject so as not to unduly frighten anyone?

b. The number of graduate students participating in your field project in Turkey this summer is greater than the number of needed trench supervisors. Since your Turkish workmen find it awkward to work for a woman, should you assign only male students to supervise trenches and have the women direct the lab work?

Notes

1. For example, see contributions to Peter Singer's "Part II: The Great Ethical Traditions" (1991).

2. This was a standard objection to consequentialist theories in their earliest formulation by Jeremy Bentham and James Mill. John Stuart Mill, the most famous of the British utilitarians, was especially concerned to reformulate the theory so as to avoid the difficulties raised by such critics. This history of debate is told in any number of excellent overviews of philosophical ethics (Craig 1998; Edwards 1967; Singer 1991).

3. This is one strategy of argument outlined by Sisela Bok, for example, in her discussion of "Deceptive Social Science Research" (1979:182–202).

4. The second "objective" set out in the SAA Bylaws is "to advocate and to aid in the conservation of archaeological resources" (1995). Principles of this kind now figure prominently in the objectives and statements on ethics of most archaeological societies. Later on, I will discuss William D. Lipe's influential argument for making an expanded conservation ethic central to archaeological practice (1974, 1996).

5. For example, the SAA has instituted an editorial policy that prohibits the publication in *Latin American Antiquity* or *American Antiquity* of any articles that rely on material "recovered in such a manner as to cause the unscientific destruction of sites or monuments; or that have been exported in violation of the national laws of their country of origin" (1992).

6. Christopher B. Donnan makes this argument in especially explicit terms: "It is tragic that looting takes place, and I know of no archaeologist who does not decry the loss of critical information that results. But to stand by when it is possible to make at least some record of whatever information can still be salvaged simply compounds the loss" (1991:498). I have discussed this example in more detail elsewhere (Wylie 1999).

7. A principle is defeasible if it is open to challenge and if it can be overridden by other considerations. Alternatively, a principle may be considered nondefeasible either on deontological grounds, as defining an intrinsic good that must never be compromised, or for utilitarian/consequentialist reasons, as requiring or proscribing action that has such profound implications it is unlikely that it could ever be outweighed by any other principle. Arguments of both kinds have been made, for example, for basic human rights.

8. In the worst-case scenario, it may be impossible to distinguish material that originated in archaeological contexts from fakes, compromising the archaeological enterprise at the most fundamental level (e.g., see Gill and Chippindale 1993). Even when these questions do not arise, Karen D. Vitelli (1996a) describes how much is lost of evidential significance when details of archaeological context are unknown.

9. For example, see discussions in which, as T. J. Ferguson puts it, "Native Americans have diverse uses for archaeology" (1996:71).

10. Roger Echo-Hawk (2000) gives a particularly nuanced appraisal of this issue. See also contributors to *Native Americans and Archaeologists* (Swidler et al. 1997) and to *Working Together* (Dongoske, Aldenderfer, and Doehner 2000).

11. This is a point made in some detail by Joe Watkins (2000) and David Hurst Thomas (2000). Consider, too, Tony Hillerman's (1989) fictional example of a Native American activist who digs up and delivers to a museum lawyer the bones of her New England forebears, challenging her to think through a role reversal in which her ancestors' remains are subject to the kind of treatment long protested by Native Americans.

12. The concept of "reflective equilibrium" was developed by Rawls and is discussed by Jamieson (1991) in connection with the methodology of ethics.

Recommended Readings
General Ethics and Ethics in Science

Beauchamp, T. L.
1982 *Ethical Issues in Social Research.* Johns Hopkins University Press, Baltimore, MD.

Bok, Sisela
1979 *Lying: Moral Choice in Public and Private Life.* Vintage, New York.

Rachels, J.
1998 *The Elements of Moral Philosophy.* 2nd ed. McGraw-Hill, New York.

Resnik, D. B.
1998 *The Ethics of Science: An Introduction.* Routledge, New York.

Shrader-Frechette, K. S.
1994 *Ethics of Scientific Research.* Rowman and Littlefield, Lanham, MD.

Singer, Peter (editor)
1991 *A Companion to Ethics.* Blackwell, Oxford.

Ethics in Anthropology/Archaeology—Some General References

Fluehr-Lobban, C. (editor)
2003 *Ethics and the Profession of Anthropology: Dialogue for a New Era.* 2nd ed. AltaMira Press, Walnut Creek, CA.

Green, Ernestine L. (editor)
   1984   *Ethics and Values in Archaeology.* The Free Press, London.

Messenger, Phyllis Mauch (editor)
   1999   *The Ethics of Collecting Cultural Property: Whose Culture? Whose Property?*
          2nd ed. University of New Mexico Press, Albuquerque.

Strathern, M. (editor)
   2000   *Audit Cultures: Anthropological Studies in Accountability, Ethics, and the
          Academy.* Routledge, New York.

MARK LYNOTT

Chapter Two

The Development of Ethics in Archaeology

The development of ethics in archaeology has followed the same general course as has archaeology as a profession. In the same way that method and theory have matured and become more sophisticated, archaeological ethics have also evolved and matured. Since ethics represent guidelines that help a specialized profession operate in the ever more complex and rapidly changing real world, it is not surprising to see that changes in archaeological ethics have been linked to events or practices outside the archaeological profession. This brief survey of the history of archaeological ethics documents the changes in archaeological ethics that have occurred in response to societal changes

Antiquarians in the seventeenth and eighteenth centuries were motivated to explore mounds, barrows, and other archaeological features by curiosity and the hope of finding treasure. Very little useful information beyond the recovery of material culture resulted from these excavations. Gradually, the more observant and thoughtful antiquarians began to realize that the archaeological record, if carefully studied, could yield important information about the past (Bahn 1996; Marsden 1974; Piggott 1989). This recognition that the archaeological record is an important source of information about the human past probably represents the earliest stage of scientific archaeology and is reflected in the first careful and systematic surveys and excavations (e.g., Lapham 1855; Squier and Davis 1848).

It is unclear when archaeology first became a profession, but the earliest attention to what might be called ethics can be seen in the late nineteenth-century concern over unscientific excavation of sites. Prior to this time, excavation of archaeological sites was aimed primarily at the recovery of artifacts for personal use or for sale to museums or art collectors. This is particularly well illustrated in the first decades of the nineteenth century when many important archaeological monuments and artifacts were removed from sites and shipped to museums in Europe. The unscientific recovery of artifacts and architectural elements from important sites can be seen in the work of Giovanni Battista Belzoni, who became well known for plundering the tombs and architecture of ancient Egypt (Bahn 1996; Fagan 1975) and in the removal of portions of the Parthenon from the Acropolis at Athens, Greece, by Lord Elgin, the British ambassador to Turkey (Greenfield 1989). Although many very important archaeological objects excavated during this period have been preserved in museums and have become important icons of the archaeological record, the debate about ownership of these items started in the nineteenth century and is ongoing today. Consequently, the first debate about archaeological ethics swirled around the unscientific excavation of sites to recover artifacts for museums or collectors.

The market for antiquities from North America did not become established until later in the nineteenth century when news about the remarkable artifacts of the American southwest became known. The discovery of Cliff Palace and other sites at Mesa Verde by Richard Wetherill in 1888 led to wholesale looting of that region to recover pots and other artifacts. In 1891, Gustaf von Nordenskiöld, with the help of the Wetherill brothers, excavated Cliff Palace and other ruins. The artifacts he recovered were sent back to Finland, where he published a detailed account of his explorations (von Nordenskiöld 1893). This created a nationalistic uproar among Americans who resented the artifacts being removed from the country. The demand for artifacts by museums and art collectors resulted in many unscientific excavations and often little useful information. This pattern was not limited to the southwestern United States. The discovery of beautiful ceramic vessels in association with burials in the lower Mississippi River valley led collectors and looters to use probes to help them plunder graves in this region (e.g., Little 1904).

The movement to preserve and protect the United States' archaeological heritage is tied to the historic preservation movement (King, Hickman, and Berg 1977) and was led by a relatively small group of easterners who saw the historical value of the archaeological record. Recognition of the need to preserve the archaeological record was not widespread at this time, and these individuals used their money and influence to encourage private and public preservation of important archaeological sites. Frederick Ward Putnam, after three years of excavating at the Serpent Mound in southern Ohio, raised private funds to purchase the site for the Peabody Museum, which later donated it to the State of Ohio (Putnam 1890). At the urging of several prominent New Englanders, land around the Casa Grande Ruins in Arizona was removed from sale and settlement, and the secretary of the interior was provided with federal funds for its repair and preservation. While this probably represents the first action on the part of the federal government to preserve an archaeological site, the government had already shown an interest in scientific archaeology with the establishment of the Smithsonian Institution in 1846. The Smithsonian Institution's commitment to archaeology is documented in its publication of *Ancient Monuments of the Mississippi Valley* (Squier and Davis 1848) as volume 1 in the series *Contributions to Knowledge*. The Smithsonian Institution also sponsored or published several other early archaeological studies, including a monumental study of the earthen mounds in the eastern United States that demonstrated conclusively that these were the work of Native American people and not a lost race of Mound Builders (Thomas 1894).

The predominant ethical principle for these early archaeologists was the need to protect sites from looting and vandalism and to excavate them in a scientific manner. After more than twenty-five years of urging the government to protect archaeological sites on government land, this principle became codified by the passage of the Antiquities Act of 1906 (Lee 2000). The passage of this act was due in great measure to the efforts of Edgar Lee Hewett (Thompson 2000), who worked to unite competing interests within the Archaeological Institute of America (AIA) and the American Anthropological Association. The Antiquities Act authorizes the president to establish national monuments to protect sites on public land, prohibits looting and vandalism of sites, and requires a permit to excavate sites on public land. The provisions of the Antiquities Act were drafted by Hewett and other archaeologists and clearly reflect the ethical concerns of archaeologists at that time.

Prior to World War II, the number of archaeologists was small, with employment limited to a few universities and museums. Archaeologists continued to be interested mainly in improving their excavation methods and publishing reports of their research. Many people who conducted archaeological excavations and published reports of their research were not formally trained in archaeology. In fact, individuals like Major William S. Webb, Dr. Clarence Webb, and Watson Smith were not trained as archaeologists, yet made significant contributions to the field of study. The AIA was founded in 1879, and its membership has always included a combination of professional archaeologists and interested avocational supporters. During its early years, the AIA maintained a significant interest in the study and preservation of sites in the southwestern United States, and was instrumental in convincing Congress to pass the Antiquities Act of 1906. The Society for American Archaeology (SAA) was founded in 1934; its membership was a blend of interested avocational and professionally trained archaeologists. Ethical concerns of the day continued to focus on the need for careful excavation and reporting of archaeological research, rather than formal training in archaeology.

At the end of the war, the GI Bill provided an unprecedented opportunity for veterans to attend colleges and universities. The increase in students produced a corresponding increase in opportunities for archaeologists to teach. This happened to coincide with the establishment of the Interagency Archaeological Salvage Program and the River Basin Surveys. These government-sponsored programs were developed in response to a nationwide program of dam building that threatened much of the archaeological heritage of the nation. The Interagency Archaeological Salvage Program and the River Basin Surveys created an expanded job market for archaeologists employed in research. The funding for these programs was authorized as a result of lobbying by archaeologists, who wished to study sites before they were destroyed by dam construction and inundation. The political activity of archaeologists continued to reflect their ethical concern for scientific study of the archaeological record, and in this case, it placed an emphasis on sites that were likely to be destroyed by development (Brew 1961; Silverberg 1967).

The postwar economic boom, coupled with an increase in employment opportunities for archaeologists, led archaeologists to talk about distinguishing between professional and nonprofessional archaeologists. Prior to this time, it was hard to distinguish between individuals who had been formally trained in archaeology and those who learned by experience. Although many avocational archaeologists continued to make important contributions to understanding the archaeological record, the increase in employment opportunities also raised pressure to define some minimal standards for professional archaeology (McGimsey 1995).

In 1960, the SAA appointed a committee to address these issues, which resulted in "Four Statements for Archaeology" (Champe et al. 1961). The first statement defined the field of archaeology. The second emphasized the importance of systematic methods and record keeping. The third is titled "Ethics" and addresses the need to publish the results of archaeological research; prohibits the buying and selling of artifacts; requires that collections and records be made available to competent scholars; prohibits an archaeologist from initiating excavations at a site where another archaeologist is working; and prohibits willful destruction, distortion, or concealment of archaeological data. The fourth statement recommends that training in archaeology should include a bachelor's degree in the arts or sciences, plus two years of graduate training combined with two years of field experience. The committee highly recommended that archaeologists obtain a master's degree. A doctorate was further recommended, but not required.

The "Four Statements for Archaeology" represents the most comprehensive and formal declaration of ethics published at that time. The nature and scope of these statements is a reflection of the nature of the archaeological profession in 1960, with a continuing focus on proper study and reporting, and a new focus on training and cooperation among scholars. During the 1960s, archaeological activity was still largely based in universities and museums. Most research was conducted through grants or field schools, and a growing number of young archaeologists urged an end to the culture–historical approach that had dominated archaeology for decades in favor of a processual approach (Binford 1962).

The 1970s witnessed an explosion of archaeological work under the umbrella of cultural resource management (CRM). Federal historic preservation legislation mandated archeological research in advance of construction for federal projects, and it often seemed difficult to find enough archaeologists to do the research that the statutes and regulations required. This often resulted in poor work or projects where no report was ever prepared. As the problem grew, interest in developing standards of professionalism in archaeology began to grow. Further incentive to address the problems came from a landmark paper by William D. Lipe (1974) that offered a new paradigm for the profession based on a conservation ethic. These developments resulted in a series of conferences and meetings in the mid-1970s that led the SAA to endorse the idea of a registry of professional archaeologists. This ultimately led to the establishment of the Society of Professional Archeologists (SOPA) in 1976. Charles R. McGimsey III (1995) presents a detailed account of the meetings and events that ultimately led to the founding of SOPA.

Once established, SOPA immediately developed its Bylaws, Code of Ethics, Standards of Research Performance, and Grievance Procedure (see Hester A. Davis, chapter 19). This immediately set SOPA apart from other archaeological organizations that viewed themselves as scholarly, rather than professional in nature. Although it was an SAA committee that led to the development of SOPA, the SAA was unwilling to become involved in the issues associated with contract archaeology in 1976. Although the SAA officially encouraged all of its members who were eligible to join SOPA, many individuals felt that the need for professional certification only applied to people working in contract archaeology. Consequently, throughout its history, SOPA's impact was limited by the relatively small size of its membership.

The SOPA Code of Ethics and Standards of Research Performance were written as minimum standards of professional behavior and addressed a wide range of archaeological activities. The Code of Ethics was written as a series of "shall" and "shall not" statements that address archaeologists' responsibility to the public; to colleagues, employees, and students; and to employers and clients. The Standards of Research Performance were equally detailed in nature and written as minimum standards.

Much of the SOPA Code of Ethics and Standards of Research Performance represent updated and expanded statements derived from the "Four Statements for Archaeology" issued by the SAA (Champe et al. 1961). These reflect a continuing concern for proper methods of study and record keeping, research reporting, appropriate treatment of colleagues, and training. Although they do not explicitly prohibit the buying and selling of artifacts, they do require support of the 1970 UN Educational, Scientific, and Cultural Organization Convention (UNESCO Convention) prohibiting "illicit import, export, and transfer of ownership of cultural property." The Code of Ethics and Standards of Research Performance also address issues that had not previously been addressed by any published statement on archaeological ethics. Most notable is the "archaeologist's responsibility to the public." This statement made explicit recognition of the public's interest in and right to knowledge about the archaeological record and reflects the belief that preservation of the archaeological record is in the public interest. It also told archaeologists to be "sensitive to, and respect the legitimate concerns of, groups whose culture histories are the subjects of archaeological investigations." Although this statement had less meaning for archaeologists when SOPA was established in 1976, it perhaps warned of the need for greater cooperation with indigenous peoples, as has become apparent following the passage of reburial and repatriation laws.

The SOPA Code of Ethics and Standards of Research Performance clearly reflect the concerns of archaeologists who were increasingly involved in the growing field of CRM. For example, the Code of Ethics warns that an archaeologist should not "[u]ndertake any research that affects the archeological resource base for which she/he is not qualified" (Society of Professional Archeologists [SOPA] 1991:I.1.2.d). This prohibition reflected one of the concerns about the growing CRM field that led to the formation of SOPA. Various parts of the Code of Ethics also reflect the recognition that much archaeology is accomplished through the business of CRM. Consequently, elements of the code address the archaeologist's responsibility to employees, employers, and clients. The Standards of Research Performance require archaeologists to find permanent curation facilities for artifacts and records from their projects. This reflects a continuing problem for CRM projects, particularly those conducted by businesses and institutions that lack curatorial facilities. Concern about compromising archaeological interests in favor of client interests is reflected in the Standards of Research Performance. "While contractual obligations in reporting must be respected, archeologists should not enter into a contract which prohibits the archeologist from including her or his own interpretation or conclusions in the contractual reports, or from a continuing right to use the data after the completion of the project" (SOPA 1997:VI.6.4).

SOPA served as the primary voice for ethics in archaeology for twenty years. It adopted its Grievance Procedure to enforce adherence of its members to the Code of Ethics and Standards of Research Performance. Using formal "Disciplinary Procedures," a grievance coordinator directed investigations of alleged misconduct. After all relevant facts were collected, the case was brought before the Standards Board, whose members were elected by the SOPA membership. If an alleged misconduct was upheld, the accused could be admonished, censured, suspended, or expelled. Throughout its existence, SOPA was the only archaeological organization in the U.S. that enforced its ethical standards by a disciplinary process. In addition to enforcing ethical behavior and good conduct, SOPA maintained a dialog on ethical issues through its newsletter, symposia at conferences, and publication of a collection of papers on ethical issues (Woodall 1990).

During the 1980s, two ethical concerns outside the mainstream of CRM began to emerge for archaeology. Indigenous people around the world became more vocal about having a voice in the study of their archaeological past, and they became insistent that they have control over the treatment of the graves and human remains of their ancestors. This increase in activism among native peoples began with the civil rights movement and gained momentum in the 1970s and 1980s. Their activism coincided with an increase in looting and vandalism of archaeological sites, which could be traced to an increased demand from the art market for archaeological objects from all over the world. The combination of these two issues stimulated the SAA to begin a discussion about ethics that has led to the development of its current ethics policy.

The relationship of archaeology to indigenous people has often been strained over the question, "Who owns the past?" Although the SOPA Code of Ethics and

Standards of Research Performance indicated that archaeologists have a responsibility to be sensitive to the "legitimate concerns of groups whose culture histories are the subject of archeological investigations," this principle was not widely discussed prior to the passage of the Native American Graves Protection and Repatriation Act (NAGPRA) of 1990. Prior to 1990, many states had passed legislation designed to protect unmarked graves from unauthorized excavation or disturbance; some states had even passed laws to repatriate human remains and associated funerary remains to tribes (Peregoy 1992); however, few members of the fast-growing archaeological community had seriously considered this issue. Consequently, NAGPRA came as a surprise to many archaeologists, who viewed the new law as antiscience and a threat to their access to the archaeological record (e.g., Clark 1996; Mason 1997). Although there are many examples of cooperation between archaeologists and indigenous peoples (Bruseth et al. 1994; Knecht 1994; Mills 1996), most archaeologists had not really considered the ethical implications of archaeological activities and ownership of the past.

Today, debate about ownership and control of the past is an international discussion. Archaeologists working where indigenous peoples still reside increasingly face demands that indigenous people have some voice in the study and interpretation of the archaeological record. This demand is most clearly articulated in the World Archaeological Congress (WAC) Code of Ethics (see the appendix), which consists of eight "Principles to Abide By" and seven "Rules to Adhere To" (Zimmerman and Bruguier 1994) and clearly reflects the view of indigenous peoples that they own the intellectual property rights to their past. The WAC Code of Ethics is markedly different from the SOPA Code of Ethics and Standards of Research Performance and reflects the differing views of the groups that developed them (see Claire Smith and Heather Burke, chapter 14). As this debate continues even today, we can only hope that it will result in more productive cooperation among all groups with an interest in the past (Goldstein 1992).

At the same time that discussion emerged about indigenous rights, the issue of ownership of the archaeological record was addressed by archaeologists in regard to looting of sites. Archaeologists from a variety of backgrounds were critical of colleagues employed by salvors who engaged in the excavation of sunken ships. The pirate ship *Whydah* received considerable attention (Carrell 1990; Elia 1992; Lees 1985). Although excavation of the *Whydah* was conducted with proper permits (Hamilton 1990; King 1985), it was feared that the collections resulting from the excavation would be sold or dispersed to benefit investors in the venture. While the ethics of collaborating with treasure salvors drew attention from archaeologists with an interest in submerged sites, a broader threat was the looting of terrestrial sites around the world.

Archaeologists working in many areas of the world found that the archaeological record was being destroyed by looters intent on recovering artifacts that could be sold to collectors through the international market. From the Mississippi

Valley and the American Southwest to the Mayan areas of Central America, looters in search of saleable objects were devastating sites (Harrington 1991; Hutt, Jones, and McAllister 1992; Pendergast 1991; Smith and Ehrenhard 1991; Vitelli 1984). Similar scenes of devastation were recorded in Southeast Asia, the Middle East, and even Europe (Brodie, Doole, and Renfrew 2001; Renfrew 2000; Tubb 1995). The worldwide nature of this problem led archaeologists to seek protection for the archaeological record through international agreements (Elia 1993; Hingston 1989), but these have hardly slowed the looting of sites and the traffic in illegal antiquities.

Within this environment, the respected journal *Science* published a story questioning the appropriateness of Christopher B. Donnan's use of looted Moche material in a *National Geographic* story (Alexander 1990). This launched a major debate about the ethics of incorporating looted data in archaeological research. In response to this debate, the editors of *Latin American Antiquity* and *American Antiquity* adopted policies that prohibit publication of papers that rely on looted data. These policies followed a precedent already established by the *American Journal of Archaeology* (Kleiner 1990). The SAA Executive Board recognized that these developments moved well beyond the published ethics statement for the society (Champe et al. 1961) and appointed a task force to update the ethics policy.

In an effort to identify the scope of the issues that needed to be addressed, the SAA Ethics Task Force organized a workshop in Reno, Nevada, in November 1993. The workshop was sponsored by the National Science Foundation, the National Park Service, and the Cultural Resource Policy Institute at the University of Nevada, Reno. Eighteen participants from a diverse range of backgrounds attended. The goal of the workshop was to generate a list of critical issues that should be addressed by the new ethics policy. After two and a half days of intense and sometimes heated discussions, the workshop participants went beyond the goal of identifying critical issues and actually generated a preliminary set of principles of archaeological ethics.

The foundation of these draft principles was the concept of stewardship of the archaeological record and the belief that preservation of archaeological resources was in the best interest of archaeology and the public. Consequently, stewardship became the first draft principle, and a commitment to the conservation ethic was at the heart of the other five draft principles. These included accountability, commercialization, public education and outreach, intellectual property, and record preservation. The draft principles were presented at a sponsored forum at the Fifty-Ninth Annual Meeting of the SAA in Anaheim, California, in April 1994.

Papers from the sponsored forum, along with a number of background papers, were published by the SAA as a special report (Lynott and Wylie 1995b). The special report was sent to all SAA members and to a wide variety of other interested individuals and groups in hopes of stimulating comments and discussion about the draft principles. In addition to the publication, members of the Ethics Task Force made presentations at regional and national meetings requesting written and verbal comments. This process was extremely productive and resulted in refinement of the six draft principles and the drafting of two additional principles. A more detailed discussion of the intent and development of the Principles of Archaeological Ethics is available from Mark J. Lynott (1997), Lynott and Alison Wylie (1995a), and Wylie (1995a, 1996).

The SAA Executive Board accepted the eight "Principles of Archaeological Ethics" in March 1996 (Kintigh 1996). The principles were not intended to be the final word on archaeological ethics, and the Ethics Task Force recommended that the Executive Board appoint a standing ethics committee to promote discussion and education about archaeological ethics. The Ethics Task Force very clearly discouraged the Executive Board from empowering the committee with enforcement responsibilities relating to the Principles of Archaeological Ethics.

While the Principles of Archaeological Ethics were being developed, SOPA and the SAA initiated discussions about the possibility of creating a registry of professional archaeologists (McGimsey 1995). These discussions eventually included representatives from the SAA, SOPA, the Society for Historical Archaeology (SHA), and the AIA. After careful discussion and negotiation, the Register of Professional Archaeologists (RPA) was established with support from SOPA, SAA, SHA, and AIA. SOPA members were automatically accepted as charter members of the RPA. The new organization adopted the old SOPA Code of Ethics and Standards of Research Performance as the basis for its Code of Conduct and Standards of Research Performance. The RPA also adopted the general Grievance Procedure that had operated effectively for SOPA for more than twenty years. All of the sponsoring organizations encouraged their membership to join the RPA, and the new organization experienced an immediate growth in membership above the old levels maintained by SOPA (see Hester A. Davis, chapter 19).

Until recently, archaeological ethics have not been a part of formal archaeological training, or even a routine topic for discussion among professionals. With the growth of the archaeological profession and the employment of archaeologists in a wide range of nontraditional jobs, the need for training in ethics is becoming acute. In response, universities are starting to incorporate ethics into archaeology curricula and books about ethics are being published (e.g., Lynott and Wylie 2000; Pluciennik 2001; Renfrew 2000; Vitelli 1996b).

Ethics are guidelines to assist professionals in meeting the specialized goals of their profession within the more complex circumstances of the greater society in which they live and work. The earliest archaeological ethics dealt with issues of site preservation, scientific study, and proper reporting of research results. While these ethical requirements are still valid today, a wide range of additional issues must also be addressed. The vast amount of public money that supports archaeology in the United States and around the world comes with responsibilities, and these are reflected in contemporary ethics. The ethical principles that archaeologists have chosen to follow are intended to help them navigate through the increasingly complex situations associated with their professional lives. This was true for archaeologists 100 years ago, and, though the specific concerns are likely to change again, it will be true for archaeologists 100 years in the future.

Discussion Questions

1. How have issues and social change from outside of archaeology affected the development of ethics in archaeology?
2. What role has government played in the development and definition of ethics in archaeology? What are the foundations of government interest and sense of responsibility toward the archaeological record?
3. What explains the interest on the part of descendant communities and indigenous peoples in archaeology? Why is the recognition of these interests a recent phenomenon in archaeology, and what are some of the issues that emerge?
4. How have nonarchaeologists influenced the practice of archaeology?
5. How have archaeological ethics changed and why? What further changes do you anticipate in the coming decades?

Recommended Readings

Brew, J. O.
    1961   Emergency Archaeology: Salvage in Advance of Technological Progress. *Proceedings of the American Philosophical Society* 105(1):1–10.
    An overview of the development and operation of the Interagency Archeological Salvage Program and other reservoir salvage programs.

Lynott, Mark J.
    1997   Ethical Principles and Archaeological Practice: Development of an Ethics Policy. *American Antiquity* 62(4):589–99.
    Explains the process that led to the development of the SAA Principles of Archaeological Ethics.

Lynott, Mark J., and Alison Wylie (editors)
    2000   *Ethics in American Archaeology.* 2nd ed. Society for American Archaeology, Washington, DC.
    A collection of papers about contemporary ethical issues and the development of an ethics policy by the SAA.

McGimsey, Charles R., III
     1995   Standards, Ethics, and Archaeology: A Brief History. In *Ethics in American
             Archaeology: Challenges for the 1990s,* edited by M. J. Lynott and A. Wylie,
             11–13. Special Report. Society for American Archaeology, Washington, DC.
     Discusses the debate about ethics within the SAA that led to the formation of SOPA.

Pluciennik, Mark (editor)
     2001   *The Responsibilities of Archaeologists: Archaeology and Ethics.* BAR
             International Series 981, Lampeter Workshop in Archaeology no. 4.
             Archaeopress, Oxford.
     A collection of papers from a seminar that addressed archaeology, its ethical develop-
ment, and its consequences as a cultural production from theoretical, intellectual, and practical perspectives.

Thompson, Raymond H.
     2000   Edgar Lee Hewett and the Political Process. *Journal of the Southwest*
             42(2):271–318.
     A historical overview of the development of the Antiquities Act and the early move-
ment to preserve the archaeological record in the United States.

PART II

Responsibilities to the Archaeological Record

NEIL BRODIE
DAVID GILL

Chapter Three

Looting: An International View

The rapacious acquisition of antiquities can be traced back for millennia. The Persian looting of Athens after its fall in 480 BC led to the forced removal of a pair of statues known as the "Tyrant Slayers" from the main public square (agora) of the city to Persia. They were later "repatriated" when the Persian Empire collapsed in the wake of the conquests of Alexander the Great. The incorporation of Greek lands into the Roman Empire during the mid-second century BC created a taste for Greek art. The sections of the Elder Pliny's *Natural History* that deal with Greek sculpture and painting list work after work on display in the city of Rome in the mid-first century AD. The rediscovery of "Greek art"—in reality Roman copies of Greek originals—by J. Winckelmann brought a desire by European elites to decorate their homes with sculptures acquired on their "Grand Tours" of classical sites in Italy.

With the rise of the great European museum collections in the nineteenth century, expeditions were arranged to augment holdings. Cultural imperialism started to impact archaeological sites as whole (or near whole) sculptural groups from buildings were acquired: the frieze, metopes, and the pediments from the Parthenon by the British Museum (Howland 2000); and the Great Altar of Zeus for display in the Pergamon Museum in Berlin (Marchand 1996:94–96). With the growing professionalism of archaeology in the nineteenth century, there was an increasing emphasis on the creation of national archaeological museums that reflected the cultural roots of modern nation-states. In the New World, the National Museum of Mexico was established in 1825. In the Mediterranean, new museums in Constantinople (serving the Ottoman empire) and Athens took shape during the 1860s.

The creation of additional museums during the twentieth century, as well as the activities of wealthy private collectors, created a new market for antiquities (Chippindale and Gill 2000; Dyson 1998:273–81; Messenger 1999). Many of the major acquisitions of the nineteenth century came from known sites and even named buildings—for example, the temple of Apollo at Bassai (Phigaleia) in Peloponnese, Greece, now in the British Museum (Jenkins 1992:78–80). This is in marked contrast to twentieth- (and now twenty-first-) century acquisitions, which are largely provided by clandestine digging of hitherto unknown or unexcavated sites, thereby losing find-spots and archaeological context.

Tastes have grown more catholic too, as developments in contemporary art have encouraged collectors to look again at the previously disparaged material of Africa, Oceania, and the Americas.

The Business of Selling Antiquities

In 1972, the Metropolitan Museum of Art in New York acquired an Athenian red-figured wine-mixing bowl. The pot, bearing the "signatures" of the "artist" Euphronios and the potter Euxitheos, was decorated with the Homeric scene of the dead Sarpedon being lifted from the field of Troy by personifications of death and sleep (Meyer 1977). This acquisition was rare "art": a "signed" piece with a price tag to match: $1 million. The acquisition was not without controversy: It is still not clear where this object was found. In spite of claims that it arrived via Lebanon, it would be unlikely (but not totally impossible) that it had been buried there in antiquity. It is far more likely to have been removed illegally from an Etruscan tomb in Tuscany and smuggled out of Italy (Dyson 1998:277–78).

Prices like this for antiquities, though perhaps modest when compared with French Impressionist paintings, help to raise the profile of the value of antiquities. Antiquities have always been sold. Auction houses like Christie's and Sotheby's in London have dispersed private collections of antiquities since at least the nineteenth century (Herrmann 1980). However, since World War II the value of antiquities has risen, and the number of objects available from "old collections" that left their country of origin before World War I has diminished (Chippindale et al. 2001). New sources of antiquities had to be found and unexcavated or partially excavated archaeological sites became a potential source of income. Etruscan cemeteries containing large quantities of intact, high-quality, figure-decorated Greek pottery have become particular targets for looting.

More recent phenomena are investment portfolios of antiquities, where ancient artifacts have been purchased with the expectation that they will increase in value over time. At the end of a set period, the antiquities are sold, and their value realized. The collectors invest without any real knowledge of the antiquities, or for that matter any appreciation of the ethical aspects, as all they are interested in is what they hope will be a good return for their investment. A recent example of such a portfolio was the "Athena Fund II." Items included a Roman "Swiss army knife" that surfaced via a Swiss antiquities dealer and passed through an auction at Christie's

(July 16, 1986, lot 121), before finding its present resting place in a major British collection (Sherlock 1988; Vassilika 1998:128–29, no. 62). The most celebrated recent case of "investment antiquities" was the so-called Dekadrachm (or Elmali) hoard of around 1,700 coins that had been discovered in Turkey in the early 1980s, removed to Germany illegally, and acquired for around $3.2 million as an investment for a group of individuals (Meier 1998). The hoard was reported to have been "authenticated" by a curator at the Museum of Fine Arts in Boston (1998). This investment was ill-founded when William I. Koch and his associates brought the court action to a conclusion by returning the coins to Turkey a week before the trial was due to begin (Meier 1998, 1999; Spiegler and Kaye 2001:122).

The need to hold regular sales at Sotheby's and Christie's—the norm has been a summer and winter sale of antiquities by both companies—means that they have had to find a regular source for antiquities. A study of sale patterns for these two auction houses—and they are two of many that have operated in London since World War II—over a forty-year period from 1958 to 1998 shows that just under 90 percent of the antiquities sampled became known for the first time when they appeared in a sales catalog (Chippindale et al. 2001:19). The 10 percent of objects with some known history often came from the dispersal of antiquities from named collections; the 90 percent often lurked behind the anonymity of the labels "property of a lady" or "property of a Belgian gentleman." It is striking that only between 1 and 2 percent of the objects can be traced from the moment that they emerged from the ground to the sale. Even general archaeological information is lacking: some 95 percent of the antiquities in the sample have no archaeological information whatsoever. In other words, the regular flood of antiquities onto the market since World War II must be linked to the destruction of perhaps hundreds of thousands of archaeological contexts and sites.

It is often claimed that these antiquities have been recycled from old collections, lying around in attics and Swiss lakeside residences for 100 years or more (see Chippindale and Gill 2000:491–92). Although this is patently true in some cases, exposés in the mid-1990s have changed the perception of the way the antiquities market works. In 1991, Peter Watson, a British journalist, was offered a series of papers by a former employee of the antiquities department at Sotheby's in London (Watson 1997). The documentation revealed the way that consignments of antiquities, especially from Italy, were received on a regular basis from what appeared to be less than secure sources. Undercover work in India exposed similar patterns of looting to feed the London salerooms (1997).

As Watson's book was going to press in early 1997, a major raid on a series of warehouses in the Geneva Freeport seized some 10,000 antiquities carrying Sotheby's labels that seemed to have been removed from archaeological contexts in Italy (Brodie, Doole, and Watson 2000:26–27). At the same time, a key middleman was arrested in Italy. These revelations led to Sotheby's closing its sales of antiquities in London and moving them to New York.

The Sotheby's "scandal" left the London antiquities dealers tarnished, and several more were identified as handling looted British antiquities from the so-called Salisbury hoard when a deposit of some 500 items from an alleged British Iron Age sanctuary was broken up on the market (Stead 1998; see also Renfrew 2000:85–89). The key thing to note is that these antiquities were still handled in spite of the auction houses and dealers supposedly following "codes of practice" (Renfrew 2000:89).

Although London may now be less important for the sale of antiquities, Sotheby's has merely shifted sales from Britain onto the Internet via its North American operations (Chippindale and Gill 2001). It now has associate dealers who offer antiquities through the Sothebys.com website. Material without history or archaeological information is being offered, seemingly without much check, on an international basis.

The International Perspective

Outside the auction houses, the antiquities trade thrives in a world of exclusive salerooms and international fairs. Cultura, the largest annual antiquities fair in the world, was established in Basel, Switzerland, in 1999. In 2000, it had 73 exhibitors and 12,000 visitors, but prices were not cheap. One U.S. dealer had 130 gold objects of the pre-Colombian Sinu culture (Colombia) on sale for $3.5 million. A particular growth area in the 1990s was "Asian art," when spolia from the Hindu and Buddhist palaces and temples of Asia began to circulate more widely. Annual Asian art weeks are now held in New York and London, when dealers, auction houses, and museums combine to present a festival of sales, exhibitions, lectures, and receptions. These are not aimed at the casual passer-by. At the gala dinner of the November 2001 London week, held in Kensington Palace in the presence of Richard Winsor, the duke of Gloucester, customers were offered the chance to rub shoulders with royalty at a cost of £400 each (in aid of the queen's Gallery Restoration Project).

This is a scandalous situation. Poverty-stricken villagers in many parts of Asia are forced to sell off their local archaeology in order to survive, but receive in exchange only a small fraction of its true worth. For them, £400 is an impossibly large sum of money. Those attending the London dinner—collectors of Asian art—wanted to be seen as part of a self-regarding cultural elite, and their consciences were eased by the assurance that their money would be used for a good cause—the queen's gallery. Yet, they could have done far more for the world's heritage by donating the price of their ticket to one of the many aid agencies operating in Asia that are in more urgent need of support than the queen's gallery.

Looting: The Scale of the Problem

Behind the glitz of the auction rooms, the sale catalogs, the Manhattan galleries, and multimedia websites lies the reality of archaeological sites torn apart in the hunt for saleable objects. Carefully stratified archaeological material loses its context and spatial dimensions forever. A sculpture displayed in a salesroom's beautifully lit showcase does not carry inherent information about its date, origin, or use, information that would have been supplied by scientific excavation. The single pot in a similar setting has also lost the evidence of its context. Its find-spot alone might have told if it was made locally or traded over a long distance. If it were known what was found with it, then more of the story would have been forthcoming. If it were found in a burial for instance, it might have cast light on beliefs about the afterlife or ways in which age and gender groups were constituted. If the pot had been carefully excavated, then scientific analysis of its contents may have allowed the identification of ancient foodstuffs or trade goods. Thus, a properly excavated and investigated pot can provide a wealth of information about ancient economies and cultural practices. This information has been forcibly stripped from the pot without context in the saleroom showcase, which remains only as a sop to contemporary notions of beauty and value, and everyone is the poorer for it.

The scale of the problem can be illustrated by a series of case studies.

The Cyclades

Marble figures from the Cycladic islands of the southern Aegean have been collected since the nineteenth century (Fitton 1995). Their simple forms were initially seen as crude, but sculptors such as Constantin Brancuşi and Henry Moore found inspiration in them. Small collections of figures, found in excavations, had been formed in Greece, and small numbers had been acquired by other European collections, often as the result of archaeological or ethnographic fieldwork in the Greek islands (Fitton 1995; Sherratt 2000).

After World War II, Cycladic figures became highly collectible. As a result, the Early Bronze Age cemeteries of the Cycladic islands were systematically turned over in the search for figures. Of the known corpus of 1,600 figures, only some 10 percent come from relatively secure archaeological contexts. The number of marble figures from graves within excavated cemeteries suggests that something like 12,000 graves have been opened in the hunt for these figures, a percentage that would imply that the funerary record of the Cyclades in the Early Bronze Age has been virtually destroyed by the hunt of one category of artifact (Gill and Chippindale 1993).

The damage to the Cycladic archaeological record is all too plain to see when walking round the beautifully displayed N. P. Goulandris Museum of Cycladic Art in Athens (Doumas 2000). Few figures in what is probably the most important collection of Cycladic artifacts have any sort of information about find-spot. The stunning monumental marble female figure, 1.40 meters high from head to toe, has no secure context (2000:154–55, no. 222); we do not know if it was some sort of early cult figure or a funerary object, and there are no large-scale parallels from secure archaeological contexts. Indeed, we cannot even be sure that it is genuine, for scientific dating techniques cannot be applied. "Unique" pieces may have their appeal to collectors (and also to dealers who can attach a more demanding price tag), but they are all but worthless to archaeologists unless they have their context. The same ambiguity of function is found with the numerous fragments of marble figures alleged to have been found on Keros that the Goulandris Museum "saved" when the Swiss Erlenmeyer collection was dispersed by auction through Sotheby's (2000:30, 168–87, nos. 243–319). Although it has been suggested that the fragments come from some sort of cult site, the evidence has been completely lost.

Tuscany

The Etruscan cemeteries of Tuscany have long been a target for unscientific excavations, as one of the major sources of Athenian figure-decorated pottery. One of the reasons is that the funerary chambers cut from the volcanic tufa have allowed the near-perfect preservation of the objects.

These Etruscan cemeteries, frequented by early tomb robbers (*tombaroli*), have been the source for many of the nineteenth-century collections of Athenian pottery. These cemeteries are now targeted by specialized gangs of *tombaroli* (see Bahn 1996:366–67 [ill.]). Pots acquired by such unscientific methods are highly desired by museums and collectors, yet their archaeological value is limited. The quantification of the find-spots of Athenian pots attributed to an anonymous personality known as "the Berlin painter" shows that only some 13 percent of the corpus come from a named find-spot (though rarely from a specific scientifically excavated grave), and some 50 percent have no recorded find-spot at all. This makes it difficult to make informed comments about the distribution of this category of figure-decorated pottery around the Mediterranean. Ancient patterns of trade and exchange for Athenian figure-decorated pottery are surely distorted and corrupted by those providing disinformation about find-spots.

Southern Italy

During the Sotheby's investigation, Watson (1997) visited southern Italy with a film crew. He was able to catch teams of diggers on camera using mechanical diggers to remove topsoil so that the chamber-tombs of Greek colonists could be entered and the highly decorated pottery removed, presumably for sale on the international market.

Ricardo J. Elia (2001) has made a study of this category of material. The corpus of Apulian pots stands at around 13,600 pieces. Although most will have been buried (and found) in Apulia, Italy, a staggering 88.4 percent of the corpus has no recorded find-spot, and only a mere 5.5 percent of the pieces come from an archaeological excavation. As in south Asia, the economic status of those involved in the looting is low and contrasts with the large sums derived from the sale of this category of antiquities.

Andean Gold

In 1992, a tractor fell into a collapsed tomb at Hacienda Malagana, just outside the town of Palmira, Colombia. The tomb contained gold, and in the weeks that followed somewhere around 160 kilograms were removed from the surrounding cemetery by more than 5,000 people. One person was murdered. It is thought that the large majority of tombs destroyed—numbering in the hundreds—did not contain gold, and only a small part of their total contents survived the frenzy. In fact, most information was obtained from the rescue excavations that followed (Bray 2000:94–95).

For collector George Ortiz, the gold from the Malagana cemetery was a "chance find," which he defines as an object "discovered as the consequence of general human activity," to be clearly differentiated from illicit digging, which is "the deliberate act of searching for remains of the past that are underground" (2001). He has some of this gold in his collection (Ortiz 1994:no. 267 bis), from the named find-spot of "El Bolo, Cauca Valley (Colombia)," although the associated entry makes no mention of the associated destruction. Nevertheless, he is clearly aware of its source. The market, he claims, has rescued it (Ortiz 1998:57).

It is well to remember, though, that rescued gold might not be everything it seems. The site of Batan Grande in north Peru, which includes the remains of twenty mud brick pyramids and extensive cemeteries, has been mined for its gold artifacts since the 1960s. Today, it boasts 100,000 looters' pits spread over a 50-square-kilometer area, including hundreds of trenches dug by mechanical diggers (Alva 2001:89–91; Toner 1999). It is estimated that approximately 90 percent of all archaeological gold attributed to ancient Peru in collections worldwide might come from this site (Alva 2001:91), although none of it is properly contextualized. A large part is thought to have ended up in the Museo del Oro, a private museum in Lima that holds something like 10,000 pre-Colombian gold artifacts, all with poor to nonexistent documentation (Toner 1999). The material was obtained (saved!) from looters—or so it was thought until recently. In late 2001, a scandal broke when a government-backed enquiry reported that many, if not most, of the metal pieces examined were recent fakes. Some were probably made from melted-down artifacts while others were made from modern gold (Chueca 2001).

The large quantities of (presumed) pre-Colombian gold now in collections around the world have done very little to advance our understanding of early Andean culture and society. Far more has been learned from the systematic study of the combinations in which gold objects are found with other materials in excavated assemblages—in other words, from the study of gold in context.

Afghanistan

In 1988, the Soviet Union withdrew its troops from Afghanistan, and by 1996 it was reported that 70 percent of the capital city Kabul's museum holdings had disappeared (Dupree 1996:42). At the same time, the country's rich archaeological heritage was being looted, while Gandharan sculpture from the area began to appear in the salerooms of London and New York (see also Chippindale and Gill 2000:483–84; Ali and Coningham 2001). It was reported that the profits from sales were being used by the various factional warlords to help keep their troops in the field (McGirk 1996). Yet, there was worse to come, and it soon arrived in the shape of the Taliban, who in March 2001 ordered the destruction of all religious idols. The famous giant stone Buddhas of the Bamiyan Valley were blown up and more destruction was visited on what was left of the Kabul museum collection.

This final Taliban-inspired iconoclasm has been used by some to justify Western collecting: if looted material had not been bought by wealthy collectors and museums, it would have been destroyed. Now, however, the Afghan heritage has been saved. But there are counterarguments. In the first place, many archaeological sites in Afghanistan would have remained untouched if there had been no market for their contents, Taliban or no Taliban. And again, there is the problem of fakes. The corpus of Gandharan sculpture has in all likelihood now been badly adulterated. Finally, the morality of buying archaeological material when the proceeds go to support an armed struggle—a struggle that touched the international community through the barbaric acts of September 11, 2001—must surely be questioned.

Professional Involvement

As the antiquities market has expanded, archaeologists have become increasingly embroiled in its activities. They have found themselves asked to identify or authenticate pieces, or to write catalog entries for exhibitions that are comprised in whole or in part of material, presumably looted, lacking a specific find-spot (see Meier 1998). Sometimes, specialists find themselves in the invidious position of having to authenticate material of dubious origin that is held privately before being allowed to study it. The dilemma of ignoring or including material that is relevant to a research project but of questionable provenance is one that now regularly faces archaeologists.

Some professionals sell their expertise on the market. They range from the materials scientist who examines metal artifacts for anachronistic alloys to the traditional connoisseur, whose experienced "eye" can, in theory, distinguish the genuine article from the fake. These experts provide the professionally validated knowledge that (it is claimed) keeps the market free from fakes and stolen artifacts. Their expertise acts to underpin the market and thus sustains the looting, but some use the money obtained from providing a commercial service to support academic research for which there would be no other source of funding. Can this be justified?

The ethical problems that such commercialization entails were thrown into sharp relief by *The African King*. This 1990 television documentary exposed the trade in looted Malian terra-cottas and highlighted the role played by Oxford University's Research Laboratory for Archaeology and the History of Art, whose thermoluminescence laboratory routinely authenticated material (McIntosh 1996:57–58). The program outraged the academic community, and the laboratory has now stopped offering a commercial authentication service. Happily, it has found that there is still life after the market.

In the past, such standards of behavior were accepted, or tolerated at least, perhaps because the market was thought to "save" the occasional object for posterity. Today, however, professional organizations deplore the destructive effects of commercial involvement and have developed codes of ethics or practice in an attempt to keep the market and professions apart.

But the effect that professional archaeologists may exert on the market goes beyond direct authentication or identification, as the study and publication of unprovenanced material will in itself provide a provenance of sorts, an academic pedigree. Once material is accepted into the validated corpus, its academic significance might translate into monetary value and provide a spur for further looting to find similar objects.

One response of the archaeological community has been to stop study and publication of material that has no verifiable provenance. The academic journals *American Journal of Archaeology* in 1978 and *American Antiquity* and *Latin American Antiquity* in 1991 decided to stop publication of papers that deal with looted or illegally exported material. Other journals followed suit. *Archaeological Reports* stopped the publication of a "Museum supplement" alongside reports of recent archaeological work in Greece, although the supplement now appears in the sister *Journal of Hellenic Studies*. However, archaeological opinion is divided on the effectiveness of this tactic (Wylie 1995a). In the first place, the publication of artifacts obtained through properly recorded excavation may also increase the monetary value of comparable looted pieces. As a corpus of material becomes better characterized, and more recognizable (and harder to fake), it is more likely to be awarded what is in this context the dubious accolade of "art," and to enter the commercial world of exhibitions and glossy catalogs. It is, in effect, commodified. Yet, it has also been argued, in apparent contradiction, that publication of looted objects in the academic literature actually has little effect on the market as it is not widely read.

Sometimes, it appears that an artifact may have an intrinsic importance that warrants its study and publication, even out of context, for the increase in knowledge that might accrue. If a modern-day Rosetta Stone appeared on the market, for example, would any right-minded individual consign it to some black market oblivion? It is always difficult to know where to draw the line. Consider, for instance, Classic Maya polychrome painted pottery. This has been very badly looted from the 1960s onwards, and most is now in Western collections, without provenance, yet some experts maintain that the study of its iconography and short glyphic texts is still valuable (see also Gilgan 2001). Others disagree by arguing that any knowledge gained through study is outweighed by the greater loss that future looting will cause.

The ethical responsibilities of archaeologists also extend to fieldwork. It is clear—in the developing world at least—that archaeological sites and monuments provide a ready (albeit unsustainable) source of income for the often hard-pressed local inhabitants. To stop the looting, it is necessary to turn these sites into something other than short-term economic resources. With this in mind, wherever possible, archaeologists should endeavour to employ, or at least involve, local people in their projects. They should also take time to explain their work and to investigate ways in which their sites may be developed into educational resources or tourist attractions. Experience has shown that when archaeological sites are seen to offer more than short-term gain they become something to curate, not exploit. Unfortunately, at the present time, public agencies in Europe and North America are not usually prepared to support this type of work, which is not considered to be research, and there is often a professional resistance to being involved in time-consuming activities that offer little academic reward.

Private Collectors and Public Bodies

Many museums now recognize that it is unethical to acquire objects that have no history. However, the situation is different when it comes to the temporary loan of antiquities from private collections. The antiquities concerned are not acquisitions; their place in the museum is temporary. But by accepting on loan antiquities that they would not ethically acquire permanently, they still add legitimacy, prestige, and "history" to the object—and legitimacy has commercial value when it comes to resale.

During the 1990s, there was a series of high-profile exhibitions in North America and in Britain of antiquities from private collections (see Chippindale and

Gill 2000). In Britain, London's Royal Academy of Arts allowed the collection of antiquities owned by Ortiz to be put on display (Ortiz 1994). Though some items did indeed come from old European collections, other items appeared to have no such distinguished pedigrees. Another British museum allowed a collection of Gandharan antiquities to be displayed (Errington and Cribb 1992). The actual owner of the collection was never identified by more than the mysterious initials "A. I. C."; it was as if the museum wished to give an indication that the collection was suspicious.

The display of antiquities from the Shelby White and Leon Levy collection in a major North American museum highlights another issue (von Bothmer 1990). The antiquities in their collection do not come from named find-spots: 93 percent have no indication of source whatsoever (Chippindale and Gill 2000:472, table 1). Moreover, 84 percent of the antiquities in the exhibition "surfaced" after 1974 (473, table 2). Yet, when Karen D. Vitelli pointed out the tension between White and Levy as collectors and as benefactors of archaeological publications (through the Shelby White–Leon Levy Publications Program), the response was both vicious and personal (Shanks 1999). The integrity of benefactors who could be seen as wishing to silence criticism through the financing of excavations and their publication was brought into question.

Conclusion

Damage to the archaeological record across the world is increasing (Brodie, Doole, and Renfrew 2001). This is a finite resource that can never be replaced. Main players in the looting, sale, and collecting of antiquities need to recognize the damage and loss of scientific knowledge that is occurring. Codes of practice for auction houses and dealers in antiquities do not seem to work (and there is a suspicion that they are deliberately ignored). The problem of legislation in what is now an international issue, freed from control by the increasing use of the Internet, requires a change of approach. The intellectual consequences of continued looting have yet to be assessed, but it is guaranteed that the loss of archaeological context is a loss of scientific knowledge.

Discussion Questions

1. In an article examining the ancient function of a particular category of artifact, your argument rests heavily on depictions of the artifact in use on several ancient pots that are in a private collection. The editors of the *American Journal of Archaeology*, to which you submitted the paper, tell you

they cannot publish the article unless you can provide information to demonstrate that it does not violate their policy on nonpublication of undocumented antiquities. What information do you need to provide? Is the journal's policy fair? Would you be able to publish the same article, without changes, in another archaeological journal (e.g., assuming the subject matter is appropriate, *American Antiquity, Antiquity,* or another journal)? If you could, would you?

2. What are the costs to scholarship (what Gill and Chippindale [1993] call the "intellectual consequences") of not studying and publishing objects that were illegally excavated? Of studying them?

3. A small but well-regarded university museum has invited you to curate an exhibit on some of its ancient objects that are usually not on view. You know that a good many of these items have no reliable archaeological context. Should you accept the invitation? Only under certain conditions? What issues do you consider in making your decision and what are the likely consequences of accepting? Of declining?

4. Jason M. LaBelle (chapter 9) suggests that all antiquities collectors are not "the same." Are all antiquities dealers alike in their practices? Does it matter? Are there "good" and "bad" dealers?

5. White and Levy are significant collectors of classical antiquities. They have also created a foundation that provides grants toward publication expenses of material from "older excavations." Would you apply to and accept funding from that foundation? Why or why not? Are there other sources of funding for archaeological work that you think raise ethical concerns for potential recipients? (See also Brian Fagan and Mark Rose, chapter 13.)

6. Some have suggested that we might contain the destruction of sites to satisfy the antiquities market by creating a legal market. The suggestions for doing so are variations on the idea of having every nation designate some sites to be excavated specifically to supply that market. The excavations would be funded by dealers, supervised by archaeologists who could record all the information they need, and could employ local people for the physical labor. The dealers would be permitted to sell the finds for whatever profit they could gain. This legal market in provenienced objects would, they argue, satisfy everyone—illicit digging would no longer be necessary on other sites, the "poor peasants" would have jobs, and even the pieces that were legally traded would have the contextual information archaeologists insist is necessary. What do you think?

If you doubt the effectiveness of such "legal supply" proposals and acknowledge that national and international laws are not stemming the tide, what alternatives can you suggest that might truly make a difference?

7. An archaeological site in a developing country is very promising as a potential tourist attraction that could provide much needed income for the locals, but conservation and development of the site and the necessary infrastructure for tourism would be time-consuming and expensive. Who should take on the job and the expenses? Do the (foreign) archaeologists have any obligation to do so?

Note

The research for this chapter has benefited from the advice and comments from, among others, Kevin Butcher, Christopher Chippindale, Jenny Doole, Jim Mintz, Colin Renfrew, and Karen D. Vitelli.

Recommended Readings

Brodie, Neil, Jennifer Doole, and Colin Renfrew (editors)
    2001   *Trade in Illicit Antiquities: The Destruction of the World's Archaeological Heritage.* McDonald Institute Monographs. McDonald Institute, Cambridge.

Chippindale, Christopher, and David W. J. Gill
    2000   Material Consequences of Contemporary Classical Collecting. *American Journal of Archaeology* 104(3):463–511.
    2002   Looting Matters! The Material and Intellectual Consequences of Collecting Antiquities, at www.swan.ac.uk/classics/staff/dg/looting (accessed April 2002).

Cranwell, Andrew
    1999   The Price of Age: An Investigation into the Illicit Trade of Antiquities. Dissertation, at www.museum-security.org/cranwell accessed (June 2002).

Gill, David W. J., and Christopher Chippindale
    1993   Material and Intellectual Consequences of Esteem for Cycladic Figures. *American Journal of Archaeology* 97:601–59.

Illicit Antiquities Research Centre at the McDonald Institute
    2002   at www.mcdonald.cam.ac.uk/IARC/home.htm (accessed December 2002).

Messenger, Phyllis Mauch (editor)
    1999   *The Ethics of Collecting Cultural Property: Whose Culture? Whose Property?* 2nd ed. University of New Mexico Press, Albuquerque.

O'Keefe, Patrick J.
    1997   *Trade in Antiquities: Reducing Destruction and Theft.* Archetype, UN Educational, Scientific, and Cultural Organization, London.

Renfrew, Colin
    2000   *Loot, Legitimacy and Ownership: The Ethical Crisis in Archaeology.*
            Duckworth, London.
Tubb, Kathryn W. (editor)
    1995   *Antiquities: Trade or Betrayed? Legal, Ethical and Conservation Issues.*
            Archetype, London.

JULIE HOLLOWELL-ZIMMER

Chapter Four

Digging in the Dirt—Ethics and "Low-End Looting"

To lend some perspective to what follows, let me begin by saying that I am a cultural anthropologist who does archaeological excavation and whose research interests include art and artifact markets, artifact diggers, and the nature of the relationships between indigenous communities and archaeological sites, objects, and practices. This chapter addresses issues surrounding archaeological ethics and "low-end looting." Most archaeologists certainly have an idea of what "looting" means, but precisely because of the connotations the term has for many archaeologists, a review of different ways "looting" gets defined is in order.

The dictionary defines "looting" as the taking of something that doesn't belong to you, based on the Hindi word *lut* meaning "pillage" or "illegal taking," but what the term actually means depends a great deal on who uses it and in what context. Broadly speaking, "looting" covers everything from undocumented excavation of archaeological sites to cases of art theft from museums and illegal export of cultural property across national borders, not to mention the actions of armies or rioters. In the context of museums and the art market, an object is often branded as "looted" if it was acquired through unmistakably illegal means; otherwise, it is simply "of unknown provenance." One museum director expressed a different outlook when he called the use of cultural heritage laws to repatriate objects from other countries held in American museums a form of looting. Most lawyers, customs officials, and international agreements avoid this rather arbitrary and loaded term altogether, preferring words like "theft," "pillage," "smuggling," or "illicit excavation."

One way archaeologists define "looting" is in strictly legal terms, as "illicit excavation" or excavation performed without the proper permits. In most places in the world, any digging for artifacts without a permit is clearly illegal, but in the United States, digging on privately owned lands is often legal, with the noted exception of human burial sites and any sites in the few states that now require excavation permits. Federal agencies in the United States actually make a distinction between a *legal* version of undocumented excavation, called "artifact hunting," and an *illegal* version called "looting," either of which might be done for commercial purposes (Hutt, Jones, and McAllister 1992:16).[1] The act and consequences of site looting are upsetting enough to archaeologists that the term has come more generally to mean whenever archaeological materials are removed from their context without proper scientific documentation, whether this is done legally or illegally, for commercial purposes or not. This (also called "pothunting") is the definition of "looting" I use here, interchangeably with "artifact digging" and "undocumented excavation."

The perspective within archaeological ethics on looting is quite different from the ethical stance held by some American Indians who see archaeologists as little more than looters who hide behind the name of science (Riding In 1992:12) or even as subhuman vultures who feast on the dead (see Joe Watkins, chapter 10). On the other hand, the destructive activities of land developers never seem to be referred to as looting, presumably because what they do is sanctioned by the state. Whatever the case, wherever and whenever undocumented excavation occurs, it destroys forever the information the earth holds about the past. From both a scientific standpoint and an ethical one, the damage is immeasurable and certainly irreversible.

Just what does "low-end looting" mean? I take it to mean undocumented excavations in which the products are not headed straight for the international art or antiquities market (see Neil Brodie and David Gill, chapter 3), but for less lucrative and often less visible markets or sometimes for no market at all. The continuum from low-end to high-end looting is less about artifact types than about looting situations and what happens afterwards. It runs from archaeologists who do sloppy science, to hobbyist collectors who would like to think they are doing archaeology, to people who dig as a purely recreational pastime, to farmers who churn up sites as they plow and developers who look the other way, to those whose main interest in artifacts is their sale value. This last category ranges from individual "subsistence diggers"[2] trying to literally pay a doctor bill to organized mafia-like squads working undercover with machine guns. Then there are all the collectors, museums, galleries, souvenir shops, auctions, exhibitions, magazines, relic shows, county historical societies, and family traditions that are part of the support system. Is it only the people who dig things up, then, who are the looters? On the other hand, certainly not all those whom archaeologists might call looters think of themselves in these terms at all.

Some archaeologists would argue that looting is looting and not a matter of high or low, better or worse, but this attitude masks the many different reasons people dig for "old things." It is not my task here to detail the wide range of activities that come under the heading of looting, and in many ways, we need to move beyond just that. The point is that for archaeologists to begin to effectively address the problems created by undocumented excavation, it is crucial to understand the economic, historical, and social contexts of different looting situations and the belief systems and power structures that make undocumented excavation a more viable and preferable alternative than conservation or archaeology for a significant number of people around the world.

It is important to admit that most early archaeologists would be considered looters by today's standards. This is not because they lacked ethics, but because significant improvements in archaeological method and analysis over the past two generations have greatly changed what it means to do "proper" archaeology. The definition of "the field" and whom it includes has also changed. As a result, the ethical responsibilities archaeologists have toward treatment of the archaeological record have changed *and continue to evolve.*

At the same time, in recent decades archaeologists have begun to acknowledge that theirs are not the only claims on the archaeological record. In many cases, archaeological concerns and claims are strongly contested by people with very different ideas about the value and ownership of archaeological sites and artifacts. Some of them carry their own resentful and (we hope) outdated stereotypes of archaeologists as self-righteous arbiters of "who owns the past," no better than so-called looters in the way they dropped in, dug, and took what didn't belong to them. Conversely, some of the stereotypes archaeologists carry of artifact diggers (or dealers or collectors) carry the same resentful overtones. To find successful solutions to the problem of undocumented excavation, archaeologists will have to move beyond the us–them thinking that has polarized and at times prevented discussion to find some common ground for problem solving and collaboration with the people they've been calling looters.

The Bad News

We now have plenty of evidence from countries all over the world documenting the destruction of archaeological sites on a global scale (see Brodie, Doole, and Renfrew 2001; Messenger 1999; Schmidt and McIntosh 1996). Most people agree that, in spite of new laws, treaties, and enforcement strategies, the overall situation is worse today than it ever was (Elia 1997; Vitelli 2000). Certain areas have been hit harder than others, and of course the effects are cumulative, since the main problem with undocumented excavation is the *irreversible* damage it causes to the archaeological record. In parts of the United States including the Mimbres valley, the mound complexes of Arkansas, the Bering Strait coastlines of Alaska, and the rock shelters and farmlands of Indiana, 80 to 90 percent of known archaeological sites have been intentionally disturbed or destroyed. The percentage appears to be comparable in archaeological hot spots around the world.

Most of the statistics we do have about looted archaeological materials come from studies of artifacts that surface on the international antiquities market, and they indicate that the vast majority—up to 90 percent or more—of these "art" objects come from illicit excavations (see Elia 2001; Chippindale and Gill 2000; Tubb 1995). Interpol's statistics on looted and stolen antiquities put their market value at $4 to $5 billion a year, similar to the arms trade and second only to narcotics. Exports of antiquities from public lands in the United States were estimated at $25 million a year over a decade ago, and looted Maya objects now bring well over $120 million a year on the art market (Dorfman 1998:3).

My own fieldwork of tracking objects from undocumented excavations in Alaska's Bering Strait has found that the artifacts in glossy catalogs and galleries on the high-end art market, though their monetary values are impressive, represent the virtual *tip of the iceberg*, usually no more than a dozen pieces out of literally tons of materials pulled out of archaeological sites in a year's time. Artifact diggers gather anything that can be reused or sold, often by the pound: old whale bones and walrus skulls, chunks of unworked walrus ivory, arrowheads, fishing tools, ivory needles, buttons, and lip plugs. Finding a piece worthy of the art market is like hitting the jackpot, a rare by-product of multipurpose and persistent digging. It seems likely that the situation is similar elsewhere. Other looted materials are recycled for local use and never reach the market. In Tanzania, villagers use the remains of ancient coral walls to build their homes (Karoma 1996), and in Central America and around the Mediterranean the ruins of temples and plazas have been a reliable source of local building supplies for centuries.

Meanwhile, the market continues to expand at both the low and high ends. The Internet has become a virtual "site" where people vicariously "dig" for literally hundreds of less expensive low-end artifacts on websites that facilitate networking among buyers and sellers in ways never before possible. In what Alex Barker calls "the vacuum cleaner effect," Internet commerce sucks up artifacts and archaeological fragments that previously had little or no market value and offers them to an ever-widening audience, turning former recreational looters into artifact buyers and sellers. In July 2000, when the Society for American Archaeology sent letters to several e-commerce companies requesting that they stop selling archaeological materials because of the connections with site destruction, eBay and Amazon.com disclaimed their liability and the ethical implications of their practices by iterating that they neither condoned nor allowed sellers to knowingly post *illegal* materials.

As for museums, they are caught between truly not wishing to support undocumented excavation and the knowledge that the bulk of their archaeological acquisitions have a checkered history. If we took all the looted artifacts out of our museums, most would be very empty indeed. Worried about funding and appearances, museums end up hiding behind honorable-sounding in-house ethical policies, yet are still unwilling to educate the public and openly address issues of how materials came to occupy exhibits and space in their institutions.

Looting may actually account for less damage to archaeological sites than erosion, agriculture, or development, but this is no consolation, only added injury. As K. Anne Pyburn (chapter 16) observes, "All sites are endangered." The global nature of the world today makes us more aware of the cumulative and far-reaching consequences of actions that deplete or pollute diminishing supplies of natural, environmental, cultural, and archaeological resources. We are left with the question of how to save what's left. Where and how do we start to turn the tide?

Who's to Blame?

A lot of energy has been spent trying to pinpoint blame for the current appalling state of affairs. Collectors are blamed for creating the demand that motivates people to dig up artifacts; the market is blamed for turning artifacts into commodities with ever-increasing economic value; diggers are blamed for being poor, ignorant, greedy, uneducated, and blind to the consequences of their actions; and countries and their legal systems are blamed for allowing any of this to continue. The problem with blame is that it tends to end in overly simplistic explanations and reproach rather than move toward a better understanding of underlying structures and the motives that drive undocumented excavation. The desires collectors have to own artifacts, for example, are provoked and sustained by a complex combination of factors including visions of themselves as stewards of the past, an association of wealth with certain standards of taste, and a great misconception of what archaeology as a science can contribute to humankind.

Blaming abstractions like the "invisible hand" of the market and the "laws" of supply and demand precludes looking more deeply at what is really happening in situations where artifacts are given economic value. The products of low-end looting tend to be less visible on the market and their scope is little understood. Their networks of dealers and collectors and the places they surface are different than those of artifacts that have been reinscribed as "art" but are just as ingrained.

Another stereotypical entity blamed for looting is the Third World peasant, supposedly ignorant of the value of heritage and exploited to supply the market. In his study of subsistence digging in Belize, David Matsuda estimates that 97 percent of the 30,000 or more artifact diggers in Belize were men, women, and children whose lifestyle made seasonal digging between agricultural activities a way to make ends meet (1998:91). The subsistence diggers I know in Alaska's Bering Strait are not blind victims of the desire of collectors, threatening dealers, or supply and demand; they are engaged and entangled in a global market for artifacts because it is the best economic option out there. Most of them quickly take advantage of seasonal wage work if it is available rather than settle for the tedium and uncertainty of digging for artifacts. On St. Lawrence Island, where the mining of archaeological sites has been an important part of the local economy since archaeologists first purchased specimens in the 1920s, the native community has made a conscious choice, for now, to prioritize the economic value of these unique resources over their value as archaeological "heritage." Until people can be convinced that preservation and scientific excavation are more worthwhile endeavors than undocumented digging, how can we expect them to change from looters to stewards?

Even in communities where subsistence digging is an ingrained way of life, local attitudes about selling artifacts vary widely. During my fieldwork on St. Lawrence Island, I found that some people loved to dig, others regarded it as a continuation of the pattern of white traders appropriating cultural artifacts, and a few blamed all the social problems in the village on "those holes people dig out there."[3] These looters may see little difference between what they do and how others extract nonrenewable resources like diamonds or oil or make a withdrawal from an inheritance or bank account. People would tell me, "Our ancestors left us these things so we could survive in a cash economy." Others recounted stories about voices telling them where to dig or when to stop because an object didn't want to be found. In Belize, the subsistence diggers observed by Matsuda (1998) called the artifacts they found *semilla*, sacred seed scattered by the ancestors to help create the future, and performed ceremonies before tunneling into temples. I am not an apologist for activities that forever destroy the archaeological record, rather I want to emphasize that to avert the problem, we need to understand it from the perspectives and the ethics of others.

It may seem to us like a forgotten era, but the memories of archaeological field collectors who descended on villages to crate up specimens for museums, hiring village laborers to dig with shovels and pickaxes, and trading store goods for desirable artifacts are still vivid in many places. Artifacts generally held little monetary value before those days. As late as the 1950s, pothunting was regarded as an admirable pastime in the United States, worthy of a ribbon at many county fairs (Canouts and MacManamon 2001:105). One of the healthiest communities of looters in the United States today was created by an archaeologist who paid residents $2 for every unbroken pot and the subsequent loss of jobs when local uranium mines closed. (You can get t-shirts here that boast "Dig San Juan County.") Many archaeologists will admit that they began their budding career with a fascination evoked by a minor looting experience. If not for the opportunity to attend college and aspire to a professional career, would some among them have become looters instead? The public deserves to understand why documentation and preservation of archaeological context is crucial to our knowledge about the world, and somehow archaeologists have to make it clear why even the ten-thousandth arrowhead is still important.

Effective Approaches to Looting

Archaeologists have been working overtime to find ways to stop undocumented excavation for over thirty years now. The primary tools enlisted in this struggle have been legal instruments, professional ethical codes, and education (see Messenger

1999). All of these have been successful to some degree, but meanwhile, site destruction continues to escalate.

Legal prohibitions, difficult to fund and enforce, have not stemmed the tide of illicit excavation, nationally or internationally. Even partial bans that allow the export of some antiquities have not reduced looting in countries like Mali (Eyo 1994). Some of the worst looting in places like Guatemala and Cambodia has been done by the military itself. In the United States, where the National Park Service has spent a great deal of money on detection, enforcement, and studies of looting behavior, laws seem to deter only the most casual looters. Still, the increase in legal actions taken against looters in countries all over the world in the last ten years indicates growing attention to the issue. The results of bilateral agreements signed by the United States with a handful of countries under the UNESCO Convention, however cumbersome and narrow, reveal that international collaboration on specific high-visibility looting problems can reduce site destruction.

It may seem that codes of professional ethics do little to directly deter looting, but they signal a sea change in attitudes and the willingness of institutions and organizations to reflect on and alter practices that support looting activities. Statements by museums and auction houses about the necessity of documented legal provenience for acquisitions or sales are important steps, but they have slippery edges and well-plotted loopholes that often serve to protect institutional liability more than ethical interests.[4] Art dealers and artifact diggers have their own codes of ethics. Should we shun them or try to understand them, find some common ground, small as it may be, and build from there?

Education is a long-term investment, most effective when it is collaborative, hands on, and responsive to the social and economic needs perceived by a community. Claiming that people should be educated about the value of "heritage" can be paternalistic, colonialist missionizing, or it can be a dialog and a learning experience for everyone involved. Every one of the archaeological projects that has successfully deterred undocumented excavation and changed attitudes of local looters has what B. Mapunda (2001) calls "participatory education" at its core. This means finding ways as archaeologists to facilitate the devolution of archaeological stewardship, research, and the knowledge it creates back into the hands of those peoples and communities closest to its source—turning the tide of "scientific colonialism" (see Zimmerman 2000:169) and making archaeology a meaningful, mutually beneficial engagement.

Examples include the programs of the Arkansas Archaeological Survey that put relic collectors to work alongside archaeologists, turning looters into stewards who in turn monitor each other (see Early 1999; Harrington 1996). In Cambodia, the Lower Mekong Archaeological Project, codirected by Miriam Stark and Cambodian archaeologist Chuch Phoeurn, has mitigated, though not eradicated, long-established looting of the site for the antiquities market through on-site community education and other forms of involvement. At Agua Blanco in Ecuador, Colin McEwan and others worked with local "looters" to build and manage a community museum, inspiring new ways of finding value in the past. These and other results suggest that participatory education should be an ethical obligation of projects and funding agencies if archaeologists are to learn better ways to protect the archaeological record.

What More Can Be Done

Looting is a complex enterprise with its own histories, market networks, and social values that extend well beyond an archaeological site. What else can be done to help turn the tide on site destruction and looting?

A handful of studies have lent some insight into the processes and motivations of the artifact market (see Brent 1996; Coe 1993; Heath 1974; Matsuda 1998; Ziedler 1982), but we need more on-the-ground ethnographies of looting that examine the economic and social contexts that make undocumented digging the choice of how people manage the archaeological remains of the past. The recent batch of quantitative studies done by archaeologists to reveal the questionable provenience of materials surfacing on the art market moves in a productive direction (see Chippindale and Gill 2000; Elia 2001; Gilgan 2001; Gill and Chippindale 1993), but more solid information is needed about how supply and demand are created, sustained, and subverted.[5] Artifact markets can be traced and understood as networks of diggers, dealers, tourists, auctions, and collectors; they are much more complex than the moment an object surfaces on the art market. Collaborating and sharing this research with communities of artifact diggers and with collectors helps everyone (archaeologists included) see the consequences of their actions in larger terms and make better-informed decisions about the future.

More information about looting and its support systems is crucial because archaeologists need to understand—not necessarily agree with—the perspectives of others who make claims on the archaeological record, especially those who damage it in doing so. Many of the claims that diggers, dealers, and collectors make about how they value undocumented materials are valid from a nonarchaeocentric perspective. Even if *none* of these claims justifies damage to the archaeological record, they cannot be discounted out of hand if archaeologists expect their own viewpoints to be considered.

Archaeologists need to continue to address the valid criticisms and the misconceptions people have about the attitudes and practices of their discipline. Subsistence diggers in Belize, for example, interpreted actions of archaeologists who wanted them to stop looting as attempts to keep them from being able to feed their families or make a little extra money (Matsuda 1998). From their perspective, archaeologists are clearly in a privileged position and are obviously profiting from their excavations, coming back every year with vehicles, fancy equipment, and a team of workers. If archaeologists want to stop subsistence digging, perhaps they have an ethical responsibility to offer economic alternatives to communities in which this is a motive for undocumented excavation.

Among the more seductive options along these lines is archaeotourism. Like tourism and like digging, archaeotourism can be done in damaging or in beneficial ways. Archaeotourism raises a host of new ethical questions—not the least of which is who really benefits from ventures like this—but from the standpoint of archaeological ethics, the greatest danger may be its blatant promotion of a consumerist valuing of the past.

Archaeological ethics can guide intentions, but actual solutions to looting will more than likely require an ethical compromise. Ethics scholars advise that the only way to move forward to the solution of ethical dilemmas is to first be open to critiquing and reflecting on one's own position and then to be willing to seek common ground with others, which usually means compromise (Moody-Adams 1997). There are times when any action an archaeologist might take, whether publishing an article or surveying a remote area, could potentially stimulate looting or increase the commercial value of artifacts. The issue becomes how to foresee, minimize, divert, or balance negative consequences. In many cases, it may not be what you do, but how you do it that matters most.

The looting of archaeological sites is part of the challenge the world faces to find less destructive, more sustainable, and more meaningful versions of resource use and economic development. Theory and practice developed in the field of conservation and development have barely been tapped in relation to site destruction, though looting has much in common with the circumstances of endangered species, environmental degradation, and common property resource use. Research in these areas indicates the vital importance of community-based decision making and locally meaningful incentives to protection and stewardship. Archaeologists may not be able to put an immediate or total halt to looting in places where it is an ingrained aspect of the local culture, but the most successful approaches seem to be participatory projects where archaeologists work in a positive and sustained manner directly with communities of looters. Like any successful grassroots development project, these initiatives require a long-term local commitment and the recognition that education is a two-way street. Once again, it appears that good archaeology is applied anthropology (Pyburn and Wilk 1995). Though each case will be different, archaeologists can begin to build a foundation of theory and praxis to inform future approaches to looting.

Discussion Questions

1. Should archaeologists focus on sites or objects or both equally in trying to prevent looting?

2. What are some of the activities of archaeologists that could potentially endanger the archaeological record or stimulate looting?

3. A month after newspapers in Los Angeles and New York carried articles about your fieldwork with the headline "Spectacular Mayan Finds Deep in the Jungle," you hear that teams of diggers have descended into the heavily forested regions near your excavation. What should you do? What might you have done differently?

4. What are the responsibilities of archaeologists toward communities of looters? What are the limits of these responsibilities? Can you suggest any incentives for turning looters into stewards?

5. On St. Lawrence Island, where undocumented digging and selling of artifacts is an important economic activity for many residents, local indigenous authorities may soon allow a field school to take place on their lands. Would you consider helping run a field school under these conditions? Would you make any conditions of your own? What if the alternative is no archaeology at all? What do the archaeologists or the St. Lawrence Islanders have to lose or gain in this situation?

6. Explain the goals and benefits of archaeology to a group of villagers, including some subsistence diggers, in Guatemala. (This could be done as a role-play.)

7. Should archaeologists participate in excavations that involve selling artifacts? Several legal scholars have proposed selling artifacts from documented excavations, both to finance community projects and to satisfy collectors, as a compromise that might lessen undocumented digging. Could archaeologists ethically make this kind of compromise? What might the consequences be? Are they worth it? In some situations and not others?

8. Some archaeologists have suggested that an injection of fakes onto the market would mitigate looting. What are the pros and cons of this suggestion?

9. I note that our archaeological ethics "continue to evolve." In this chapter, I suggest ways that current archaeological society codes might need to be revised. Suggest new wording for such a revision, considering carefully the implication of your choice of phrasing. What challenges do you anticipate such a proposed version would encounter from the society membership? How would you respond to them?

Notes

I want to thank Larry J. Zimmerman and Karen D. Vitelli, for involving me in this worthy project and encouraging me to write this chapter. Thanks also to K. Anne Pyburn, David Matsuda, and Vitelli for their suggestions on this manuscript. Finally, thanks to the National Science Foundation's Office of Polar Programs for its support of my research and of Bering Strait archaeology.

1. The differential treatment of public and private property in the United States has created a double standard that certainly muddles legal and ethical definitions of "looting." Some wonder how the United States can criticize other nations for their laxity toward looting when it is actually legal within our own borders. On the one hand, the justice system must prove artifacts came from public lands before taking legal action against a supposed looter; on the other hand, unless a state law supercedes, private landowners can, and in several instances have, opened their land to recreational or for-profit artifact digging. To archaeologists, this is looting of the worst kind, no matter how legal it is, whereas landowners might perceive the standpoint of archaeological ethics as an erosion of private property rights.

2. A subsistence digger, as defined by David P. Staley (1993:348) and David Matsuda (1998:96), is a person who uses the proceeds from artifact sales to support a subsistence lifestyle.

3. I interpret this comment to mean that the gaping holes left by diggers did not show the proper respect to the spirits of the people who once lived there, and this was upsetting the cosmological balance of the community.

4. The International Council of Museums Ethics Code is the only code I know of that goes beyond denouncing illicit excavations to condemn *any* unscientific damage to sites. At Sotheby's, the policy is not to sell anything known to be illegally looted and to try to avoid selling "recently" looted material.

5. Sometimes, the best results come from unexpected directions. For example, the marketing of Viagra has greatly decreased trade in rhinoceros horn (personal communication, A. Early, March 23, 2002).

Recommended Readings

Brodie, Neil, Jennifer Doole, and Colin Renfrew (editors)
2001   *Trade in Illicit Antiquities: The Destruction of the World's Archaeological Heritage.* McDonald Institute Monographs. McDonald Institute, Cambridge.

Cameron, Catherine (editor)
1997   Special Issue on the Loss of Cultural Heritage—An International Perspective. *Nonrenewable Resources* 6(2).

Hutt, Sherry, Elwood W. Jones, and Martin E. McAllister.
1992   *Archaeological Resource Protection.* Preservation Press, Washington, DC.

Messenger, Phyllis Mauch (editor)
1999   *The Ethics of Collecting Cultural Property: Whose Culture? Whose Property?* 2nd ed. University of New Mexico Press, Albuquerque.

Meyer, Karl E.
1977   *The Plundered Past.* Atheneum, New York.

Schmidt, Peter R., and Roderick J. McIntosh (editors)
   1996   *Plundering Africa's Past.* Indiana University Press, Bloomington.

Smith, George, and John E. Ehrenhard (editors)
   1991   *Protecting the Past.* CRC Press, Boca Raton, FL.

Tubb, Kathryn W. (editor)
   1995   *Antiquities: Trade or Betrayed: Legal, Ethical and Conservation Issues.*
          Archetype, London.

Vitelli, Karen D. (editor)
   1996   *Archaeological Ethics.* AltaMira, Walnut Creek, CA.

GEORGE F. BASS

Chapter Five

The Ethics of Shipwreck Archaeology

Why should there be a separate chapter on the ethics of underwater archaeology? Since I learned to dive for archaeology in 1960, I have objected to the label "underwater archaeologist." We don't refer to mountain archaeologists, jungle archaeologists, or desert archaeologists. That an archaeologist who excavates a shipwreck thirty-five meters deep wears scuba gear seems no more important than the excavator of a habitation mound who may reach his or her site by a four-wheel-drive vehicle. The terminology of ships is specialized, but so is that of Greek architecture.

It might seem, then, that the ethics of underwater archaeology should be exactly the same as the ethics of terrestrial archaeology. There are, however, areas in which underwater archaeology does differ from dry-land archaeology, which presents special ethical concerns.

Ownership of Shipwrecks

In Mediterranean countries, ancient shipwrecks have long been treated like any other archaeological site. Regardless of its origin, an ancient shipwreck belongs to the nation in whose territorial waters it lies. To disturb it in any way, a foreign or national archaeologist must have the proper credentials to obtain official permission from the archaeological service of the government of that nation. Because in the last century so many antiquities were taken from these countries to foreign museums and collections, this approach developed as a safeguard. Thus, there has been less treasure hunting in the Mediterranean than in many places, although illegal looting of antiquities does occur under the Mediterranean as on surrounding lands. (Turkey, where I dive, is *still* rich in ancient wrecks because most diving is allowed only in specified areas and only with local guides.)

Archaeology versus Treasure Hunting

Elsewhere, legal treasure hunting has long been allowed because international admiralty law holds that salvors have certain rights to wrecks, rights that distinguish wrecks from traditional archaeological sites on land. Although looting of sites on land has long been both unethical and illegal, the law of salvage and the law of finds gave legal permission to those who believed it ethical to plunder historic shipwrecks for monetary gain. These laws, derived from laws dating back to at least the time of Hammurabi, were established to provide incentives to salvors by offering compensation for their services. By sharing the spoils of salvage, both ship owners and salvors profited. Although the laws were not designed to encourage treasure hunting, the concept of "finders-keepers" has been used successfully by treasure hunters, especially since the advent of scuba made diving commonplace. Countries from the Caribbean to the Far East, especially developing countries, still issue salvage permits to treasure hunters for wrecks in their waters, often in the misguided belief that their shares of promised treasures will provide vast sums to local coffers. In reality, treasure hunters have probably made more money by enticing investors than by finding treasure. And it has been shown that states that work with archaeologists gain greater financial rewards.

The raising, conservation, and display of the warship *Vasa* from Stockholm Harbor in 1961 cost many millions of dollars, but that seventeenth-century vessel has since become the main tourist attraction for Sweden, and the Vasa Museum the most visited museum in the nation. The Museum of Underwater Archaeology in Bodrum is the most popular archaeological museum in Turkey, drawing over 250,000 paying visitors a year. For better or worse, it was this museum that drew the first tourists to Bodrum, turning a little town of 5,000 people into a city whose population swells to over 200,000 every summer. Visitors to such museums bring more to the economy than the price of entrance tickets, for each visitor may well spend another night in a local hotel, eat additional meals in local restaurants, buy souvenirs, take local taxis, and in other ways enrich the local economy. Humanity gains, too, for the wrecks in these museums are published thoroughly in popular and scholarly books and articles.

Treasure hunters have also established museums, which is commendable. Archaeologists could find no fault with these if it could be established that their contents had been excavated and conserved properly, and that the excavators were not engaged in selling artifacts from the sites. Sales of artifacts are the crux of this matter, for we have not even considered here the illegal treasure hunters who damaged almost every known early ship of exploration in the New World before they were studied by archaeologists.

Are there any circumstances under which artifacts might ethically be sold? I am asked why duplicate amphoras from excavated wrecks should not be sold, but they are not true duplicates; archaeologists return to them in museum storerooms decades later with new questions and new techniques and gain from them new knowledge of past economies. But what about objects made after the Industrial Revolution allowed true duplication of artifacts? Society must decide if it is worth the cost of curating thousands upon thousands of lead bullets or glass bottles made in the same molds. Should we keep every plastic ashtray manufactured today since each will in time be an antique?

I might find little fault with a treasure hunting group that published its finds more thoroughly than some archaeologists and kept the finds together by selling them to one owner who will curate and display them as a collection, which he or she has willed to the government. What I cannot know, however, is how much attention was paid on the seabed to items of little sales value. Because treasure hunters must make a relatively quick profit in order to repay investors, they are not likely to care for the concretions and wooden scraps from which archaeologists learn so much and are not likely to spend decades on conservation, about which I will discuss in more detail.

Mythology

In campaigning for legislation to protect underwater archaeological and historic sites, archaeologists have had to counter myths spread by those who wish to profit monetarily from those sites. Treasure hunters, for example, say they save shipwrecks from destruction by storms, whereas it has been established that even shallow wrecks are stabilized to the extent that any damage they suffer is usually at the hands of humans. Treasure hunters claim that only through sales of artifacts can the sums needed for underwater salvage be raised, whereas the most exemplary shipwreck excavations have not depended on the sale of a single artifact; on the contrary, treasure hunters never have spent the funds needed for full conservation. Treasure hunters say that hulls in the New World need not be carefully excavated because they are shallow and are already broken to bits by waves, whereas their own photographs often show these hulls as well preserved as those in deeper Mediterranean waters. They further insist that hulls of New World wrecks need not be studied because detailed plans of even the earliest exist in the Archives of the Indies in Spain. They do not. They say that they deserve whatever profit they can make because they risk their lives, as if archaeologists did not take the same risks. They wrongly claim that they invented 90 percent of the equipment used in underwater excavations. They say that they are the only ones who go out and find wrecks, ignoring the more than 100 ancient wrecks located off the Turkish coast by the Institute of Nautical Archaeology (INA) alone. When treasure hunters wave the flag of "free enterprise," implying that there would be nothing wrong with selling for profit the bits and pieces of an American Revolutionary War ship, one can ask why it is not then ethical for an entrepreneur to dismantle Mount Vernon or the Alamo to sell their bricks as souvenirs in the name of "free enterprise." Is a ship less important as a monument simply because it lies under water?

While testifying in 1987 before a Senate subcommittee considering an act to protect historic shipwrecks, I asked: "If those opposed to the Abandoned Shipwreck Act have a reasonable case, why must they resort continually to falsehoods?" (U.S. Government Printing Office 1987:159). The full Senate accepted the premise that archaeology is simply archaeology, whether on land or under water, and voted in favor of the act.

The Media

The Senate may have been convinced, having heard all the arguments, but the general public probably is not. The story of the little guy who strikes it big against great odds has human appeal. The undeniable romantic attraction of shipwrecks continues to separate underwater from terrestrial archaeology in most minds. Both print and television media, even those that campaign against the looting of archaeological sites on land, tend to sympathize with treasure hunting as long as it is under water.

Some prominent journalists say that archaeologists should work with treasure hunters because treasure hunters have accumulated valuable historical artifacts that can reveal much about the past. But archaeologists are not asked to cooperate with tomb robbers, who also have valuable historical artifacts. The quest for profit and the search for knowledge cannot coexist in archaeology because of the time factor. Rather incredibly, one archaeologist employed by a treasure hunting firm said that as long as archaeologists are given six months to study shipwrecked artifacts before they are sold, no historical knowledge is lost! On the contrary, archaeologists and assistants from the INA needed more than a decade of year-round conservation before they could even catalog all the finds from an eleventh-century AD wreck they had excavated. Then, to interpret those finds, my colleague Frederick van Doorninck had to learn Russian, Bulgarian, and Rumanian, without which we would never have learned the true nature of the site. Could a "commercial archaeologist" have waited more than a decade or so before selling the finds?

Are we not thankful that King Tut's tomb was excavated by archaeologists instead of treasure hunters, its contents kept together for the enjoyment of the hundreds of thousands of people who have seen it in exhibits around the world instead of being split up and sold off to the highest bidders? Why is a shipwreck different? Why should society, which does not allow people to excavate ancient habitation mounds for artifacts to sell, allow them to sell similar shipwrecked artifacts? To convince the public of the answer, more archaeologists should, by the example of their own work, set standards for comparison instead of simply criticizing treasure hunting.

Legislation

Many nations in recent decades have passed legislation to afford underwater sites the same protection as terrestrial sites. Portuguese law now prohibits the sale of any artifact taken from its waters. The Australian Commonwealth Historic Shipwrecks Act came into effect in 1976. In the United States, the aforementioned Abandoned Shipwreck Act removes *abandoned* shipwrecks from the laws of salvage and finds and passes ownership of these wrecks to the individual states, each of which can decide what kind of law it wants as long as the law provides some kind of private-sector access to the wrecks.

Sovereign Immunity

A separate issue concerning ownership, perhaps unique to shipwrecks, is that of sovereign immunity. Government-owned noncommercial vessels are immune from normal laws of the sea. Like embassies, which cannot be entered by the police of the state in which they are situated, warships cannot be boarded by local police when in foreign waters. Furthermore, if they sink no one can salvage them without permission of the navy that owns them. Thus, an American warship remains U.S. real estate even if it has sunk in Chinese or French or Argentine territorial waters. This forced an agreement between France and the United States before excavation off Cherbourg of the CSS *Alabama,* a Confederate warship that became U.S. property when the Confederacy was defeated. Similarly, before Canadian authorities could draw up plans for the eventual disposition of the *Hamilton* and *Scourge,* armed schooners lost in Lake Ontario during the War of 1812, they had to receive permission from the U.S. Navy, which simply transferred title to the vessels to the city of Hamilton, Ontario.

Sovereign immunity remains in perpetuity. It allowed France to claim René La Salle's ship *La Belle,* sunk in 1686 in Matagorda Bay, Texas, while the great explorer was looking for the mouth of the Mississippi River. As in the case of the *Alabama,* an accommodation had to be reached to allow the State of Texas, whose archaeologists located and excavated the ship, to continue *La Belle*'s conservation and restoration for ultimate display in a new museum of Texas history in Austin. Efforts of a commercial firm to salvage the remains of the frigate *Juno,* sunk off the coast of Virginia in 1802, were stopped by the decision of a federal court that the vessel still belonged to Spain, and Spain did not want the vessel disturbed.

Does sovereign immunity protect only warships or does it cover royal vessels such as Spanish galleons that were owned by the Spanish Crown and carried royal property as well as having military functions? The U.S. government's concern with sovereign immunity for its own ships usually involves warships and other military vessels, because the United States never had a monarch. The recent history of *Belle* and the court decisions involving Spanish ships illustrate that for ships that were in the service of a monarchy at the time they sank, the principle that they remain the property of that nation can also apply (personal communication, James Goold, Esq., 2002).

Wrecks in International Waters

Nongovernmental ships lost in international waters present still another problem of ownership that is unique to underwater sites. Who, for example, should be allowed to excavate the remains of an ancient merchantman in the middle of the Mediterranean?

UNESCO Convention on the Protection of the Underwater Cultural Heritage

To preserve and protect shipwrecks and other archaeological sites in international waters, the UN Educational, Scientific, and Cultural Organization (UNESCO) adopted the Convention on the Protection of the Underwater Cultural Heritage. This in effect removes underwater cultural heritage from the purview of the salvage laws that allow salvors to keep whatever they find on ships abandoned in international waters. (A ship is not abandoned if its owner or insurer can still be located and has not given up its interest in the ship, in which case the salvor must reach a settlement with that owner or insurer.) Basic to the convention is: "The commercial exploitation of underwater cultural heritage for trade or speculation or its irretrievable dispersal is fundamentally incompatible with the protection and proper management of underwater cultural heritage. Underwater cultural heritage shall not be traded, sold, bought or bartered as commercial goods."

This UNESCO convention could not run counter to the UN Convention on the Law of the Sea (UNCLOS). To understand the UNESCO Convention, therefore, let us familiarize ourselves with some of the concepts established by UNCLOS. In nonlegal terms, UNCLOS says that a nation's territorial sea includes waters up to 12 nautical miles from shore, the contiguous zone may extend out to 24 miles, and a nation's exclusive economic zone (EEZ) may extend out 200 miles. The continental shelf of a country may extend beyond its territorial waters, but that country has sovereign rights to natural, but not cultural, resources on that shelf. The seabed outside these limits, that is, the high seas beyond national jurisdiction, is called the Area. UNESCO considered extending the cultural heritage zone into the EEZ, but this would have upset the balance of economic and other interests in UNCLOS.

The UNESCO Convention sets high standards for archaeological investigations in international waters in order to "preserve underwater cultural heritage for the benefit of humanity." Ships of signatory nations are obliged to report any discoveries or illicit activities, whether in their waters or in the Area, and those nations "shall take measures to prevent the entry into their territory, the dealing in, or the possession of, underwater cultural heritage illicitly exported and/or recovered" partly by prohibiting use of their ports "in support of any activity . . . which is not in conformity with this Convention." This should be applauded by archaeologists, but unless all nations sign the convention it will remain a limited instrument, for ships engaged in unethical practices can simply use the ports of nonsignatory nations. Currently, the United States is not even a voting member of UNESCO.[1]

Common Sense

Conventions and laws are drafted by people and can be changed by people, so people must strive to determine the right thing to do. Robert Neyland, the director of the *Hunley* Project that will be briefly discussed later on, told me of his favorable impression of a meeting of U.S. Navy officials who organized the discussion of the recovery of archaeological artifacts around three main topics: "laws either domestic or international that were violated; Navy regulations that might have been ignored; and lastly standards of human decency, or ethics" (personal communication, Robert Neyland 2002).

Human decency, common sense, and the attempt to do the right thing all bear on the ownership of shipwrecks, for even the UNESCO Convention does not address the central question of who should own, say, a Bronze Age shipwreck found in international waters.

For a while, there were efforts by some nations to have any shipwrecked artifacts salvaged from international waters returned to the "land of cultural origin." That this plan is unfeasible can be demonstrated by three wrecks I have worked on in Turkey. More than forty years after my excavation of a Bronze Age shipwreck at Cape Gelidonya, scholarly publications still debate the origin of the ship, some saying it was Cypriot, others that it was Canaanite, others that it was Mycenaean Greek. What would a jury decide? And if a judge or jury decided the ship was Canaanite, would its contents be returned today to modern Syria, Lebanon, or Israel? Similarly, how would one divide objects from the Uluburun shipwreck of around 1300 BC? The lands of "cultural origin" of the wreck's 18,000 cataloged items include Iraq, Egypt, Rumania, Italy, Greece, Cyprus, somewhere in tropical Africa, somewhere on the Levantine coast, and perhaps Afghanistan! The eleventh-century AD wreck at Serçe Limani, we know after years of research, was sailed by Hellenized Bulgar merchants living by the Sea of Marmara not far from Constantinople, who picked up a cargo of

Islamic ceramics and glass at an unknown Near Eastern port, perhaps Caesarea in modern Israel. Should the glass, the largest collection of medieval Islamic glass in existence, be given to Israel or to an Islamic nation on the Levantine coast? If the latter, which one? Presumably the Bulgar merchants had paid for the glass. Should Turkey give it to Bulgaria? And the ship's hull? We don't even know the nationality of its owner.

Perhaps those who believe artifacts should be returned to the land of cultural origin think a Greek statue would simply be sent to modern Greece, whereas that statue could have been cast in southern Italy or on the west coast of Turkey in classical times.

There was an outcry in the Italian press when ocean explorer Robert Ballard with a team of professional archaeologists raised artifacts from a deep Roman wreck in international waters and brought them to the United States. What was the basis for complaint? Has anyone shown that those artifacts came from Italy rather than from some modern North African state, or even from as far away as the United Kingdom?

Common sense must play a role in determining ownership. Some archaeologists complain about the court decision that awarded to a salvage group 90 percent of the estimated 21 tons of gold on the steamer *Central America* that sank more than a mile deep 200 miles off South Carolina in 1857. But could archaeology alone possibly justify, now or in the future, gambling millions of dollars just to locate a 150-year-old wreck? That was the cost to the salvors—treasure hunters—who then carefully raised to the surface some of its gold and artifacts. Furthermore, I learned more about the *Central America* from publications inspired by its salvage than I know of wrecks excavated by some of the archaeologists who object most vehemently to the court decision.

Some nations would like to extend their claims over ancient and historic shipwrecks onto their continental shelves and even across the entire 200 miles of their EEZ. On what ethical basis? The average width of the Mediterranean is less than 500 miles, which means that, especially when one takes islands into consideration, virtually the entire sea would be claimed by one state or another. Is a Minoan wreck in the Libyan EEZ any more a part of the culture heritage of Libya than of Venezuela? Why should states that have shown little interest in shipwrecks and no expertise in underwater excavation have greater claim to them than states with proven records? Why, on any ethical grounds, should such states be able to stop work of high professional standards, perhaps to excavate the sites badly and never publish them? The UNESCO Convention attempts to preserve wrecks for the benefit of humanity and not for any particular state, especially one unrelated to the history or culture of the wrecked ship.

Controversially, I suggest that anyone able to meet the high standards for excavation, conservation, curation, and publication demanded by the UNESCO Convention should have the right to own an ancient wreck found in international waters. Would it be unethical for the Metropolitan Museum of Art, the Louvre, or the British Museum to own and display such a wreck?

Age

Regardless of depth, how many wrecks should be protected? Under the UNESCO Convention, it includes all those "having a cultural, historical or archaeological character which have been partially or totally under water, periodically or continuously, for at least 100 years." There are millions of shipwrecks. How many have a "cultural, historical or archaeological character"? I was told how the sinking of an old vessel near Annapolis, Maryland, caused an immediate hue and cry over raising money to save and preserve this historic monument. At that very moment, however, the vessel's sister ship was being cut up for scrap on land, the normal fate of old ships that are not lost at sea. Had the undeniable mystique that surrounds shipwrecks simply led to an emotional reaction?

Is age a sufficient criterion for saving a wreck? The UNESCO Convention's "at least 100 years" reminds me of the question of how many whiskers does it take to make a beard. Of course, arbitrary lines must be drawn, but why should a wreck of no significance on December 31, 2001, possibly become a historic monument one day later on January 1, 2002?

Conservation

Conservation presents another ethical concern specific to shipwreck archaeology. Unknown to the public, which sees dramatic photographs of diving archaeologists in wet suits, those archaeologists must spend far more time and money on unglamorous conservation than on seabed excavation. This is in addition to such expensive equipment as compressors, generators, underwater cameras, recompression chambers, sets of scuba gear, and sometimes even ships and coffer dams. Without denying the vast sums spent on the ongoing restoration of ancient cities, or the infinite patience required to conserve frescoes and mosaics, I suggest that no branch of archaeology demands more of conservation than shipwreck archaeology. Virtually everything taken from water, with the exception of gold and precious gems, demands instant treatment to prevent disintegration. Ceramics, metals, glass, ivory, bone, and other organic remains including wood must first be desalinated to prevent later decay. Most require the mechanical removal of hard and often thick layers of calcium carbonate, called concretion, that build up on objects in the sea. Many demand subsequent chemical treatment.

It clearly is unethical to disturb a shipwreck site without the commitment and means to conserve it, no matter the cost. When civic-minded but misguided individuals in the early 1960s arranged for what proved to be the rather brutal salvage of the Civil War ironclad *Cairo,* until then perfectly preserved in the Yazoo River of

Mississippi, they were surely unaware of how quickly the timbers would rot and the iron would corrode. They had neither the plans nor the funds for conservation. By the time the National Park Service assumed responsibility of *Cairo* from the State of Mississippi, for restoration in the Vicksburg National Military Park, only 15 percent of its hull remained.

Compare the contemporary treatment of the *Vasa* to that of the *Cairo*. Housed first in a temporary museum, its hull was sprayed with polyethylene glycol for seventeen years while 5,000 iron bolts were manufactured to replace those that originally held its timbers together. Items from clothing to foodstuffs to iron armaments stretched the conservators' skills. Finally, thirty years after being raised, *Vasa* became an awe-inspiring display in the new museum designed for the only extant seventeenth-century ship.

Similarly, ongoing conservation of King Henry VIII's sixteenth-century warship *Mary Rose* at Portsmouth, England, is expected to require more than twenty years, as did conservation of the *Bremen Cog* in Germany. Year-round conservation and restoration of the hull and contents of the eleventh-century Serçe Limani shipwreck, including three tons of broken glass, occupied a conservation staff for two decades. Exemplary excavation of a ship that sank around 300 BC off Kyrenia, Cyprus, required only two summers of diving, but five years of conservation and restoration. Conservation of the twenty tons of Bronze Age artifacts raised from the Uluburun shipwreck, including objects of pottery, tin, copper, bronze, silver, glass, ivory, bone, shell, bitumen, stone, and wood will take decades.

Conservation is expensive. The excavation of the 1554 fleet off Padre Island, Texas, cost the state $250,000, but subsequent conservation cost $500,000 (personal communication, J. Barto Arnold 2002). Conservation of La Salle's ship *Belle* at the Texas A&M University Conservation Research Laboratory will cost between $4 and $5 million before the ship becomes the centerpiece of a new museum (personal communication, D. L. Hamilton 2002). This is stretching state funds to the limit. Conservation costs for the Confederate submarine *Hunley* in Charleston, South Carolina, are running even higher; conservation of an iron artifact of its size and complexity, never attempted before, will run seven times the cost of recovery and may total $17 million (personal communication, R. Neyland 2002).

Safety

The ethics of underwater archaeology demand safety above all on a field project. Fatal accidents have occurred on land excavations, but having colleagues and students working twice a day under more than 35 meters of water for months at a time presents unusual hazards. The INA tries to always have an expedition physician as well as a dive master at remote sites. Each dive is controlled by a timekeeper on the surface who alerts the divers with an electronically generated signal two minutes before the end of their dive, and with a separate signal when it is time for them to come up. Oxygen decompression tables designed specifically for the INA's use by Duke University have a built-in safety factor, but we still have a multiperson double-lock recompression chamber on site; we do not make deep dives without one. In addition to one or more air-filled plastic hemispheres in which a diver can breathe in case of equipment failure, we place extra sets of scuba gear around each deep wreck. In camp, we turn off the electric generator at 10 PM each night to encourage a good night's sleep and allow no more than one alcoholic drink an evening, before or with dinner. Even so, there were several cases of bends, all treated in the chamber, in 22,500 dives to between 45 and 60 meters at Uluburun.

Site Locations

Perhaps more than on land, locations of underwater sites should be kept secret. We are recording with the Global Positioning System the location of each of more than 100 wrecks we have found off the Turkish coast. Published, this information could lead wreck looters directly onto isolated wrecks only intermittently watched by the Coast Guard.

Deep-Sea Archaeology

Work in the high seas has given birth to "deep-sea archaeology," claimed by some engineers who say that they should be the ones to direct deep-sea operations since they design and operate the equipment. This claim will last about as long as the old claim that underwater archaeology could only be conducted by professional divers. Archaeology is archaeology. Technicians must assist the archaeologists, not the other way around.

The ethics of underwater archaeology are basically the same as those of good archaeology in any environment. As the previous discussion has shown, however, a few important aspects of shipwreck archaeology do call for special ethical considerations.

Discussion Questions

1. How do concepts of ownership support or undermine the archaeological ethic of stewardship in relation to underwater archaeological sites?

2. Should artifacts from underwater excavations be sold to support the high costs of research and conservation? Why or why not? If so, under what conditions?

3. How do we reconcile the concept that archaeological sites are "owned" by a person or a nation with the idea that the archaeological record belongs to all of humanity?

4. Do you see any way to strike a compromise between commercial salvage and archaeology?

5. Is it worth the cost of curating multiple examples of objects dating from the post–Industrial Revolution that have been made in molds? How does one decide? (See also Alex W. Barker, chapter 6.)

6. If treasure salvors create a museum for exhibiting their finds, do archaeologists have a legitimate complaint with the rest of their work?

7. What are the ethical differences between terrestrial and shipwreck archaeology? Do the same differences exist between terrestrial and other kinds of underwater sites? Do we need a separate code of ethics for underwater archaeology?

8. Should anyone able to meet UNESCO standards be allowed to own an excavated shipwreck? Is ownership of shipwrecks different from ownership of terrestrial sites?

9. What alternatives to age can you suggest as criteria for determining whether a shipwreck should be saved or not?

10. Look at some of the websites for underwater archaeology. Who sponsors each, and what attention does each give to ethical concerns?

Note

1. I enjoyed discussing the UNESCO Convention with J. Hall, a member of the U.S. delegation that attended the UNESCO deliberations as an observer.

Recommended Readings

Bass, G. F., and W. F. Searle
    1988   Shipwrecks and Society. In *Ships and Shipwrecks of the Americas: A History Based on Underwater Archaeology,* edited by G. F. Bass, 256–59. Thames and Hudson, London.

Carrell, Toni L. (editor)
    1990   *Underwater Archaeology Proceedings from the Society for Historical Archaeology Conference, 1990.* Society for Historical Archaeology, Tucson,

Arizona. (See especially papers by J. R. Halsey, P. Throckmorton, G. F. Bass, W. A. Cockrell, and D. H. Keith).

Delgado, James P. (editor)
1997 *Encyclopedia of Underwater and Maritime Archaeology.* British Museum, London.

Kluwer Academic Publishers
2002 The Plenum Series in Underwater Archaeology, edited by J. Barto Arnold III, at www.wkap.nl/prod/s/PSUA (accessed June 2002).

Ruppé, Carol V., and Janet F. Barstad (editors)
2001 International Handbook of Underwater Archaeology. *The Plenum Series in Underwater Archaeology.* Kluwer Academic, New York.

U.S. Government Printing Office
1987 *Hearing before the Subcommittee on Public Lands, National Parks and Forests of the Committee on Energy and Natural Resources.* U.S. Senate, 100th Cong., 1st sess. on S. 858, September 19, 1987.

ALEX W. BARKER

Chapter Six

Archaeological Ethics: Museums and Collections

Stewardship

The twentieth century witnessed a steady growth in the importance of university archaeology in defining the focus of the discipline, and the simultaneous decline in the role of museum-based archaeology except at a few major research museums. While none can deny the advancements in both research and teaching this shift has offered, it also reduced the training afforded students in the use, care, interpretation, and potential of that other portion of the archaeological record, the portion already curated in museums or other repositories.

In situ materials from the past are a fragile and shrinking resource, because of excavation of sites as well as other destructive processes both natural and anthropogenic. Site excavators must weigh the potential benefit of greater knowledge gained against the sure cost of site destruction. Curated collections, by contrast, represent a growing resource whose long-term integrity and utility is enhanced rather than diminished by responsible use. Once excavated, that portion of the archaeological record is gone, except as curated collections and associated records. Rather than being subtractive, however, study of these curated collections and records is additive, with research by successive generations of scholars increasing the utility of these portions of the archaeological record for future analysis. Museum curators, then, have a special and distinct role as stewards of the past.

This is not to say, of course, that we'd be better off digging everything up and packing the archaeological record off to the nearest museum. The curated portion of the archaeological record includes only those objects, records, and data recorded by researchers at the time of recovery and hence is a poor substitute for the extant, in situ record. Nor are processes of decay and disorder banished by museums, but at best they are held at bay through professional training, focused research, and considerable effort. Just as understanding the basic concepts of collections management and curation is necessary for all archaeologists to ensure that as little as possible is lost in the transition from in situ to curated record, so an understanding of broad issues of museum and collection ethics will help archaeologists appreciate the dynamic, complex, and contested ethical issues attendant on collections.

Museum ethics is a separate area, broader in many respects than archeological ethics, and already the subject of many volumes several times the length of this one. Here, my goal is not to cover all ethical issues impacting museums focusing on cultural history, but simply to raise a few representative topics at the intersection of archaeological and museum ethics.

Acquisition and Disposition

Should museums purchase collections of archaeological objects? To some, museums that refuse to purchase archaeological objects or collections are missing valuable opportunities to preserve the past. If museums don't buy these collections, it is argued, the objects simply go to private dealers and collectors, and the potential to learn from these objects or interpret them for a broader audience is lost. These are powerful arguments that have led more than one museum trustee to doubt the competence (or even the sanity) of curators reluctant or unwilling to enter the antiquities marketplace.

There are, however, equally powerful arguments against institutional participation in the buying and selling of archaeological materials. First and foremost is that commercial trade in antiquities drives the destruction and looting of archaeological sites, threatening the integrity of the resource. How can an institution that directly contributes to the commercial demand for antiquities fulfill its ethical obligation to avoid the commercialization of the archaeological record? While a host of other objections to museum purchases of antiquities can be cited—the lesser intellectual and interpretive value of unprovenienced collections, potential legal or regulatory issues relating to the export or looting of materials, questions of authentication, and whether scarce resources would be better spent supporting primary fieldwork—none are as compelling as the responsibility of archaeologists to avoid the commercialization of the archaeological record and contributing to site looting and destruction.

Unlike most repositories, museums have a mission-based obligation to manage their collections in relation to a broader set of institutional objectives. Frequently, these objectives include not only the maintenance of collections, but their judicious development to meet the five core museum functions: to collect, to conserve, to study, to interpret, and to exhibit.[1] Museums must be more deliberate in their acquisitions than many repositories (whose mission is to serve as a storehouse for collections and records, and who frequently charge a fee-for-service for the acceptance of collections) because they have a responsibility to manage their collections to further specific, mission-based purposes. As a result, curatorial ethics also involve considering whether acquisition of a collection advances that institution's mission. A given archaeological collection from the American southwest may be of considerable scientific interest, but may be inappropriate for a museum with a mission-based charge of studying the civilizations of southeast Asia.[2]

Both archaeologists and museum professionals recognize a growing curation crisis, as most museums or repositories lack the space to continue to accept collections at the rate that research, mitigation, and cultural resource management projects are generating materials (see Michael K. Trimble and Eugene A. Marino, chapter 8). Available resources continue to be aimed more at the recovery of collections than at their long-term organization, conservation, and preservation. The growth of the cultural resource management (CRM) industry has not resulted in a concomitant growth in trained staff, space, or funding at museums and repositories to accommodate the resulting collections. This, in turn, leads to difficult ethical dilemmas for collections-holding institutions.

If all appropriate collections cannot be accepted, how should decisions be made regarding which to accept or to decline? If collections contain large volumes of material of lesser-perceived research value (e.g., hundreds of boxes of plate glass from a historic site), should the museum or repository accept only representative voucher specimens of these materials for permanent curation? The same problems affect the management of extant collections, as museums and repositories struggle with the issue of deaccessioning parts of existing collections to make room for new collections or to better care for remaining objects.

Museum acquisitions are generally presumed to be permanent, and while deaccession—the removal and disposition from a museum of portions of its cataloged or accessioned collections—is a necessary and accepted tool of collections management, it is a difficult process. Ethical issues arise not only in deciding what collections or parts of collections should be deaccessioned, but also in establishing the museum's clear title to dispose of the collection and, most importantly, in deciding on the method of disposition. Museum collection policies clearly describe these procedures and explicitly define acceptable forms of disposition. These generally include donation or transfer to a peer institution, trade or exchange with peer institutions, return to the donor or previous title holder, sale, or destruction. Proceeds from sales are restricted by both the American Association of Museums (AAM) and the International Council of Museums codes of professional ethics[3] to use for additional acquisitions or direct care of remaining collections. As many institutions have policies against the sale or purchase of archaeological materials, method of sale and use of proceeds may be moot.

Title and Access

Title is a complex and in many respects problematic concept, actually representing a bundle of separable rights of ownership that may or may not be transferable. More generally, title is rooted in a Western, Lockean tradition of private property whose translation into the contested world of cultural property is at best problematic.[4]

Assessments of title generally consider both completeness, or the degree to which all of the associated rights of ownership are or may be transferred, and quality, or the degree to which a possessor may enjoy those rights undisturbed, as well as assurance that the object acquired is as represented.

Restricted titles, or restricted gifts, represent a significant ethical problem in museum practice. In some cases, a donor may give a gift with explicit or implicit understandings regarding its use. Perhaps, the most common such understanding is that the object(s) will be used for display. As only a small percentage of most museum collections are displayed at any given time, this can frequently lead to disappointment and disillusionment, and demands that objects be returned to the donor. Most museums employ a deed of gift form, in which the donor both warrants that he or she has clear and unrestricted title to the object(s) being donated, and that he or she conveys this title fully and without restriction to the museum or repository.

The growth of collections generated by entities with an interest in restricting access to archaeological materials raises new ethical concerns regarding appropriate levels of access. Sometimes, access restrictions are based on sovereignty, as in the case of Native American tribes or other entities asserting control over cultural materials generated from work on tribal lands. Significant ethical questions surround the generation of archaeological collections that will not be generally available for further study or examination. The general rule is to seek the broadest possible access to the results of any archaeological study, including the material collections and associated records, documents or reports, and in those rare cases where access is restricted the conditions, limitations, and justifications for exclusive or restricted access should be clearly agreed and stated. Generally, the person or entity holding the title to a collection may establish rules of access, but this does not absolve archaeologists of the ethical responsibility to seek the broadest possible access.

Title is also implicated in another key problem facing the discipline: the future of orphaned collections, particularly those generated by university professors in the course of their research. After the retirement of a faculty member, his or her collections may lose their perceived research value and be viewed as a liability to the department or college. In some cases, this leads to responsible arrangements with appropriate museums or repositories that protect collections from the vagaries of departmental interests and changing capacities to store and care for collections. In other cases, collections are viewed as private property, to be taken away at retirement and disposed of as that faculty member wishes. Collections vanish or are rediscovered, in partial form and often missing their accompanying documentation, in attics or garage sales years later. If archaeological research leads to the recovery of collections, ethical practice requires that appropriate arrangements be made for appropriate levels of care for those collections at an appropriate facility, either a museum or archaeological repository. Some academic departments now require that research designs include explicit arrangements for the curation of collections generated by the project.

Unclear title can leave collections in perpetual limbo. Museums and repositories are limited in their ability to accept, transfer, or otherwise manage collections for which they cannot establish clear title, but it is relatively common for archaeological collections to lack clear transfers of title. Although a researcher may have obtained all the necessary permissions from a landowner, such verbal agreements may not be sufficient to allow transfer of clear title to a museum or repository.

Federally associated collections present special problems. Museums hold significant federally associated collections, which they have preserved, conserved, and curated, sometimes for a century or more. Federal agencies retain title, however, leaving both the future of those collections at that institution—and the wisdom of those long-term investments in collections management and care—uncertain.

Archaeological collections include not only the physical objects themselves, but also associated notes, records, photographs, and other documentation giving meaning and significance to the objects. Neither the objects nor the associated records are the property of a given researcher, scholar, or contractor. It is the responsibility of all archaeologists to make adequate and appropriate arrangements for the curation and care of all collections—in the broadest sense of the term—at competent repositories, museums, or other institutions, and to identify the location and accessibility of these collections in publications or other reports.

Value and Values

Museum acceptance or display of objects impacts the ways an object is perceived or valued in the commercial marketplace. Exhibiting objects from a private collection may considerably increase the commercial value of the objects displayed—no small problem in art or anthropology museums where increasing value is likely to lead to increased antiquities trafficking and looting of sites to meet market demand. While this concern may seem remote to many nonmuseum archaeologists, publishing objects or collections may have the same net effect.

Beyond the potential of increasing commercial value of collections, a concern explicitly identified in the Society for American Archaeology's Principles of Archaeological Ethics, exhibition or publication of collections demands a careful consideration of the character and provenance of the collections themselves. If the provenance is unknown, the provenience is still less certain. Not only does this call into question interpretations based on the assumed cultural context and associations of the object or collection, as these may be in error, but without adequate provenience there is cause to question whether the material itself is genuine. As a result, there is a real and considerable potential to obstruct rather than to advance our understanding of the past by building constructs or arguments on false foundations. Some journals have established policies against the publication of objects or collections of unknown provenance, from or contributing to the looting of sites, or that were acquired or exported illegally.

At the same time, however, anyone who can fake an artifact can probably fake a provenience for that artifact with equal ease. Deciding whether to record information from a given collection or artifact where the provenience is less than certain becomes a difficult issue, balancing the prospect of better understanding the past by using all available lines of evidence against the perils enumerated earlier.

As previously noted, many museums are either reluctant or unwilling to purchase archaeological material; stipulations against purchase of archaeological collections except in extraordinary circumstances are not uncommon in institutional collections policies. As a result, one of the few benefits museums can offer donors is tax relief for charitable contributions. Significant claimed tax benefits, however, require an outside appraisal to establish the fair value of the objects, and hence the value of the charitable contribution a donor might claim. Museums themselves cannot appraise items offered to them since they constitute an interested party to the transaction. This introduces a number of problems. First, it involves museums in establishing values for artifacts or collections, albeit indirectly. Second, it means that potential donors must first consult with persons involved in or conversant with the antiquities trade to receive the full benefits of donating to a public institution. In many cases, this means deciding whether to receive a tax benefit for the value of an object or the actual cash value by selling it on the market. Some advocate doing away with the tax benefit for charitable donations entirely, arguing that it promotes commercialization. Others feel it is the only mechanism by which museums can offer some benefit to individuals wishing to preserve their objects or collections through donation to a public institution for future study.

Similar but increasingly esoteric problems arise in establishing the value of an object or collection for insurance purposes, since the main values employed are fair market value or replacement value. The former is, once again, based on established commercial value of like items or collections, while the latter is an artificial estimate at best, as by nature most archaeological collections are unique and irreplaceable.

Conservation and Care

The conservation of archaeological materials represents a distinct, growing field that requires unique kinds of training and expertise. Ideally, conservation, whether in the field or in the museum, should be performed by or under the immediate supervision of a trained archaeological conservator. As a separate discipline, separate codes of professional ethics have also been established for conservators.[5] Many larger field projects now employ the services of an archaeological conservator to ensure that materials are adequately stabilized in the field and to coordinate object care and transport between field and museum. In practice, however, the services of a professionally trained conservator may be beyond the means of smaller field projects, and even many museums.

Formal conservation, however, is based on intrinsic properties of an object and how ambient environments, external hazards, and inherent vice may affect these properties. It does not generally consider the cultural context or social construction of an object or the different kinds of culturally mandated care possibly necessary for the social maintenance of the object.

From the standpoint of object conservation and basic principles of collections management, for example, dried plant material represents a significant risk for introducing mold, insects, increased acidity, humidity, or other threats to the long-term stability of an object. From the standpoint of more holistic care, however, certain dried plants may be necessary for the longer-term care and maintenance of both specific, socially constructed and construed objects and more generally the social practices that animate and give meaning to those objects. Native tribes and consortia of multiple tribes or bands have begun to develop handling and storage protocols for many kinds of archaeological and ethnographic objects.

As a result, many museums have developed hybrid or holistic care protocols that combine principles of object conservation with traditional care mandated by native or descendant groups. The Cultural Resource Center at the National Museum of the American Indian has a separate room used for smoking of objects, the Milwaukee Public Museum allows groups to wrap specific objects in cloth bundled with cedar, sage, and other sacred plants, and the Museum of Indian Arts and Culture in Santa Fe builds storage cases with open vents so kachinas can "breathe."

In addition to considering how an object is stored, concerns may also arise over the location of storage or the kinds of materials with which it is stored. Preferred storage for many kinds of archaeological materials is underground, while groups may prefer that other items, including ethnographic objects like drums, be stored aboveground. Some groups specify that human remains and associated funerary objects should be stored together, and that no other objects should be housed in the same room.

Balancing these sometimes conflicting needs can be difficult, particularly when resources are scarce. In a perfect world, sufficient resources—time, space, staff, and money—would be available to address both object conservation and cultural care priorities on an ongoing basis; if such a perfect world exists, it has no museums.

Some groups specify that only men handle some categories of objects or may prohibit women from working in or near storage rooms while menstruating. Here, traditional care protocols run up against applicable legal codes. From an ethical standpoint, balancing between hard-won rights of women to equal treatment in the workplace and an equally hard-won voice for native peoples in the care and treatment of objects created by their ancestors is difficult at best. Ethical practice in such cases—as in most other cases as well—is based on maintaining clear and open processes for reaching a resolution, rather than on achieving one or another particular outcome.

Interpretation

As archaeologists, we often talk about studying the past. We don't, really. We study the present—those latter-day bits and pieces of the past that survive, those perduring lines of evidence still accessible to us today that allow us to draw inferences about what happened yesterday. Susan Pearce, one of the major authors addressing issues of archaeological curatorship, uses Ferdinand Saussure's distinction between *langue* and *parole* to illustrate the complexity of interpreting that obscured past. From the wide range of unstructured possibilities are drawn a set of forms that a society's communication systems, material culture, and other cultural forms may take. To be culturally intelligible, these forms must be used in apposite ways informed by culturally constructed rules. These rules of use creating structured, meaningful action are the langue. Parole represents everyday behaviors—utterance, making a tool, or cooking a meal—drawn from the langue, the physical actions expressing the semiotic structure. Even in ethnographic cases we don't directly observe the langue, but we may be able to draw inferences about it based on observed parole, the actual structurally informed behavior of people in their daily lives. Archaeology is still another step removed, as the behavior itself is only indirectly available to us as the result of a series of inferences.

Our understanding of the past relies on a similarly structured series of choices. These paradigmatic structures constrain what kinds of problems are worthy of research, what qualifies as credible evidence or methodology, and what kinds of conclusions are warranted given culturally acceptable forms of data.

Finally, a third set of structural filters influences the way this understanding of the past is communicated to museum visitors. The broad range of possible ways of representing the past is structured through the organization of current theories regarding visitor learning, pedagogy, aesthetics, and canons of interpretive exhibition and representation, and from this structured langue individual choices are made and a physical exhibit—the application of rules in a specific case, or parole—is created.

Lindow
man
L? could
also be
applied
other
to

Visitors, of course, must interpret the actual installation of the exhibit through their own sets of rules and constructs, and thus still more layers of signification and meaning must be considered. All of these points are equally valid in other museum contexts, of course, but they have special resonance in anthropology and archaeology because our purpose is to portray other ways of being human, other ranges of possibility, other langues.

Pearce's point is that representations of the past are the result of a long series of distillations and selections regarding what's important and what's relevant in understanding past events or processes. And most of those distillations and selections are influenced more by the dynamics and politics of the modern world than those of the world we seek to portray. As a result, museum interpretations of other times and other cultures often reveal more about the culture creating the display than the culture ostensibly being displayed. A lack of critical reflection has led many museums to perpetuate racist, ethnocentric, or paternalistic views, or ethnic, gender, or other stereotypes. Ethical practice enjoins archaeologists to accurately portray and interpret the past for a diversity of audiences, explicitly and critically reflecting on biases that may influence their interpretations, rather than colonizing the past with our own stereotypes or assumptions, naive or otherwise.

From an ethical standpoint, it is worth extending Pearce's argument beyond the point she intended. This approach, recognizing the various lenses, filters, and differently structured information that inform the viewpoints of different groups (Native American groups, interest groups, archaeologists, educators, exhibit designers, and so on), helps illustrate the complex ethical dilemmas involved in the use, care, and interpretation of collections. Because exhibits or interpretive materials are the physical expression, they draw the criticism. But the problems may be based not on a particular installation so much as the underlying assumptions and structures informing choices made in the presentation of collections or interpretation. Each subsequent iteration of a design may share the same underlying flaws because, however different, each reflects the same deep-seated structures of meaning and expression by the group or groups engaged in the design. Critics thus feel that their concerns are never addressed, designers feel that revisions never satisfy the critics, and all parties leave feeling dissatisfied with both process and outcome.[6]

While the ethical issues raised are real, they are not for the most part based on intentional acts. Simplistic views of ethics focus on conscious choices, resulting in a passive approach where ethical consideration is only given to clearly defined issues of appropriate versus inappropriate behavior. I would advocate a more active approach to ethics, recognizing contingencies and consequences to almost all choices made, and requiring an acknowledgement that critical self-reflection and careful consideration of possible biases and of the potential impact of any course of action is a continuing professional responsibility.

Museum Research and the "Mañana Mentality"

Archaeological sites represent a finite, nonrenewable resource. As every beginning archaeology student learns, the very act of excavation results in the site's destruction. The proportion of material already excavated (or looted) from any given period is steadily increasing, albeit slowly. Thus, the proportion of the archaeological record housed in museums or similar institutions—and hence of the research universe available for substantive archaeological inquiry—increases each year. Unfortunately, this is not simply because of the growth of museum and repository holdings but because of the loss of intact materials to looting, development, and other destructive processes as well.

Archaeology has long implicated museums in a kind of "mañana mentality," a sense that because museums held their collections for posterity, curated collections were already safe, freeing the discipline to focus on fieldwork and research generating new collections.[7] Systematic, collections-based research, emphasis on the research value and utility of extant collections, and careful consideration of the strengths and weaknesses of the collections curated in museums and repositories as subjects for substantive, relevant research were viewed as tasks for another day.

That day is here. Probably the most pressing ethical questions posed by archaeological collections in museums and repositories are simply these. If existing collections are adequate for addressing key questions of culture history and social process, does excavating new sites and generating new collections to address these questions represent best ethical practice? And if they are not sufficient, if new fieldwork is almost always required to address substantive research questions—in other words, if existing collections are insufficient in quality or character to sustain substantive, innovative research on the archaeological record they document—then are we paying adequate attention to the transformation of the in situ record into the curated record? If the destruction of sites to address research questions does not result in collections, records, and associated documents of sufficient quality to allow future generations of researchers to interrogate these data with new questions, new problems, and new viewpoints, are we truly serving as responsible stewards of the archaeological record?

Discussion Questions

1. An important, perhaps unique collection is available for your study, but it is made up of looted artifacts. Which should take priority, the desire to salvage all potential information from the archaeological record or the desire to avoid promoting activities that may further damage the archaeological

record through increasing commercialization or lead to mistaken or misleading results?

2. Consider a distinction between what I have termed "active" and "passive" ethics. Passive ethics involves behaving in an ethical manner when confronted with a clear-cut ethical choice. Active ethics refers to recognizing that all activities may have ethical or practical consequences and considering these potential consequences as part of one's professional responsibilities. Which is more important in dealing with collections issues? Why?

3. A local collector approaches you to establish the value of her collection so she may receive a tax write-off for her donation to a nearby museum. If unable to receive a tax benefit, she is determined to sell the collection on the open market. What should you do?

4. In preparing an exhibition about a specific American Indian tribe, you find that your interpretation of the tribe's past based on archaeological evidence is fundamentally at odds with the tribe's own interpretation of its past based on transmitted knowledge and tradition. How should these conflicting viewpoints be reconciled?

5. A collector offers his collection to your museum, with the condition that he can control who has access to the materials. Do you accept the collection? A utility company makes a similar offer. Now what? What if an American Indian tribe made the same offer? Is your decision the same in each case? Why or why not?

6. As part of an archaeological project several years ago in the little-known country of central Myopia, you excavated a series of important hoards of Bronze Age goods. At the time, your agreement with the government allowed you to retain a portion of the hoard for your museum with clear title. Now a new government claims the material as cultural patrimony, saying export permission was given only because the previous regime was starved for the hoard (... er, hard) currency your project provided. How will you respond? What factors will you consider in weighing your options?

7. Are there situations where the purchase of artifacts or collections on the commercial market is justified? Why or why not?

8. Because museums hold their collections as a public trust, and for the benefit of diverse, sometimes conflicting constituencies, it can be argued that the mission of archaeological museums is concerned as much with the future as the past. What issues may affect the ability of museums to preserve the curated archaeological record for the benefit of future generations? Are there specific populations with a greater or lesser stake in that future? Who benefits from the curation of the archaeological record?

9. If existing collections are inadequate to address relevant, significant research questions, why? What can be done to ensure that collections being generated today have continuing utility and meaning for the discipline?

Notes

1. Noted museum essayist Stephen Weil suggests that these traditional core functions are evolving into three: 1) to preserve, 2) to study, and 3) to communicate. His approach has the advantage of being simpler and of embracing the responsibilities of both formal, exhibit-based museums and repositories. All museums share an educational mandate, and the American Association of Museums specifically calls on member museums to place education at the center of their public service roles.

2. For the same reasons, curators need specialized knowledge not only of the material culture, ethnography, and archaeology of a region, but also of cultural property law, international conventions or treaties, and intellectual property statutes specific to that area. These are detailed and rapidly changing areas of knowledge, specific to individual regions or countries, and lie beyond the modest scope of this chapter. Many are covered, at least in abbreviated form, elsewhere in this volume.

3. AAM not only established its Code of Ethics for museums and museum professionals, but institutions accredited by AAM are also required to have established a formally adopted code of ethics outlining appropriate procedures and policies relating to collections, governance, and other core areas of museum practice.

4. Communal ownership or other shared rights of title or possession are poorly served by the partitive orientation of Western private property traditions, whose primary function is to define and circumscribe an individual's rights in opposition to those of the wider group or groups.

5. For example, see the Code of Ethics and Guidelines for Professional Practice of the American Institute for the Conservation of Historic and Artistic Works, revised 1994.

6. Or, to put it more simply, we may start out confident we have addressed all conceivable ethical concerns, but end up "not Saussure" after all.

7. Some scholars recently noted that this may reflect an underlying gender bias as well. Fieldwork was viewed as a male activity, while women were relegated to laboratories and cataloging collections "made" by their male counterparts.

Recommended Readings

American Association of Museums
    1991   Code of Ethics for Museums, at www.aam-us.org/aamcoe.htm (accessed April 2002).

American Institute for the Conservation of Historic and Artistic Work
    1994   AIC Code of Ethics and Guidelines for Practice, at aic.stanford.edu/pubs/ethics.html (accessed April 2002).

Edson, Gary (editor)
    1997   *Museum Ethics*. Routledge, London.

International Council of Museums
    1986   ICOM Code of Ethics for Museums, at www.icom.org/ethics.html (accessed April 2002).

Malaro, Marie
    1998   *A Legal Primer on Managing Museum Collections.* 2nd ed. Smithsonian
    Institution Press, Washington, DC.

Messenger, Phyllis Mauch (editor)
    1999   *Ethics of Collecting Cultural Property: Whose Culture? Whose Property?* 2nd
    ed. University of New Mexico Press, Albuquerque.

Pearce, Susan
    1990   *Archaeological Curatorship.* Smithsonian Institution Press, Washington, DC.

Phelos, Marilyn
    1998   *The Law of Cultural Property and Natural Heritage: Protection, Transfer, and
    Access.* Kalos Kapp Press, Evanston, IL.

CHRISTOPHER A. BERGMAN
JOHN F. DOERSHUK

Chapter Seven

Cultural Resource Management and the Business of Archaeology

American cultural resources represent the historic and living heritage of the people of the United States. Cultural resources include a variety of properties and objects, such as buildings and structures, sacred places, historic documents, museum collections and individual artifacts, and historic and modern landscapes. According to Tom King, "cultural resource management" (CRM) is a term coined in the 1970s to describe the process by which cultural properties and objects are treated with respect to various federal environmental and historic preservation laws such as the National Environmental Policy Act (NEPA) and the National Historic Preservation Act (NHPA). The past two decades of the twentieth century bore witness to an explosion of CRM-related archaeological consulting—the "business of archaeology."

In terms of cultural resources, NEPA represents an umbrella policy requiring federal agency oversight of undertakings "to consider all environmental impacts, on all aspects of the environment," including sociocultural concerns. The NHPA is exclusively concerned with the sociocultural environment, specifically historic resources and other cultural properties.

The enactment of the NHPA in 1966 initiated the development of various institutions vital to national historic preservation concerns including

- the maintenance and expansion of a National Register of Historic Places (NRHP) that includes properties of "significance in American history, architecture, archeology, engineering, and culture";
- the creation of an Advisory Council for Historic Preservation (ACHP) that is responsible for overseeing the NHPA, providing historic preservation education and training, and serving the needs of Congress and the president; and
- the establishment of State Historic Preservation Officers (SHPOs), a group that conducts state- or territory-wide inventories of historic properties,

nominates properties to the NRHP, maintains state- or territory-wide preservation plans, and participates in Section 106 of the NHPA reviews.

Section 106 of the NHPA embodies the rules that govern the manner in which cultural resources are treated during any undertaking involving a federal lead agency, federal funding, or federal lands. These regulations were formally issued in 1979 by the ACHP and codified as 36CFR800, that is, Title 36, Part 800 of the Code of Federal Regulations. Section 106 has been amended in 1986, 1992, and 1999, and it requires federal agencies to

- "take into account the effect of the undertaking on any district, site, building, structure, or object that is included in or eligible for inclusion in the National Register"; and
- "afford the Advisory Council on Historic Preservation . . . reasonable opportunity to comment with regard to such undertaking."

Section 106, at least in practical terms, is most easily explained as a series of steps involving data collection, punctuated by consultation and decision making. These steps represent a logical framework by which data can be gathered and interpreted, allowing for informed decisions regarding effects to cultural resources during an undertaking. The steps in the process may be broadly summarized as identification, evaluation, and mitigation. In the parlance of U.S. archaeological cultural resource studies, these are referred to as Phases I, II, and III of investigation, respectively. The identification phase considers the presence of cultural properties within an Area of Potential Effect (APE). Evaluation tests those cultural resources against a series of criteria that gauge NRHP eligibility, whereas mitigation develops measures that offset adverse effects to any NRHP-eligible or -listed properties.

The preceding paragraph greatly oversimplifies the complexity (and sometimes frustrations) of implementing Section 106. In fact, it requires numerous skilled professionals, among them archaeologists, architectural historians, and preservation planners, to shepherd both public- and private-sector clientele through the compliance process. According to the 1994 Society for American Archaeology (SAA) census, more than two-thirds of the archaeologists practicing in the United States today are involved in Section 106–mandated archaeology.

Ethics and CRM

As highlighted elsewhere in this volume, ethics is concerned with morality—what is good and bad and what comprises moral duty and obligation. The French existential philosopher Jean-Paul Sartre remarked in 1945, "The Good must be done." For Sartre, the Good results from choices; it is an objective reality that results from human efforts and at the same time transcends them. Ethical behavior references a generalized condition; when one makes a choice for oneself specifically, one chooses for all universally. If we believe it to be "good" to behave deceitfully in a given situation, then we must acknowledge it is equally "good" for others to do so in similar situations (all things being equal). It is in this manner that the notion of responsibility becomes embedded in our choices.

In general, law and supporting regulation drive the CRM process, but the forces of development and production motivate it. As a client of ours once remarked, "We are in the business of construction, not archaeology." His pithy comment hints at an important problem associated with ethics, that of value. Some person, thing, or situation that is desirable and has worth is considered to have value; that which is deemed valuable is good. Human beings impose value on the world; gold, for example, is simply a heavy, ductile metal and yet, as we all know, it has an assigned social value beyond its material composition. From the perspective of our client friend, construction is good and archaeology is simply okay. The perception of what has value is therefore highly relative.

The ethical dilemmas of the cultural resource manager center on balancing values that are often at odds with one another, such as development and preservation or compliance and research. To undertake this task, the CRM practitioner needs to

- understand federal, state, and local cultural resource regulations;
- identify any specific permit requirements of the lead regulatory agency or agencies;
- understand the nature of the client's industry, financing, and schedule;
- know the specifics regarding a proposed project's horizontal and vertical APE;
- know the limits of personal and corporate professional capability;
- adapt archaeological methods to meet the client's compliance needs;
- ensure the proper identification and treatment of a variety of cultural resource types; and
- be able to negotiate the resolution of conflicts.

Earl Derr Biggers's fictional detective Charlie Chan, a master of aphorisms, once remarked that an expert was merely a "person who make correct decisions quickly." CRM is a consulting industry that relies on experts who routinely act as crisis managers. When a client has a problem, consultants are engaged, and the expectation is a speedy resolution of potential delays to the project. In assisting a client, the consultant is faced with a variety of technical issues that impinge on ethical considerations, such as whether or not to survey, the type and intensity of investigation, the significance of sites encountered, and the treatment of significant sites. In the following sections, we will examine a variety of areas where ethical considerations and CRM archaeology come into contact. This discussion is not meant to be all inclusive, but rather an overview of the types of situations that confront consultants and regulators during the cultural resource compliance process.

The Archaeological Discipline and CRM

The archaeological discipline embraces a wide variety of topics and professional settings. CRM consultants use the practical skills of archaeological, historical, and architectural inquiry to assist their clientele with meeting the requirements of Section 106. Since the outset of CRM in the 1970s, an unfortunate attitude has persisted in the archaeological community emphasizing differences between investigations conducted as research and investigations conducted as CRM. This mind-set has its origins in a kind of elitism that juxtaposes the purity of academic research against quick and dirty compliance investigations. (Indeed, much of the early CRM was in fact salvage archaeology conducted under very difficult scheduling and funding constraints.) It has resulted in professional and political divisions between academia and those practicing CRM, as well as the intellectual marginalization of CRM studies as "gray literature." Surprisingly, some CRM professionals accept this prejudicial devaluation and pass it on to their practice. The oft-repeated statements, uttered by consultants and regulators alike, that "CRM archaeology is just compliance work" or "this is not archaeology, but CRM" herald this acceptance.

The concept "just compliance archaeology" implies application of a certain set of standards that fall below those normally employed in investigations conducted under other auspices. Typically, CRM studies, at least archaeological ones, follow agency-mandated "cookie cutter" guidelines for fieldwork, analysis, and reporting. These guidelines set the minimally acceptable standards to allow an investigation to pass through the review process. The net result is lots of reports with homogenized results that often only cover basic data description: how many units dug, how many strata identified, how many artifacts recovered, and so on. These reports lack the kind of data synthesis needed to describe one of the fundamental aspects of archaeological study: understanding past behavior. It seems an act of bad faith to excuse a less-robust approach to CRM fieldwork and analysis by falling back on the argument that CRM is "just compliance archaeology." The whole situation becomes even more inexcusable from an ethical standpoint when one considers that modern CRM investigations are usually better funded than research programs.

It must be admitted that university faculty, consultants, and regulators do not take their responsibility to archaeology, practiced as CRM, seriously enough. This is especially significant when one considers that most archaeological inquiry in the United States is now conducted as CRM, rendering CRM virtually synonymous with American archaeology. We suggest that the first step to achieving a more responsible attitude is recognition by the profession at large that there simply are no necessary qualitative differences between CRM and other types of archaeological inquiry. There may be differences in the type and source of funding, but beyond that the methodology, technical applications, and goals should be the same.

CRM practitioners need their colleagues teaching in anthropology departments to promote greater emphasis on the practical applications of archaeology. We are not just referring to the fact that students will likely require preparation for a career outside of academia such as CRM, but they must also be able to relate to archaeological problems from more than just a theoretical perspective. In our experience as CRM archaeologists, it is woefully obvious that newly graduated students frequently possess a limited understanding of basic field and analytical techniques. As James Adovasio remarked during the 1997 SAA meetings, "[G]enerations of theoretically elegant students . . . have been streaming from American graduate schools since 1970. Unfortunately, most are methodologically incompetent and, as the saying goes, could not excavate their way out of a sack!" At a time when public- and private-sector clients routinely voice concerns over project costs, it is inappropriate for them to shoulder the burden of training that logically should be incorporated into university classroom and field school curricula.

CRM principal investigators (PIs) are responsible for the practical implementation of Section 106–mandated archaeology. It is important that these individuals understand that their vision of what constitutes good archaeology has a direct effect on the quality of the data generated in CRM studies. If compliance with Section 106 is narrowly interpreted as minimum effort, then data recovery excavations with gross artifact proveniencing units or simplistic analyses like categorization of prehistoric lithic materials solely into primary, secondary, or tertiary flakes will invariably result. These methodologies diminish the quality of the data obtained, limit their usefulness, and are disproportionate with the financial outlay provided by clients. This, in turn, fuels justifiable criticism over the high-cost/low-research benefit ratio ascribed to many CRM undertakings.

Agencies overseeing the Section 106 process should move away from investigative guidelines that may be termed "cookie cutter." In the context of Phase II evaluation or Phase III mitigation, for example, establishing *quantity*-based standards (e.g., a fixed percentage of an impact zone must be excavated) as the means for achieving compliance is common practice by many SHPO offices. Although this approach simplifies the process of developing a research strategy, it downplays more qualitative considerations, such as the manner in which the artifacts are recovered, the validity of research issues related to the NRHP eligibility of a site, and the goals of data recovery as a mitigation measure.

On occasion, alternative mitigation practices, such as "mitigation banking" or excavation outside a zone of impact, may be in the best interest of the cultural resources. Consideration of such alternatives requires agency personnel to maintain an open mind toward the methods applied during the preparation of a treatment plan. Like CRM PIs, agency personnel must ensure that their understanding of archaeological investigation is on a par with current methodologies. In 1990, when inquiring as to whether a certain SHPO office (nameless to protect the innocent) would like us to conduct deep testing along the floodplain of a major river, we were told that although it "might be informative," it was not necessary. More than a decade later, geomorphological studies are still underutilized in CRM investigations, although the situation is improving.

The CRM Profession

The successful cultural resource manager is a problem solver, a person who can balance competing interests, successfully achieving both the ends of the client and meeting (hopefully also exceeding) the demands of Section 106. In almost all cases, the balancing act involves compromise. In the ethical arena of black and white, compromise represents a gray zone we like to think of as the "realistic." Recognizing that the ideal is wholesale preservation of resources, the CRM professional must develop strategies that minimize effects to cultural materials in the face of a reality that proposed development is likely to proceed in the majority of cases. From our experience, the ability to compromise is critical to the CRM profession. Knowing how often, when, and where to compromise requires good judgment based on an unfailing sense of the responsibility of dealing with a nonrenewable resource.

Former president Calvin Coolidge once commented, "The business of America is business." CRM from the business perspective is intimately linked with development-oriented clientele. In providing advice on Section 106 compliance, the service a CRM consultant provides is closer to an attorney–client relationship than that of a police officer. A common misunderstanding of novices to the world of CRM consulting is what role to play. Regulators and law enforcement agencies ensure that an applicant complies with the regulations, whereas the cultural resource manager's job is to provide sound advice that guides the client toward making the right decisions. Advising the client begins with an assessment of whether the proposed action will trigger Section 106 or not. If a proposed project triggers Section 106, it will be necessary to develop a program to identify and evaluate the effects on cultural resources. Some clients, such as the natural gas industry regulated by the Federal Energy Regulatory Commission, are extremely savvy regarding the process. Others, such as the burgeoning wireless communication industry or the coal industry, simply don't understand why Section 106 is "victimizing" them. One private developer we worked with in 1993 exclaimed in a fit of pique that having to do CRM "was an uncompensated taking." A fair amount of time can be spent by the CRM professional, sometimes on the receiving end of verbal abuse, explaining why a particular client must comply with Section 106. This aspect of the job is best considered part of public education, and if it keeps a client from running afoul of the law and helps protect cultural resources, then it is time well spent and ultimately a good business practice.

CRM PIs must balance the conflicting interests of cost effectiveness and scheduling, research methodology, and the quality of results obtained. In simple terms, there seem to be two approaches utilized by CRM operations to conduct projects. The first may be termed the "assembly line," whereas the second may be termed the "craft shop." The assembly line involves fragmentation of an investigation into specific tasks such as fieldwork, geomorphology, lithic analyses, or ethnobotany. The results are then patched together with little or no interaction among the individuals conducting the studies. Although compartmentalization may provide a measure of economic efficiency, it produces disjointed results lacking proper synthesis, an anathema for our critics in academia. The craft shop approach is based on a single person, or a small team of individuals, directly overseeing the work effort from project planning to fieldwork through analysis and reporting. Our experience suggests that this can be more labor intensive, involving one or more senior personnel commanding greater salaries, but it has the advantage of producing greater resolution in the results. Deciding what is best highlights the relative nature of the perception of good. The assembly-line approach may represent the best solution for a client in that it achieves acceptable results with cost efficiency. The craft shop, although not always to the client's economic advantage from a strict bottom-line mentality, is most likely to produce meaningful results archaeologically.

Decisions regarding what methods will yield the best results are one problem; selecting the right personnel can be another. While driving through Gettysburg one day, a member of Pennsylvania's Bureau of Historic Preservation pointed out that a prehistoric archaeologist had directed investigations at one of the Civil War field hospitals. Apparently, the archaeologist had overlooked some important details in the excavations and our colleague stated that it seemed inappropriate for prehistorians to direct activities on historic sites and vice versa. One misconception confronting CRM professionals, especially those within large multidisciplinary firms, is the expectation that any archaeologist can excavate any site at any time. This position is motivated by monetary concerns, as few businesses like to admit they are out of their league and should pass off work. In the case of Phase I survey, it may not be so important what the area of expertise of the PI is (assuming he or she understands the dynamics of site location within a given landscape); however, for evaluation and mitigation it is essential. Applying the right professional skills to a specific investigation ensures not only proper treatment of cultural resources, but also that a client's project gets done efficiently and correctly. The Register of Professional Archaeologists, currently a 1,500-member professional standards organization, is very clear on this matter, stating that we should "recommend to employers or clients the employment of other archaeologists or other expert consultants upon encountering archaeological problems outside [our] own competence." Competent professionals making informed decisions about the treatment and significance of cultural resources are critical to the historic preservation process as will be seen in the next section.

Treatment of Cultural Properties and Materials

Donald L Hardesty and Barbara J. Little correctly describe the NRHP as "the key to cultural resources evaluation within the U.S. Federal regulatory framework." There are four criteria used in assessing NRHP eligibility:

- Criterion A concerns properties that are associated with events that have made a significant contribution to the broad patterns of our history;
- Criterion B concerns properties that are associated with the lives of persons significant in our past;
- Criterion C concerns properties that embody the distinctive characteristics of a type, period, or method of construction, that represent the work of a master, that possess high artistic value, or that represent a significant and distinguishable entity whose components may lack individual distinction; and
- Criterion D concerns properties that have yielded, or may be likely to yield, information important in prehistory or history.

These four criteria represent the terms used to assess the significance of cultural resources. They are not the only yardsticks; a property must also display integrity among other considerations. Criteria A to D are vague, leaving plenty of room for subjective interpretation and argument. At the root of most disagreements regarding eligibility is the problem of significance, another assigned value based on relative perspectives. A noteworthy example of this problem concerns the decision surrounding what constituted the eligible portions of Mount Shasta in California. The keeper of the NRHP confined the property boundaries to only the upper slopes without consulting Native Americans who were petitioning eligibility for the entire mountain. According to the keeper, timber harvesting at the base of the mountain compromised integrity, a view not shared by Native Americans, who considered the condition of the forest as inconsequential. This situation clearly highlights the potential for biased interpretation, not just in the wording of the NRHP criteria and standards themselves, but also in their application.

In Pennsylvania, we have been engaged in a five-year argument, just about to erupt again, regarding the eligibility of upland plowzone lithic scatters. One side of the argument contends that these sites lack potential for yielding high-quality interpretive data and, based on lack of integrity, are not eligible for the NRHP. In our opinion, this belief incorrectly considers upland plowzone sites to be inherently flawed, damaged by decades of agricultural activities. In fact, it is more likely that the perceived poor quality of such sites results from inadequate field and analytical methodologies. In other words, it is not plowzone sites that are flawed, but rather the investigative techniques used to interpret them. For example, at the Early Woodland West Runway site (15Be391) in Kentucky careful excavation techniques combined with experimental and microwear studies helped to define prehistoric activity areas in a shallowly buried plowzone setting. The refitting efforts at the early Paleo-Indian Nobles Pond site in Ohio and the late Archaic site (36So106) in Pennsylvania not only clearly indicate that the reassembling of artifacts is possible at sites largely confined to plowzone contexts, but also that this methodology can isolate activity zones in similar occupations lacking pristine preservation. Outside of the United States, there is a growing body of literature, some of it CRM generated, that also warns against the devaluing of archaeological sites composed of surface or near-surface lithic scatters.

Beyond the more esoteric arguments related to site significance lies the treatment of artifacts recovered during CRM studies. These issues include identification of ownership and the need for proper curation on completion of a project. Recently, a federal agency involved in the Section 106 compliance process indicated in a proposal request that an arrangement had been made with the site's landowner concerning the final disposition of an artifact sample. The final deal stated that the landowner would hand over the bulk of the collection in exchange for having the artifacts appraised. Any artifact, including funerary objects, deemed to have a value beyond a certain dollar amount would be retained by the landowner. Certainly, the attempt to gain control of a large number of artifacts for museum curation, mostly prehistoric lithic debitage of little interest to a private collector, is a laudable end. However, this end does not seem justified by the means that involved an explicit statement that artifacts have monetary value as collectibles. In a day and age when archaeologists are trying to discourage looting and damage to sites, the compromise developed here sends the wrong message to the public.

Without a doubt, the public is an important consumer of the intellectual output of archaeologists. The following section reviews some issues related to CRM practice that result from differing perceptions of value by various ethnic groups making up the American national identity.

The Cultural Heritage of Others

According to the 1994 SAA census, the majority of archaeologists (over 90 percent) practicing in the United States are of European ancestry. Based on this statistic, it is clear that the majority of CRM professionals are routinely dealing with the cultural heritage of others. In our own careers, this has involved the study of prehistoric and historic period Native American sites and nineteenth-century African American settlements.

In the summer of 2001, we made a trip to a reconstructed late prehistoric village along the banks of the Great Miami River in Ohio. Among our party were a Choctaw woman and a Sicangu Lakota woman and her son who expressed an interest in seeing the site. While touring the reconstructed houses and other facilities, it became clear that both women displayed a reluctance to enter the interiors of the structures. In fact, it was only after the Lakota woman's son cajoled his mother that they finally entered one of the houses. Later, we inquired if there was a problem, and the response from both women was that they had no idea who had occupied these structures in the past and were concerned about lingering "bad influences." Their observation contains an important consideration for CRM practitioners. Our empirical way of seeing things may hold little validity for those whose cultural heritage we are studying and, if we don't learn to ask, there may also be important avenues of research entirely missed by CRM studies as typically configured.

As emphasized many times previously, CRM is at its heart a consultative process. Section 106 is about dialog. Nowhere does this seem more essential than when dealing with the prehistory and history of groups outside the dominant culture. It is our belief that many of the laws (e.g., the Native American Graves Protection and Repatriation Act) enacted in the late twentieth century, as well as the continuing air of acrimony (e.g., the "Kennewick Man" fracas), can be partly attributed to the failure of archaeologists to listen to and consult with Native Americans. Simply put, Native American feelings regarding their cultural patrimony have not consistently been taken into consideration and are routinely subordinated to the pursuit of science. Once again, we encounter the thorny issue of value: science is good and Native American feelings are simply okay—to some archaeologists anyway.

The development of the role of Tribal Historic Preservation Officers (THPOs), resulting from amendments to the NHPA in 1992 and 1999, increased the participation of tribal groups in the Section 106 process. The office of the THPO is an important step toward empowering Native Americans in matters of historic preservation. Other positive developments are a small, but hopefully steady, increase in the number of Native Americans working in the CRM sector along with other minority groups in the United States. In this regard, education clearly plays an important role in encouraging such individuals to consider CRM as a career path, as well as making archaeology accessible to a wider and more diverse public.

CRM and the Public

Every archaeologist has a continuing responsibility to public education. Our cultural heritage is subject to mixed ownership, both private and public and at the local, state, and federal levels. The concept of ownership, a keystone of American economic and political structure, implies privileged control with a potential disregard for interests beyond those of the immediate owner. Given this mind-set, it is hardly surprising that the citizenry lacks a developed sense of custodianship regarding historic resources. This inevitably leads to situations such as those witnessed at Slack Farm in Kentucky, or the GE Mount Vernon Hopewell Mound in Indiana, among many other tragic examples that hit the headlines in the 1990s. Any interest in improving the current situation must be founded on a well-informed public actively involved in historic preservation issues. If the archaeological community feels a lack of support for the time and money required to maintain the historic preservation process, it may be a reflection of the relative lack of effort directed toward public education.

In terms of CRM archaeological investigations, public education means that all mitigation projects should incorporate serious and effective outreach programs to be presented in popular articles, videos, posters, open-site visitation days, and so on. Many federal lead agencies and SHPOs are now actively encouraging such outreach as part of Section 106 compliance and require mitigation plans to stipulate measures for involving the public. It is clear that archaeology is an easy sell; when questioned as to the profession we pursue as archaeologists, the response is usually one of enthusiastic inquiry. It is a mistake not to capitalize on the natural interest people have in the past and use it to benefit the archaeological profession and historic preservation.

Conclusion

There is no doubt that each one of us has an idea of what constitutes the Good (*sensu* Sartre), however much we may differ in our individual perspectives about what is good for us. In the previous discussion, we have deliberately avoided calling attention to business practices that are obviously inappropriate, such as "lowballing" competitive bids to get work or unjustifiably inflating a scope of work as a means of increasing revenue. Undoubtedly, there are immediate financial benefits to such practices (a personal good), otherwise people would not resort to them. However, such activities clearly represent a disservice to the Good of the CRM profession, resulting in work that doesn't get done due to lack of funding or angry clients who rightly feel they have been gouged.

Turning to the larger picture, it seems to us that the Good in the context of historic preservation and CRM is achieving a proper balance between the exigency of development and the need to identify and protect cultural resources. As populations continue to grow, the national and global demand for industrial expansion and economic development will continue to accelerate. At the same time, the importance of historic preservation in the face of development is paramount; the inexorable pace of construction, consuming vestiges of the past, is gradually but persistently erasing monuments of national and personal identity.

The current milieu in which North American archaeology finds itself might be described as a "house divided" and, as we all have heard, divided houses do not stand. A wide diversity of opinion exists as to the value of Section 106–mandated archaeology and its implementation through public and private CRM programs. The past few years have seen continuing antagonism between academics and CRM practitioners, especially within archaeology, as well as the appearance of various watchdog groups aimed at protecting the political and financial interests of CRM firms and their employees. Although such interest groups may signal attainment of a previously unknown level of sophistication, their emergence betrays the entrenched nature of vested concerns in the nonresearch aspects of archaeological and other CRM practices in the United States.

If achieving balance in the face of competing values represents the Good in terms of clients, historic preservation, and development, the same could be said for the archaeological community as a whole. Given the volume of archaeological studies conducted as CRM (over $300 million in contracts and an average of forty-four reports per firm in a five-year period), it is imperative to find ways to improve the quality of these investigations. All archaeologists, regardless of their employment situation, have a role in this undertaking. Universities must improve the quality of student field and analytical training and encourage their graduate students and faculty to exploit the copious data available from regional CRM studies. CRM firms must develop and implement research designs that maximize data quality, while regulatory personnel must improve the vision and standards of what comprises compliance. This is a tall order, requiring a new level of cooperation among very differently situated professionals, but the payoff will be a revitalized CRM, part of a holistic archaeological profession that enhances the value and quality of our nation's intellectual and social life.

Discussion Questions

1. In what ways is preservation a goal of CRM (or not)? How can preservation be built into a CRM project? How does CRM work provide a challenge for the ethic of stewardship?
2. How do differing perceptions of value affect the manner in which cultural properties are treated?
3. How do varying perspectives toward the CRM profession affect the quality and type of research produced in Section 106 investigations?
4. Does compromise seem appropriate when considering damaging effects to a nonrenewable resource?
5. Do the NRHP criteria provide an adequate measure for gauging site significance? As written, do they reflect a bias toward the cultural heritage of certain sectors of American society?
6. In what ways can education and efforts to involve the public in CRM provide benefits to national historic preservation efforts?
7. How do corporate interests, in terms of issues like profitability, result in potential conflicts for the CRM professional in a business setting?

8. What are the ethical consequences of adopting business practices such as "lowballing" project bids?
9. What is the role of government in CRM?
10. Who benefits from CRM?
11. How is CRM different in other countries?

Recommended Readings

Advisory Council on Historic Preservation
    n.d.   Protecting Historic Properties: A Citizen's Guide to Section 106 Review. Pamphlet. Washington, DC.

Baker, Joe (editor)
    2000   The Pennsylvania Cultural Resource Management Symposium. *Journal of the Middle Atlantic Archaeological Conference* 16.

Green, William F., and John F. Doershuk
    1998   Cultural Resource Management and American Archaeology. *Journal of Archaeological Research* 6(2):121–67.

Hardesty, Donald L., and Barbara J. Little
    2000   *Assessing Site Significance*. AltaMira, Walnut Creek, CA.

King, Thomas F.
    1998   *Cultural Resource Laws and Practice*. AltaMira, Walnut Creek, CA.

National Register of Historic Places
    2002   Listing a Property: What Is the Process? at www.cr.nps.gov/nr/listing.htm (accessed April 2002).

MICHAEL K. TRIMBLE
EUGENE A. MARINO

Chapter Eight

Archaeological Curation: An Ethical Imperative for the Twenty-First Century

In the course of studying and practicing archaeology, we constantly come across a familiar parable that has been with us since early graduate school lectures and is still heard today at professional meetings. This parable states that 1) archaeology is, first and foremost, a science grounded in basic research methods and 2) that, as a science, all archaeological data should be saved for future study and educational purposes. Though often proclaimed, we don't think that many archaeologists really listen to its message. In fact, the parable has become a sort of social science "pseudo babble" that justifies constant excavation while doing little to further the use of existing collections for either scientific research or general educational purposes. There are exceptions, but on the whole, archaeologists value new material over old even though they often argue the opposite position.

We, therefore, feel justified in stating here that ethical practice within this discipline should include the care of archaeological collections as a priority. These collections should be valued, curated, and studied, not just by archaeologists, but by everyone with a professional interest and the results of those studies should be made widely available. If, as Ned Woodall suggested to one of the authors thirty years ago, a discipline is judged by how it treats its data, then we as a discipline have an ethical responsibility to treat our data much better than we have thus far.

Background

Archaeology, like other disciplines, has spent serious time and attention during the past thirty years developing its own set of ethics, or guiding philosophy, with respect to various aspects of the profession (see the appendix for various codes of ethics). The Antiquities Act of 1906, the National Historic Preservation Act of 1966, the

Archaeological and Historic Preservation Act of 1974, and the Archaeological Resources Protection Act of 1979 all mention, in varying levels of detail, the importance of professionally maintaining archaeological collections for the future and underscore the importance of the conservation ethic in archaeology. However, for the past century collections generation has far outweighed collections management, especially with respect to time and funds expended. If curation resources are not adequate, then reinterpretation and reproduction of results—fundamental tenets of science—become impossible. If archaeologists and museum professionals do not adhere to a strict code of conduct for the long-term care of these materials, then everything else they espouse, such as education, outreach, and scientific explanation, is moot.

Curation—The 1970s, 1980s, and 1990s

Since 1976, a number of major symposia on archaeological curation have taken place at various professional meetings. All the papers have acknowledged, in one form or another, a crisis within American archaeology and that the crisis relates directly to the condition of archaeological collections. Some topics discussed at early events focused on the use of regional centers for curation (Farnsworth and Struever 1977:13–15; Hester 1977:4–10) or examined the proper ways to store collections (Ford 1980:55–62), the growing use of computers for collections management (Wilcox 1980:43–52), and the ethics of curation itself (King 1980:10–18). Many of the topics first mentioned almost thirty years ago (Marquardt 1977) and further explored in recent years still elicit similar discussion points, and they are still valid. Though topics may vary, each time archaeological curation is discussed a common theme quickly surfaces: something should be done and done quickly to address the long-term care of archaeological collections.

For most of the past century, collections care, albeit nonstandard and unevenly applied, has centered on objects. By the 1980s, those advocating the care of *everything* associated with an archaeological collection (e.g., associated documents) finally began to be heard. Andrea Lee Novick (1980:35) notes that it is easy to forget the quantity of documentation generated from archaeological investigations (fieldwork and research), but that the documents are no less important than the objects and no less protected by legislation. Richard I. Ford (1984:135) notes that it is important to remember that an archaeological collection is not just objects, but documentation *and* objects. Thus, in the last few years artifacts and records were, at least implicitly, united forever in terms of importance and necessity. Sydel Silverman (1992:1) points out that for anthropology, records are more than historical references to events; they are primary data and stand for objects and associations that are unique and, in some cases (as in archaeology), no longer available for examination.

With the publication of 36 CFR Part 79 by the National Park Service in September 1991, definitions, standards, procedures, and guidelines were established for federal agencies, for the first time, to preserve prehistoric and historic cultural materials and their associated documents—an important step in and of itself as it explicitly tied records to objects. This regulation, though an unfunded mandate, authorized archaeologists to build costs for curation directly into their contracts with the agency sponsoring the investigation. It established guidelines to ensure the proper maintenance of these collections in perpetuity and created a link between federal cultural resource managers and museum professionals and archaeologists. It also defined an archaeological collection as including associated documents (field notes, photographs, background information, and "administrativia"), forever connecting the artifacts to the records generated during their excavation. For federal collections, artifacts and records remain the property of the government and both are required to be adequately managed.

Discussion

Our aim here is to draw attention to a process through which practitioners of archaeology can begin to ascertain whether they are approaching long-term collections care with ethics in mind using what Joseph Fletcher (1966:26–39) calls an empirical set of inquiries that are neither too simplistic nor too specific in scope, but grounded on specific, case-based needs.

Ethics are, after all, about making choices. Good choices—particularly those that benefit long-term care and use of archaeological collections—require a systematic approach and critical analysis of available options. This last point cannot be emphasized enough.

Our process for making such choices begins with a basic statement: proper care for archaeological collections should take a balanced approach. For example, we have encountered many curation facilities with exemplary computer systems and database abilities for recording information about their collections, but with collections stored in buildings with no fire-suppression systems or no security of any kind. Some collections are stored in state-of-the-art buildings or in the best museum-quality cabinets that money can buy, but lack a system to adequately track the materials, have no user-friendly way of allowing access to the materials by interested researchers, and have only temporary staff to assist them. In many cases, curation facilities are merely snapshots of a particular interest on the part of their staff. They often do not reflect a coherent understanding of what is important for proper curation but exhibit a separatist zeitgeist characterized by overdevelopment of one aspect of collections care and complete disregard for another.

Proper Curation—A Critical Assessment

Adequate curation requires examination at two levels. The first level deals with curation planning, prior to and during fieldwork. The second focuses on basic long-term collections management issues.

Curation Planning

Curation planning and execution are best summed up as a review of choices made at the preexcavation phase of a project. A set of field curation and collections management protocols should be in place before any excavation begins. These protocols need to be mutually agreed on by the principal investigator and the institution that will house the materials and should be flexible enough to allow their transition into a long-term management plan. Archaeological projects that institute rigorous sampling protocols before excavation begins greatly increase their chances that a long-term facility will accept their collections.

The reality of the current environment, however, is that the number of professionally adequate repositories that actually have space for collections seems to be dwindling by the day. This being the case, we need to make ethical choices to alleviate the burden placed on the facilities. This can only be done through aggressive management of what is being excavated. In short, archaeologists who are involved in active excavation programs need to make better decisions about how much is enough when it comes to excavation. Additionally, we need rigorous criteria that focus first on intensifying the existing archaeological record for an area or region to guide the decisions of where to dig, and how much and what kind of material to recover. In terms of state and federal archaeological investigation, we are not far from the point where contracts must be more stringent about the kinds of materials we recover (e.g., Archaic, Woodland, Historic) based on what we already know about an area. For example, why should archaeology in the Midwest continue to focus on Mississippian materials, while the Archaic and Woodland periods are still vastly underreported? Similarly, we may soon have to decide when it is appropriate to deaccession materials that we already have, even if they have not been examined. Countless cubic feet of soil samples that have never been analyzed and, in all likelihood, are no longer useful may be better removed from a collection to make room for additional material classes.

Would such positions signify an end to excavation? No, but they would illustrate the intention of the archaeological community to seriously address collections management responsibilities. In the end, the best curation practices cannot compete with an unchecked collections generation paradigm. Ethical decisions on both sides of the house must be made—now.

Long-Term Management

Long-term collections management requires a systematic approach that takes the long view and examines curation facilities along several fronts. A review of the overall completeness of the facility and its staff provides a solid baseline from which to gauge organizational abilities to care for collections. This review includes an examination of the building first, followed by an assessment of the curation system, and finally an examination of the administrative infrastructure of the organization. This multitiered approach is the only way to adequately gauge the professionalism and accountability of a curation facility. We also believe this analysis system should be used by individual archaeologists to ensure their collections receive the best long-term care.

Building Assessment

One of the most basic requirements for adequate curation is a structure or repository constructed with that purpose in mind or updated to accommodate specific curation needs. Using 36 CFR Part 79 as a guide, we suggest that adequate curation, at the building level, includes fire detection and suppression systems, environmental controls and security systems, sound building construction and structural adequacy, plumbing, building egress, handicap accessibility, regulatory and site issues, and space availability and use.

Adjustments can be made during the construction or retrofit phase, for example, moving pipes so they do not hang above collections or readjusting the placement of gas lines or electricity to allow for a specialized use area, but all this needs to be considered early in the design process to avoid costly reconfigurations later on. Similarly, adequate size to hold current and future collections must be considered as early as possible to ensure that the facility is not filled to capacity by the time it opens.

The composition of a collection is the driving force behind the level of environmental attention necessary for a facility. At a minimum, a curation facility must have regulated heat and air conditioning and be accompanied by at least some basic form of humidity and temperature monitoring and control system. For some types of collections, a well-maintained heating, ventilating, and air conditioning (HVAC) system may be enough to provide adequate environmental control. In some cases, the complexity of an archaeological collection may demand more. Zoned control of spaces for specialized types of collections is the most efficient use of an HVAC system.

We also place janitorial and pest programs under the umbrella of environmental control. Without aggressive integrated pest management plans that include both monitoring and control, the best-planned facility will experience rapid deterioration of its collections by insects, mold, dust, and other pests.

Fire detection and suppression are a must for any facility holding archaeological collections. Suppression cannot be equated merely with the presence of fire extinguishers. While not specifically laid out in any regulation or guide, proper fire detection and suppression has come to consist of an electronic fire alarm system that notes increases in heat, presence of smoke, and can transmit notification to the personnel of the building and to the local fire department or a central monitoring station able to dispatch fire services. Training on the system for *all* employees of the facility should include training and equipment for hearing and other physically impaired personnel. The same applies to security systems in terms of the priority given to both detection and deterrence and their applicability to all employees.

Facilities possessing these characteristics—characteristics that we consider to be the minimum—represent a solid base from which to build a well-rounded curation program. Again, one of the biggest problems nationwide is overemphasis on one system over another. Ethical curation seeks balance of all needs.

Curation System Assessment

The second basic ethical requirement for any repository is consistency within the curation system being used. Adequate curation includes flexibility—to accommodate the needs of a particular collection—and a logical, delineated baseline of repository protocols—to create continuity of management for all materials. At a minimum, the following points should be considered for proper curation.

Labeling   Artifacts will be consistently labeled with a simple system, described in protocols, to ensure protection of provenience and other identification information. The system should make sense and enable someone unfamiliar with a collection to easily understand it. Labeling systems should not be "personal codes" decipherable by only one or two individuals. We do not suggest that each and every specimen always be labeled. Again, use a system that combines efficient use of time and funds. We do, however, advocate the use of archivally stable products. Acid free, polyspun paper inserts may be included in the bag holding the artifact to reinforce the bag label. Labels should be written using archival-quality pens or laser-quality printers. Record collections need to be properly labeled as well, using archival, permanent ink or laser print on labels and archivally stable products, such as foil-backed labels for materials like photographs.

Housing   Acid-free boxes with telescoping lids are excellent primary containers for housing archaeological collections. Placing box labels within inert plastic sleeves affixed to the front of the box will greatly increase the life of the container, maximizing its usefulness and cost. Because collections are stored in perpetuity, but with the goal of being used for research, containers that will support the wear and tear of use are very important to the longevity of the materials. For internal containers, inert plastic four-milliliter bags are a minimal standard. Because longevity is a concern, better-quality storage materials only increase the level of care for the materials. Records need to be stored in archival folders and kept within acid-free, banker-type boxes with exterior labels identical to those used for artifact boxes.

Documentation   Records, notes, reports, catalogs, related historical documents, and photographs are all integral components of an archaeological collection. Proper curation requires 1) submission of all original documents with the artifacts for permanent curation and 2) a repository capable of managing this documentation in addition to any artifacts it receives. Submission of at least one full copy of all records is recommended, although two are preferred for safety. Paper documentation must be on acid-free paper. Associated documentation accompanying a collection of artifacts should include

- Ownership document (legal title) for archaeological materials and a complete listing of all components of the collection including the number of containers, their contents and associated provenience units, and all accompanying documentation.
- A catalog of the artifacts by provenience unit. While recognizing that there are different levels of cataloging, minimally all should include an identification of the object, material of manufacture, and quantification (count and/or weight). A discussion of how the catalog system was composed and how it operates is mandatory.
- A description of the artifact classes according to the best-current levels of professional knowledge is recommended. Notation regarding artifacts stored outside of their provenience unit should be included.
- A copy of the final report, site location data, project scope of work, and any relevant historical documentation pertaining to the site.
- A statement indicating whether conservation treatment was performed, a list of those objects treated, and a complete description of the treatments used. If conservation was not complete, a list of those objects requiring immediate attention must be included.
- An archivally stable photocopy of all original field and laboratory documentation.
- A master set of permanent black-and-white photographs, negatives, color slides, and videotapes using the best current standard films and papers. All photographic material needs to be, minimally, labeled using archivally stable methods, with the site, provenience, and catalog number. A catalog describing the images of all photographic materials must be included in the collection.
- Electronic data (tape, disks, and so on) may accompany the documentation and should be accompanied by a statement describing the system (including a schedule for backing up the data) and software used and the content of each disk, tape, and so on. Standardized methods for the storage of electronic data will likely be developed in the future.

As noted earlier, records should be stored in a similar manner to objects, using archivally stable boxes, folders, labels, and inks.

Conservation   All archaeological excavation carries the professional obligation to preserve the objects and records generated through both proper curation and appropriate conservation treatments. Conservation of perishable material is an ethical responsibility and an essential element in the archaeological process. Although conservation is under the purview of a separate group of professionals (objects and document conservators), the responsibility for securing the services of such experts falls to the managing archaeologist. Conservation treatments must be appropriate to the material and its condition and should reflect the best-current standards in methodology and materials. All treatments should be carried out by or under the supervision of an adequately trained professional. All treatments must be fully documented; this documentation becomes a part of the site's permanent archive.

Policies and Procedures   A discussion explaining how artifacts and records are organized and cataloged should accompany the materials. It is important to make clear how a curation system works so that others can easily interpret it and access the collections. In addition, it is important that a repository possess written protocols and procedures that outline all of its capabilities with respect to archaeological collections. Such items include, but should not be limited to, discussions of the following policies:

- Accession files—files that list all materials formally accepted as part of the collection.
- Location identification—a finding aid that shows where collections are stored within the storage area.
- Cross-indexed files—files that tie collection information to one or more salient characteristics (e.g., information pertaining to a particular collection is linked to the archaeological site that generated the collection).
- Published guide to collections—a report that lists holdings of the museum, to be used as a reference guide only.
- Site-record administration—a policy that allows for the integration of state site forms or reports that pertain to archaeological sites that generated the collections.
- Computerized database management—a policy that sets forth a particular database to be used to record the holdings of the museum, the frequency with which the database will be updated and backed up, and the extent of information that will be available for museum staff and researchers to use.
- Minimum standards for acceptance—a policy that clearly defines and outlines the types of collections the museum will accept.
- Curation policy—a policy for museum personnel to follow when a collection has been offered to the museum for permanent, long-term care.

- Records management policy—a policy that outlines how records will be maintained by museum staff; this includes records that are donated and accessioned by the museum, as well as those documents generated by museum staff.
- Field-curation guidelines—guidelines created by a repository and sent to archaeological contractors and used to adequately prepare collections for placement in that facility.
- Loan procedures—a policy that outlines how the museum will honor any loan requests for a collection or collections.
- Deaccessioning policy—a policy that outlines how the museum will remove a collection from its holdings (there is currently no deaccessioning rule for Department of Defense collections; all parts of its collection are currently required to be maintained in long-term storage).
- Inventory policy—a policy that outlines how the museum conducts an inventory of its holdings, with what frequency it executes the inventory, and the pertinent individuals who are notified of the inventory and its results.

A curation system that encompasses the aforementioned points will make it easier to store and manage materials. Such a system satisfies minimal curation standards, and institutions with such a system in place that also emphasize a multidisciplinary approach to curation are strong curation partners and able to ensure a healthy long-term care environment for collections.

Infrastructure Assessment

Proper archaeological curation cannot simply consist of using the best products available or of creating a staff of capable professionals in collections management and conservation. Though integral to a successful curation program, one cannot forget that the best-laid plans for curation will not come to fruition without funding or a well-executed museum business plan. The last basic need for adequate curation is, thus, an infrastructure that is well rounded and aggressive in creating programs that bolster the curation component of the repository through a strong administrative unit cognizant of the needs of the collections and aware that the collections cannot sit undisturbed on a shelf. Collections must be preserved and used to reach their full potential. The administrative capability of a museum can be summarized as the ability to excel in fund-raising and outreach programs, to be open to partnerships, to engage in cooperative agreements, and to have a secure grasp on budget and real estate issues.

Curation facilities have borne the brunt of costs for curation for years. Even though the passage of laws like the Archaeological Resources Protection Act of 1979 and regulations such as 36 CFR Part 79 have supported more planning for curation at the budget-programming level, additional funds are still required. Although new contracts often carry some healthy funding for curation, older collections still lack the requisite attention. Only those curation facilities with developed programs that use their collections to create revenue for neglected materials and their long-term care will thrive as professional centers of collections management. Healthy outreach programs that use a repository's holdings to educate and stimulate interest in archaeology by the public will succeed in garnering support for *all* programs. Obtaining funding for curation is exceedingly difficult for, while donors are quite apt to provide money for expeditions to recover new material or for building new wings to display their collections, they are reluctant to provide monies for the less "sexy" side of archaeology. Buying boxes and bags for artifacts or providing funds for databases to record repository information just isn't glamorous enough for some donors. Outreach programs have become very good sources of fund-raising for collections facilities. While the majority of those funds need to go into developing additional outreach programs, some should funnel into other programs included in the institution's mission. Not only do these programs succeed in securing funds, but they also succeed in tying the materials to the public and making them real to the average person. Collections sitting in a box on a shelf do not intrigue people, but collections available for people to touch or examine excite the mind and make archaeology interesting on a whole new level.

An aggressive commitment to securing cooperative agreements with other agencies or groups must also be the goal of a professional curation facility. Many repositories hold materials from a variety of state and federal agencies. In some cases, they have done so for a very long time with little or no remuneration for their effort. Creating agreements that bind these agencies together to help with the costs of proper collections management not only helps the repository, but also creates a partnership between the facility and the particular agencies that can grow and serve everyone. Costs can be absorbed, building additions can be planned and constructed, and collections can receive care that begins to reflect the monetary effort used to excavate them in the first place.

Critical examination of the administrative infrastructure of a repository is important because it allows one to understand the institution's capabilities in the more business-oriented aspects of curation. Institutions with a strong administrative and financial understanding of collections management and a strong vision of their mission are best suited to serve as long-term curation facilities.

Conclusion

Many of the examples we have used and the references we make to specific instances are driven by our personal experiences and focus on federal collections identified in the United States. It is important to note, however, that ethical choices are faced by all practicing archaeologists regardless of what part of the world constitutes their research area. Colleagues working in other countries may work with different laws and regulations, but still have a responsibility to preserve the archaeological record as best as they can. In fact, internationally, the challenge is often greater. Although we have limited funds for curation in the United States, such funds are practically nonexistent overseas, thus making ethical decisions all the more acute.

As stated earlier, ethical curation for us means the ability to accurately and critically identify those institutions that can offer well-rounded, professional care for archaeological collections. The multiaspect focus we advocate illustrates the need to examine *all* systems of a curation facility from the building to the curation system, the staff, and the administrative infrastructure. It is our intention that the guidelines we suggest for curation planning and long-term management be applied to any example of ethical collections management. Even though every situation cannot possibly be accounted for in any one approach, the same issues tend to arise everywhere. We are strongly committed to this multitiered examination and suggest that proper curation and ethical treatment of the archaeological record can only be done by institutions that adopt such an approach.

It is clear that, at this point, there exist within the discipline individuals and institutions that excel at cleaning and stabilizing collections. It is equally clear, given recent research, that many of the institutions that currently house archaeological collections do not meet even the minimum guidelines set out in 36 CFR Part 79. Many within the archaeological community still focus on excavation and pay little attention to curation. This is unethical and our profession can no longer endorse the practice. It is time to admit that the only way we can guarantee that our national collections will receive long-term, professional care is to develop national guidelines that outline minimum standards required for professional archaeological repositories and their supporting infrastructure. To that end, we have suggested the basics that such a system should entail. They are minimal considerations, but keeping them in mind will help ensure that ethical choices are made that benefit all concerned.

For far too long, archaeological collections have been treated as one-dimensional with respect to their needs. For far too long, *any* manner of building has sufficed as an archaeological curation facility, as long as it has had open shelf space and someone to unlock the door. National research over the last decade by a variety of parties indicates that archaeological collections do not simply require clean bags and new boxes. The bar must be raised with respect to long-term care so that the discipline can meet the challenges of legislative mandate and the rigors of scientific research. Proper care requires that. Only those institutions and those professionals that effectively meet the multiple needs should be considered proper stewards for these nonrenewable resources.

Ethical curation is the responsibility of the entire archaeological community. It can no longer be an afterthought or left to nonarchaeologists to pursue. Curation is everybody's business and all of us, everywhere, need to contribute to the solution.

Discussion Questions

1. Should archaeologists stop digging, study what is already excavated, and bring curation up to the minimal standards suggested in this chapter? How realistic is this scenario?
2. Discuss some of the ramifications of adopting a reduced excavation/ increased curation paradigm in archaeology.
3. Reduced excavation is not enough. Most museums are probably going to have to deaccession some of the material they currently house. Given this, is there a need for national—or international—deaccession regulations, and, if so, who would be best qualified to examine current collections to determine what should be deaccessioned?
4. You received slightly more than half the funding you had requested to cover the full expenses of your field project. As a thoughtful, ethical, long-term planner, you calculated that your curation and collections management costs amount to almost one-third of the original budget! How will you adjust your project to the decreased funding?
5. Do archaeologists have an ethical responsibility to sample all material classes before handing the materials over to a museum? What form should this sampling take? Should archaeologists submit only a sample of all materials classes for curation by a museum? If so (or if the museum will only accept a sample), how should the sampling be done?
6. If all records are an integral part of an archaeological collection, should museums refuse a collection if all record groups are not transferred with the objects for long-term care?
7. Should the curation of collections be subject to international standards? To national regulations? Why or why not? If you think we need standards, who should establish them? Who would/could enforce them?
8. Do you think graduate institutions should require classes in field curation, collections, and records management? Should graduate students be required to work with and write up one or more collections before receiving a degree? Why or why not?
9. Is our discipline at a point where we will no longer be relevant unless we begin, on a national level, to integrate archaeological collections and the story they have to tell into primary and secondary school curricula? What might be the costs and benefits, and to whom, of making archaeological

collections and their stories an integral part of all primary and secondary school curricula?
10. Brainstorm some creative ways to fund curation.

Recommended Readings

Appelbaum, B.
1991 *Guide to Environmental Protection of Collections.* Sound View, Madison, CT.

Cronyn, J. M.
1990 *The Elements of Archaeological Conservation.* Routledge, London.

Eiteljorg, Harrison, II
1998 Archiving Archaeological Data in the Next Millennium. *CRM* 21(6):21–23.

Ford, Richard I.
1980 A Three-Part System for Storage of Archaeological Collections. *Curator* 23(1):55–62.

King, Mary Elizabeth
1980 Curators: Ethics and Obligations. *Curator* 23(1):10–18.

Magio, Barbara
1991 *Buried in Storage.* The Alexandria Archaeology Collections Management Project. Technical Leaflet 178, American Association for State and Local History, Nashville, TN.

Moyer, C.
1986–1987 Archaeological Conservation Forum. *Society for Historical Archaeology Newsletter* 19–20.

Novick, Andrea Lee
1980 The Management of Archaeological Documentation. *Curator* 23(1):35.

Odegaard, Nancy, and Grace Katterman
1992 *Guide to Handling Anthropological Museum Collections.* Western Association for Art Conservation, Los Angeles.

Pearce, S.
1990 *Archaeological Curatorship.* Smithsonian Institution Press, Washington, DC.

Pearson, C. (editor)
1987 *Conservation of Marine Archaeological Objects.* Butterworths, London.

Robinson, Wendy
1998 *First Aid for Underwater Finds.* Archetype, London.

Silverman, Sydel, and Nancy Parezo
1992 *Preserving the Anthropological Record.* Wenner-Gren Foundation for Anthropological Research, New York.

Singley, K.
  1981   A Conservation Manual for the Field Archaeologist. *Historical Archaeology* 15(1):36–48.

Society for Historical Archaeology
  1993   Standards and Guidelines for the Curation of Archaeological Collections, at www.sha.org/curation.htm (accessed June 2002).

Sullivan, Lynne P.
  1992   *Managing Archaeological Resources from the Museum Perspective.* Technical Brief no. 13. National Park Service, Department of the Interior, Washington, DC.

PART III

Responsibilities to Diverse Publics

JASON M. LABELLE

Chapter Nine

Coffee Cans and Folsom Points: Why We Cannot Continue to Ignore the Artifact Collectors

Surface hunters, artifact collectors, pothunters, and looters—whatever name you would like to call them—have had a profound impact on the archaeological record in terms of the sheer quantity of items picked off the surface of sites over countless decades. Many artifacts and sites have gone unrecognized or have disappeared, wrested from their homes among the fields and creeks only to end up in cigar boxes or glued to felt and placed in old wooden frames. As upsetting and frustrating as this is to most archaeologists, the greater tragedy lies in our own failure in slowing the loss of this irreplaceable knowledge. Several factors contribute to the overall problem, including the general lack of communication between archaeologists and artifact collectors, with the two communities becoming increasingly alienated from one another over the past thirty years. As well, there is the failure of archaeologists to produce public education programs that specifically address this community and the role it plays in significantly altering the archaeological record.

As professionally trained archaeologists, it is our ethical duty to interact with these individuals because they possess a tremendous knowledge of local sites, artifacts, and other collectors. It is foolhardy to dismiss or ignore surface hunters. Although some might think otherwise, the past clearly does not belong to a chosen few with university degrees, but instead belongs to a rich patchwork of communities, including the people who left the material originally, their descendents, the modern local community (including collectors), and interested researchers, who often are from very distant lands, both politically and geographically. Developing a dialog with all of these groups certainly strengthens our discipline as a whole.

Surface hunters are either despised or praised by professional archaeologists, of course, depending on whom you ask. But either way, ignoring their influence is simply not productive because the collecting community is quite diverse in its actions, attitudes, and membership. Segments of the surface hunters' community are not about to stop collecting, as they firmly believe they are salvaging artifacts from plowed fields and river bottoms, items that would be lost to time without their care. Never mind their belief that most archaeologists are not interested in even examining their finds. Many other collectors have a fascination with artifacts, but have little or no access to information concerning proper ways to study archaeology. Still others catalog and store their collections to high standards that professional archaeologists themselves sometimes fail to meet. Interaction with all of these groups remains our best pathway for preserving and learning about the archaeological record.

In what follows, I would like to relate some of my thoughts about dealing with collectors from the Great Plains. I think a good case can be made for working with "low-end" artifact collectors[1] because the interaction benefits professional archaeologists and the public alike. But before I begin, I have an important point to mention. It is a sad fact that some artifact collectors buy and sell items and/or destroy sites with uncontrolled excavations. In my experience, however, most surface hunters do not engage in these activities and view those who do so as the real "looters" of the past. Our professional response to people who illegally excavate sites or engage in the artifact trade is another matter, beyond the scope of this chapter, but one that must also be addressed though aggressive interaction.

The Great Plains: A Haven for Collecting

I work mostly within the central and southern Great Plains of North America. Archaeologically, the region has often been treated as a peripheral zone, removed from the masonry and adobe buildings of the Southwest and the large and complex mound groups to the east. Many people fail to recognize that although the region may not have what most think of as "spectacular" archaeological sites, people have nearly continuously inhabited the area for at least 10,000 years. They left an abundance of remains, ranging from small ephemeral campsites to large fortified villages scattered along old riverbanks. The Great Plains is a culturally rich and dramatic land, a region deeply influenced by the abundance or lack of water on its surface or in its vast and deep underground aquifers. Over countless millennia, the Great Plains has suffered numerous droughts, some much more severe than even the historic 1930s Dust Bowl. Through this erosion, traces of the past have slowly been exposed across the region. Local individuals have been collecting artifacts from the surface of their fields and their homes for the last hundred years, with new finds appearing after each strong windstorm or turn of the plow.

Nearly every small town across the plains has a collector or two, and most communities have many more. As the land becomes increasingly deflated, the collections increase in size (as does the number of collections), no doubt from the greater exposure provided in sandy country. Often, these collections are a family affair that began as a simple hobby, but sometimes evolved into near obsession.

From my observation, the most active collectors are middle aged or older; fewer young folks are as interested today. Artifact collections can range from a pile of flakes and points thrown into a bucket, to mounted artifacts on a frame or two, to an entire basement filled with glass cases stuffed with tens of thousands of stone tools. Some collectors even have private museums filled by a lifetime's worth of walking fields.

My own research focuses on the Paleo-Indian period, the earliest occupation of the region, which occurred at the end of the last Ice Age and shortly thereafter, nearly 10,000 to 12,000 years ago. Paleo-Indian tools are among the most sought after artifacts within the collector community, largely for two reasons. First, these stone tools are perceived as rare finds, and complete specimens are especially coveted. A stone spear point that has lain in the soil for 10,000 years has an almost addictive attraction for collectors (and archaeologists alike) and many are proud of their favorite specimens. But what makes Paleo-Indian tools even more desired is their exquisite craftsmanship. Prehistoric knappers took considerable care to flake their tools in very regular and patterned ways from exotic and beautifully colored stones. Their design and execution go well beyond the needs of a purely functional tool, to what some think is true art. That these specimens can (and regularly do) sell for thousands of dollars on the artifact market attests to their popularity among collectors and artifact dealers alike.

The Professional and the Amateur, Yesterday and Today

Today, there is a definite split between the world of the "professional" and the "amateur" archaeologist, the differences defined by education, experience, motive, and paid employment. The division has not always been so distinct, however, and is the result of the professionalization of the discipline during the mid- to late-twentieth century. Yet, at one time cooperation was the norm and was to the great benefit of both communities. A brief overview of the history of Paleo-Indian studies illustrates this point.

Modern Paleo-Indian research began with the excavation of the Folsom type–site in northeastern New Mexico between 1926 and 1928 (Meltzer 1994; Meltzer, Todd, and Holliday 2002). With the discovery of an easily identifiable type artifact, the Folsom point, a rapid race was on within the professional community to find additional Folsom sites (Figgins 1934, 1935; Renaud 1931, 1934). Immediately, professional archaeologists began corresponding with individuals throughout the Great Plains. E. B. Renaud, a French archaeologist from the University of Denver, began a series of monumental reconnaissance surveys that took him and his students across the archaeologically unexplored Great Plains for nearly seventeen years (Renaud 1947). Local informants were Renaud's bread and butter, guiding his exploration and fieldwork to small towns, wind-eroded fields, and old prehistoric campsites. With the help of these locals and their artifact collections (often bulging at the seams because of rapid erosion afforded by the Dust Bowl), Renaud was able to quickly construct a typology and general patterns of prehistoric cultural history.

Through interaction with Renaud and other prominent university-trained archaeologists, several families made contributions to the study of Paleo-Indians, or "Early Man" as they were referred to at the time. These families included the Andersens of Yuma County, Colorado, and the Bakers of Cimarron County, Oklahoma (see fig. 9.1). Elder fathers led both families, searching for mammoths and spear points while trekking across the sand dunes and abandoned farms of their drought-blighted counties. The families each had sons of college age, Harold Andersen and Ele Baker, respectively, who worked the fields with their fathers, together amassing large Paleo-Indian artifact collections.

During the Great Depression and the Dust Bowl, few people went to college and even fewer received archaeological training. Harold and Ele were among the exceptions, as both were able to attend school and eventually direct archaeological fieldwork. Sadly, they were never able to make lasting professional careers in archaeology despite their great love and enthusiasm for the science, generated by artifact collecting. Their passion and discoveries were displayed in regional museums and at large international archaeological conferences and served as type specimens for an increasingly robust typology emerging in the research world of the mid to late 1930s. To the Andersen and Baker families, their hobby went well beyond a novelty, as they knew that they were contributing to science as amateurs and their results were incorporated into the burgeoning field. Both collections were eventually donated to museums, held in the public trust for preservation and future research. Yet, with a quiet irony, the collections and family legacies slipped into relative obscurity over the many years, stored in cabinets where only a few archaeologists knew of their existence.

I stumbled onto the collections while carrying out a regional study of Paleo-Indian raw material use on the central Great Plains. When I began the research, I specifically chose areas that were hit hard by the Dust Bowl and other notable droughts, because through such harsh erosion, these areas offered good visibility of late Pleistocene and early Holocene landscapes.[2] I was aware that a few large sites were known from these dune fields, but was not prepared for the substantial number of unreported sites.[3] During the project, I came to learn the lost stories of the Andersen and Baker families and began assembling their history from their old notes, brief mentions of their collections in the early Paleo-Indian literature, and from a few recollections of old-timers (LaBelle 1997).

Several field projects were born from the Andersen and Baker collections, including my test excavation of the Slim Arrow site, a bison bone bed in northeastern Colorado (LaBelle in press), and a multiseason excavation effort at the Nall site, a large Paleo-Indian campsite in the Oklahoma Panhandle (LaBelle, Holliday, and Meltzer, in press). Tom Westfall and I have also begun to relocate the Andersen sites using the notes from their splendid collection. Westfall, a very knowledgeable local collector, is well acquainted with the area, having attained (with the help of his family and friends) a very sizable collection of Paleo-Indian artifacts from the sand hills and gravel bars of northeastern Colorado (Westfall 2002).

We had a tremendous number of visitors to the Slim Arrow site and many of these families have large artifact collections themselves. We were able to view their collections and learn about still other unreported sites. Several public presentations on our work at Slim Arrow led to invitations for coffee and chances to record additional collections. The overall response was wonderful, with great enthusiasm for our project and a desire to contribute to our study and the story of Yuma County. The same can be said for Cimarron County, Oklahoma, where our field projects greatly benefited from the cooperation of local collectors and interested townspeople. I quickly learned that short-term research visits can easily snowball into multiyear projects when you actively embrace local collectors.

The Nature of Colorado Archaeological Research

I believe that it is in our best interest as a discipline to continue working with surface hunters. There are a tremendous number of collectors, compared to archaeologists, and they live and collect in areas that archaeologists might only visit on rare occasions. They possess a vast knowledge of local sites that few professional archaeologists could attain without months, if not years, of archaeological work in the same area. Without interaction and cooperation, we will never benefit from their knowledge accumulated over years of artifact hunting. In fact, willful ignorance of their activities leads to a very biased perspective on the archaeological record, because they are actively altering the surface by removing cultural material much as other natural processes do.

Yuma County provides a good example of the use of a well-documented collection, as well as the response of an interested local community when invited to contribute to a research project. Both groups benefited from the interaction, leading to increased awareness of and respect for the archaeological record. But why bother working with collectors, especially when evaluating their collections can be seen as inappropriate professional behavior?

The nature of archaeological research in Colorado demonstrates the continued benefit of working with collectors. There is a notable geographic bias in Colorado archaeology, fueled by research interest, landownership, development, and money available for field projects. For example, the state is well known for the pueblos and cliff dwellings in the southwest, such as Mesa Verde and Hovenweep National

Parks. Quite justifiably, large amounts of time and money have been spent surveying, testing, and stabilizing these ruins and others. Other areas of Colorado experienced large amounts of fieldwork through cultural resource management (CRM)
projects involving energy research and development. But eastern Colorado, already
known for the large number of Paleo-Indian sites (as well as sites from all other periods), has not fared so well.

The magnitude of the problem is well illustrated with counts of the number of
absolute dates available for each of the counties in Colorado (Rayne 1997) (see fig.
9.1). Dates provide a good proxy measure of the intensity of research activity conducted in counties as well as regions, as dating is fairly cost prohibitive and usually
occurs in the testing and excavation phases of fieldwork.[4] The dates in these county
tallies are primarily radiocarbon and dendrochronological, although other types of
dates are also included, such as archaeomagnetic, obsidian hydration, and thermoluminescence.

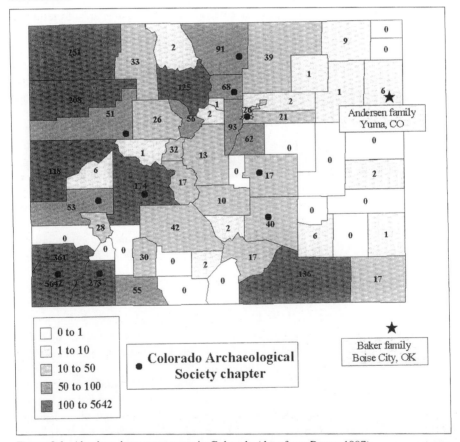

Figure 9.1. Absolute dates per county in Colorado (data from Rayne 1997).

Most of the counties in eastern Colorado have less than two dates per county, while eight counties have no dates whatsoever. Compare this to the southwest, where Montezuma County has over 5,600 dates; 1,500 dates are available from Mesa Verde alone. Other counties, such as along the Front Range or in northwestern Colorado, have experienced large numbers of CRM projects since the 1970s. Unfortunately, many of the counties in eastern Colorado remain virtually unknown except for generalizations drawn from broader regional studies. Collectors provide the best available data source in these regions, yet they remain a relatively undervalued resource.

We should also consider where our data come from. One hundred forty Paleo-Indian sites are recorded in eastern Colorado (personal communication, Mary Sullivan, Colorado Historical Society, 2001), which would be a very impressive total if the sites were the large bison kills or campsites so well known from introductory textbooks. Instead, most of these are small lithic scatters, often mixed with more recent materials. Only a small number of these sites (16 out of 140, 11 percent) are among the more important Paleo-Indian sites considered pivotal to interpreting the early prehistory of the plains (see table 9.1).

These sites were discovered throughout the twentieth century, most since the rise of CRM studies. Yet, despite an exponential increase in the amount of fieldwork, the majority of the sites (thirteen out of sixteen, 81 percent) were discovered by amateurs and reported to archaeologists for subsequent excavation, analysis,

TABLE 9.1

Notable Paleo-Indian Sites in Eastern Colorado

Site Name	Cultural Complex	Site Type	Year of Discovery	Discovered by a Professional Archaeologist?
Lindenmeier	Folsom	campsite	1924	no
Claypool	Cody	campsite	1932	no
Dent	Clovis	mammothbone bed	1932	no
Powars	Folsom	campsite	1935	no
Olsen-Chubbuck	Cody	bison bone bed	1957	no
Fourth of July Valley	Allen	campsite	1960	yes
Lamb Spring	noncultural?; Cody	mammoth bone bed; bison bone bed	1960	no
Fowler-Parrish	Folsom	bison bone bed	1962	no
Gordon Creek	late Paleo-Indian	human burial	1963	no
Frazier	Agate Basin	bison bone bed	1965	yes (by a geologist)
Jurgens	Cody	3 separate campsites	1965	yes (by a geologist)
Jones-Miller	Hell Gap	bison bone bed	1972	no
Dutton	noncultural?; Clovis	mammoth bone bed	1975	no
Selby	noncultural?	mammoth bone bed	1975	no
Drake	Clovis	tool cache	1978	no
Frasca	Cody	bison bone bed	1978	no

and publication. Professional scientists discovered only three of the sites (19 percent) and the same geologist discovered two of those! This pattern of amateur discovery of Paleo-Indian sites is not unique to Colorado; it is common across most of the United States (for a more detailed analysis of Paleo-Indian site discovery, consult Seebach 2000). A great deal of Paleo-Indian research must continue in this cooperative realm.

Our Stated Goals: Public Interaction and Education

Despite their tremendous contributions to Paleo-Indian site discovery, there has been a general drift in the mainstream archaeological community away from interaction with surface hunters. Instead, the focal point of public education is now placed in cultural resource stewardship. While this focus is certainly laudable and a path we must advocate, we also have to realize that lawful collecting of archaeological resources continues unabated. At least part of our public education programs ought to address this specific community. But even our greatest allies in public education, the amateur societies, have distanced themselves from collectors.

Amateur societies, including the Colorado Archaeological Society (CAS), which began in 1935 with the publication of its journal *Southwestern Lore,* have a long and rich history. Artifact collectors were once welcome among state societies, at times probably forming the majority of the membership. Although members were encouraged to catalog their personal finds, no explicit effort was placed on cultural stewardship or the transfer of their artifacts to more permanent and public holdings. Amateur societies continue to flourish today, providing forums for members to view presentations on local and exotic digs, as well as to participate in ongoing projects. But the groups have moved in concert with the professional community toward concepts of preservation and away from artifact collecting. CAS has even established its own ethics code, discouraging the personal and undocumented collection of artifacts (Colorado Historical Society 2002).

Many state societies also train amateur archaeologists either through society field schools or state-sponsored programs. In Colorado, the Office of Archaeology and Historic Preservation offers nondegree training in the Program for Avocational Archaeological Certification (PAAC). PAAC, which began in 1978, offers classes in lithic technology, site survey, research designs, and rock art recording, among other topics (Colorado Historical Society 2002). As of March 2002, 197 members of CAS had completed at least some coursework in PAAC (Colorado Historical Society 2002). Most of the members are certification candidates (142 out of 197, 72 percent), having completed coursework in site survey and Colorado archaeology. There are also some very experienced amateur archaeologists in the program, with nearly 8 percent (16 out of 197) having completed the thirteen courses in the program (as well as several hours of field and laboratory experience) and attaining the status of a "Colorado archaeology scholar." PAAC members are a valuable and knowledge-able group, serving as local archaeological stewards, as well as potential volunteers for projects throughout the state. PAAC is an excellent example of a sound public education program, channeling the enthusiasm and dedication of amateur archaeol-ogists toward productive and cooperative work. But do PAAC and CAS reach all those in the state who are interested in archaeology?

CAS has ten active chapters (see fig. 9.1), primarily located in the large urban areas, such as along the Front Range (the Ft. Collins–Denver–Pueblo corridor), or in the small mountain and southwestern communities with associated colleges or sig-nificant archaeological districts (the Gunnison and Durango areas). Eastern Col-orado is underrepresented in CAS chapters, at least in part due to the rural population on the Great Plains. Several of these towns are large enough to draw chapters, but they have yet to formally organize.

There is a great interest in archaeology in eastern Colorado, but it is firmly rooted in artifact collecting. For example, an archaeological club has been formed in Yuma County, independent of CAS. Semiregular meetings draw between forty to sixty members from well over a 100-mile radius, including folks from Nebraska and Kansas at times (personal communication, Westfall 2002). Collectors show off their latest finds at the meetings, as well as listen to the occasional professional archaeol-ogist discuss current research. The talks tend to focus on Paleo-Indian topics, which are quite popular among the group. In many ways, the Yuma Club is much like other CAS chapters, save for the one important distinction: people bring their artifacts to show at the meetings. This sort of activity is discouraged within CAS[5] and is also in violation of the ethics code established for PAAC participation.

The Struggle: Collectors and/or Ethics

We have reached a challenging ethical dilemma. Just what exactly are professional archaeologists to do? How can we work with people who collect artifacts, and at the same time preach values of cultural stewardship? CAS and PAAC are not to blame for pushing collectors out of their fold because undocumented surface col-lecting *is* a destructive practice. At the same time, excluding surface hunters from an active archaeological dialog only worsens the situation. We must step forward with continued interaction and education, addressing these multiple communities through public programs. Most importantly, we can influence the present and fu-ture actions of surface hunters by teaching them the value of documenting their collections.

Some archaeologists might be surprised to know that surface hunters have es-tablished their own ethics code in regard to collecting. C. G. Yeager, who organizes the annual Loveland Stone Age Fair in Colorado (first begun in 1934), published a list of ten rules in his *Arrowheads and Stone Artifacts:*

1. Always obtain permission
2. Inform and communicate
3. Only surface hunt on privately owned land
4. Respect the land and other private property
5. Report noteworthy or unusual archaeological sites
6. Be humble and appreciative
7. Never dig or excavate
8. Catalog and document
9. Continue to educate yourself
10. Respect the feelings and opinions of others (2000:5–9)

Whether or not to follow these rules is obviously left to the individual—some probably disregard the rules and dig sites or illegally collect artifacts. But as I've already mentioned, others clearly do not. We must accept the fact that collecting artifacts from private property is legal, and likely will remain so in the future.

Given that, wouldn't it be more constructive for our goals as archaeologists to accept some collectors as potential teammates? I think we can look to the Society for American Archaeology's (SAA) Ethics Code for some guidance on this issue. The SAA Principle on Commercialization (principle 3; Society for American Archaeology 1996) rightly points to the connection between the buying and selling of artifacts and the destruction of archaeological sites, and states "archaeologists should abstain from any activity that enhances the commercial value of archaeological objects." Professional archaeologists seem to have taken this to mean that they should have nothing to do with any collectors, ever. I've argued here that, by tarring all collectors with the same brush—treating them as all of one kind—we are failing in our role as stewards of the archaeological record (principle 1), are ignoring a significant "affected group" (principle 2), and have been too limited in our educational outreach (principle 4). There are differences among collectors. Those whose legal activities are motivated not by financial gain, but by a genuine interest in their local past, share many of our own passions and have the potential to contribute to our discipline in significant ways. If we made a genuine effort to respect their knowledge, learn from them, and provide them with the kinds of information they need to share in the true goals of stewardship, I believe it would, as principle 2 exhorts, "be beneficial to the discipline and to all parties involved."

Conclusion

I feel a sense of excitement when I drive down little back roads and see an old arroyo cutting deep into the surface, exposing ancient and buried soils. When I spot that lone butte, or those wind-blown fields, I wonder if there is any archaeology exposed over there. Chances are, I will never get to walk that spot of land, but you can bet the locals have, and they have probably collected an artifact or two already. It sure would be nice if archaeological sites were never disturbed, if everything was still there in place where it was once dropped. But that is surely an unrealistic dream. Many different taphonomic processes have already differentially altered the sites, and chances are humans have been salvaging items from them ever since prehistoric times. Wouldn't it be better to know what has been removed from a site in recent times at least, than to pretend those removals never happen? Shouldn't we at least listen to all those who share an interest in the past?

Discussion Questions

1. What sort of bias might artifact collecting introduce into a CRM survey of an area? Should CRM archaeological crews actively consult with local collectors? Why or why not?
2. What would you say to a collector who told you that artifacts would be lost forever if he or she didn't pick them out of the river bottoms or plowed fields?
3. What types of sites do archaeologists tend to excavate? What types of sites do artifact collectors tend to hunt? Are they the same types of sites? Are there differences in the kinds of sites each group tends to focus on depending on location (part of the world) and time period? How might the focus of each group be affecting our understanding of the larger picture?
4. Archaeologists who specialize in the Paleo-Indian period tend to work with artifact collectors more frequently than others. Why don't more archaeologists work with surface hunters?
5. Discuss the contradictions between the SAA Principle of Commercialization and those of Stewardship and Public Education. How can we begin to resolve the dilemma?
6. To what extent are surface collectors active in the area in which you work? Have you ever consulted them? Was the interaction friendly? Productive? Do you agree that archaeologists should pay more attention to interacting with such collectors?

Notes

Like most, this chapter grew from thoughts and discussions shared with collectors and fellow archaeologists alike. Many thanks are due to all those friends willing to share their collections over the hood of a truck or with a warm cup of coffee. I would like to thank Tony Baker in particular, as he diligently continues the work his grandfather began over seventy years ago. The Baker family deserves ample recognition for its contributions to the archaeological community. This chapter benefited from the comments and suggestions of Brian Andrews, Tony Baker, Hilary Chester, Julie Hollowell-Zimmer, Kit Nelson, John Seebach, Karen D. Vitelli, Tom Westfall, and Larry J. Zimmerman. I thank you all.

1. "Low-end" refers to collectors acquiring items for their own personal collection. For a more in-depth discussion of the topic, see Julie Hollowell-Zimmer, chapter 4.

2. The epicenter of the Dust Bowl was Cimarron County, Oklahoma, where up to ten to twenty feet of sediment was removed in some areas, revealing glimpses of the distant past after each windstorm.

3. The two collections greatly contributed to our Paleo-Indian database, yielding over sixty-six Paleo-Indian localities in the Andersen collection and over thirty in the Baker collection.

4. The actual number of recorded sites per county (a measure of survey and testing) shows similar patterns in eastern Colorado.

5. This is not to say that there aren't any CAS members actively collecting artifacts, but few people openly admit to or talk about collecting artifacts.

Recommended Readings

Arrowheads.com
    2002   at www.arrowheads.com/main.htm (accessed April 2002).
    This website is a springboard into the depths of artifact collecting over the Internet. Most of the links from the site are to artifact dealers. The scale of this problem truly eludes our collective imagination.

Baker, Tony
    2002   Paleoindian and Other Archaeological Stuff, at www.ele.net (accessed April 2002).
    Tony Baker's website is often updated with new Paleo-Indian research conducted by this well-known amateur archaeologist.

Colorado Archaeological Society
    2002   Objectives and Code of Ethics, at
            www.coloradoarchaeology.org/statecode.htm (accessed April 2002).

Colorado Historical Society
    2002   Office of Archeology and Historic Preservation, at coloradohistory-
            oahp.org/programareas/paac/paacindex.htm (accessed April 2002).

Indian Artifact Magazine and Prehistoric American
    Indian Artifact Magazine provides a forum for artifact collectors to tell their own stories of artifact discovery, as well as submit photos of recent finds. The editor keeps collectors abreast of current research and publications within the professional community. *Prehistoric American* provides a slightly different view of the collector world, with the articles focusing more on exquisite (and expensive) artifacts from North America.

LaBelle, Jason M.
    1997   "Uncle Bill" and Panhandle Paleoindians. Paper presented at the Fifty-Fifth
            Plains Anthropological Conference, Boulder, CO, November, at
            www.ele.net/LaBelle/unc_bill.htm (accessed December 2002).

Hofman, J. L.
    1989   An Ode to Collections Lost. Newsletter of the Oklahoma Anthropological
            Society 37(1):6–7.

Peotone: Caught in the Middle
    2002   at www.dirtbrothers.org/Peotone/ (accessed December 2002).
    This website advocates salvaging sites from proposed development. An interesting case
study includes the area around Peotone, Illinois, where local amateurs are trying to save archaeological sites from the possible construction of a new airport.

Society for American Archaeology
    1996   Principles of Archaeological Ethics, at
            www.saa.org/Aboutsaa/Ethics/prethic.html (accessed December 2002).

Westfall, T.
    2002   Mostly Sand and Gravel: Artifact Adventures on the High Plains. Writer's
            Showcase, San Jose, CA.

Yeager, C. G.
    2000   *Arrowheads and Stone Artifacts: A Practical Guide for the Amateur
            Archaeologist.* 2nd ed. Pruett, Boulder, CO.

JOE WATKINS

Chapter Ten

Archaeological Ethics and American Indians

Should the interest in scientific knowledge and education outweigh the religious, civil, and sovereign rights of American Indians? Is there anything in the archaeological record that would allow anyone to define the "rights" of any person or group of people who wishes to deal with cultural materials created by people in the past? Even more importantly, who has the "right" to determine the fate of the cultural materials, human skeletal remains, or items buried with those individuals themselves: the ancestors of the people who produced those items or scientists?

In order for this discussion of ethics to be meaningful to everyone, we must look beyond archaeology as only a series of methods driven by a set of theories reflected in a research design that define what a researcher wants to study. Scientific objectivity has a role even in the practice of the social sciences, but the ethical practice of science must involve a thorough examination of the relationship between the scientific community and those with claims on the information so carefully sought by the scientist. In the case of archaeology, it is imperative for archaeologists to be aware that American Indians are one of the primary stakeholders in a complex and multifaceted past owned by no one but controlled by many.

Archaeologists have the power to influence large segments of the population concerning the many different ways that the past is interpreted, discussed, and presented. Although many archaeologists don't realize this power or its broad influence, their decisions and interpretations are often accepted over those of untrained populations (including, in most instances, those of local and descendant communities). In contrast, most other stakeholders often feel powerless to influence local decisions. Even in rare instances where nonarchaeologists have economic or political control over a situation, they more often rely on people with the proper "credentials" for information on which to base their decisions.

A Stormy History

Perhaps it is only coincidental that until the 1969 publication of Vine Deloria's book *Custer Died for Your Sins,* American Indians shared an uneasy truce with anthropology and its subdiscipline of archaeology. Anyone who examines the history of the conflict between archaeologists and American Indians will note that troubles flared during the general political unrest of the late 1960s and early 1970s. Maybe the social and political unrest of the times spurred American Indians to action, but American Indian protests for the period 1969–1979 as reflected in American Indian newspapers such as *Akwesasne Notes* and *Wasaja* showed that their distrust of archaeology and archaeologists revolved primarily around the perceived threat to their ancestors and human remains. Political groups such as the American Indian Movement organized to stop or impede the excavation of archaeological sites (such as the disruption of excavations at Welch, Minnesota, in 1971), protested the display of American Indian human remains and sensitive material in museums and other exhibits (the occupation of the Southwest Museum in Los Angeles in 1971), and addressed the desire for the repatriation of human remains and artifacts (the fight for the return of the Onondaga wampum belts in 1969 from the State Museum of New York).

Archaeologist Bruce Trigger feels that the Euro-American stereotype that portrayed American Indians as "unprogressive" influenced the development of archaeology to a great extent. He argues that Euro-American scholars defined "history" as studying themselves and anthropology as the science of allegedly simpler peoples. In a more critical history of archaeology, Alice Beck Kehoe argues that archaeology treats American Indians as belonging outside of science and that archaeologists act as if they are the only ones capable of understanding the processes that led to the development of American Indian culture and prehistory. While Trigger and Kehoe feel that the conflict between archaeologists and American Indians is rooted in the very way archaeologists define what it is they do, archaeologist Joseph C. Winter's view of the controversy seems more to the point: "This confrontation is basically a conflict of values in which the representatives of competing cultures hold radically differing views of resource definition, ownership, significance, and use" (1980:124).

Throughout the 1980s, American Indians continued to proclaim that they were tired of the remains of their ancestors being treated as nothing more than scientific specimens to be studied, stored in museums, and then forgotten. With the development of compliance archaeology and cultural resource management (CRM) as a business, more and more archaeologists came to understand that their actions had impacts beyond the collection of scientific data from excavated archaeological sites. Tribal groups made it known that the archaeological sites were the physical remnants of their ancestors and that the scientists had failed to consider the social and cultural impacts their excavations had not only on the cultural landscape, but also on existing tribal members. As a result of vigorous lobbying by tribal groups, California and a few other states have gone so far as to require that companies and agencies utilize American Indian personnel to monitor the impact of construction projects on cultural resources or sites of cultural significance.

Christopher A. Bergman and John F. Doershuk discuss the development of archaeology as a business in chapter 7, and the reader should be aware of the impact that various federal legislation has had on the relationships between American Indians and archaeology. Thus, archaeologists are bound by federal statutes to undertake certain relationships with American Indian groups when certain issues are involved, but what, then, are some of the ethical issues that practicing archaeologists should be aware of when dealing with American Indians?

American Indians and Archaeological Ethics

In chapters 1 and 2, respectively, Alison Wylie and Mark Lynott present the history and the philosophy underlying the development of archaeological ethics as codes of conduct to help guide archaeologists' efforts as stewards of a public trust—a past "managed" for the benefit of the entire world. In contrast, the Vermillion Accord on Human Remains (passed in 1989 at the Inter-Congress on Archaeological Ethics and the Treatment of the Dead in Vermillion, South Dakota; see the appendix) attempts to combine good archaeological practice with the concerns of indigenous populations. Both the Society for American Archaeology (SAA) Code of Ethics and the Vermilion Accord attempt to govern the way that archaeologists approach the management of the past, but the Vermillion Accord has as its orientation an emphasis on "respect":

- Respect for the mortal remains of the dead regardless of origin, race, religion, nationality, custom, and tradition.
- Respect for the wishes of the dead concerning disposition whenever possible, reasonable, lawful, and when they are known or can be reasonably inferred.
- Respect for the wishes of the local community and of relatives or guardians of the dead whenever possible, reasonable, and lawful.
- Respect for the scientific research value of skeletal, mummified, and other human remains (including fossil hominids) when such value is demonstrated to exist.
- Agreement to the disposition of fossil, skeletal, mummified, and other remains by negotiation on the basis of mutual respect for the legitimate concerns of communities for the proper disposition of their ancestors, as well as the legitimate concerns of science and education.
- The expressed recognition that the concerns of various ethnic groups, as well as those of science, are legitimate and to be respected.

Both of these written statements help guide the way that archaeologists conduct their study of the past, but the underlying tenets of each are different. The SAA Code of Ethics has as its underlying premise the idea that the past belongs to everyone, that the information in the past is to be collected, preserved, and presented to the public, and that archaeologists are the most qualified to perform these functions. The Vermillion Accord, on the other hand, recognizes the interrelationships between the materials from the past and the cultures of the present, and calls for negotiated agreements between scientists and indigenous populations. Both documents are praiseworthy in that they seek to place limits and boundaries on the way that the materials from the past are managed, studied, and protected, but it is important that we all recognize how these different perspectives might influence archaeological practice (see Claire Smith and Heather Burke, chapter 14).

Numerous authors have asked, "Who owns the past?" but perhaps the most pertinent question is not one of ownership, but rather one of control over the presentation of the past. Doesn't everyone (or anyone) have the right to present his or her perception of the information held in the past? During the first half of America's existence (1770s through the 1870s), some argued that American Indians were inferior to civilized men to rationalize the seizure of Indian lands. Eventually, racial myths grew to supplant other myths about the Indians as a justification for waging war on the Indians and violating their treaty rights. As an example, the "Mound Builder controversy" arose out of attempts to explain the presence of numerous mounds across the Midwestern and Southeastern United States.

The Mound Builders were believed to have been a non-Indian race, possibly related to the prehistoric Mexicans, Danes, or even Phoenicians, who had withdrawn from eastern North America or had been exterminated by the newly arrived Indians. Most writers of the period hypothesized that these Mound Builders had constructed the enormous mounds, because people believed that the Indians of North America were not capable of such feats of engineering. But the controversy was not only a scholarly debate. As Don Fowler notes, "The Myth of the Moundbuilders was never official government policy, but it did bolster arguments for moving the 'savage' Indians out of the way of white 'civilization'" (1987:230). The extermination of American Indians by westward-moving settlers of the United States was made morally easier by the apparent primitiveness of the natives, and the controversy served well as a justification for exterminating the American Indian groups that had destroyed North America's only "civilized" culture (Willey and Sabloff 1980:40).

American Indians and Historic Preservation

A brief review of the historic preservation movement in the United States makes it clear that early historic preservation efforts were based primarily on upper-class values applied to Euro-American concepts of history practiced by nationalist-focused groups. Perhaps, Trigger's implication that anthropology has become the study of allegedly simpler people while history has become the study of groups that evolved into civilizations is also implicit in the term "historic preservation," since it seems to focus on saving those things whose purpose was fulfilled primarily in the past. Yet, in spite of this Euro-American focus, the Navajo Tribal Council passed a resolution enacting an antiquities preservation law for the Navajo Reservation in January 1972, becoming one of the first attempts to extend tribal protection over cultural resources on tribal lands.

The Navajo have had a long relationship with archaeology and archaeologists, starting with Richard Wetherill's excavations at Chaco Canyon in 1896. Since that early involvement, the tribe has come to exert tribal control over cultural resources on the Navajo reservation within the overall management of environmental issues. The establishment of the Navajo Tribal Museum in 1956 was the beginning of tribal involvement in archaeological and historical research programs. With the establishment of the CRM program in 1977, the Navajo Nation became one of the most administratively advanced American Indian groups relative to the discovery, description, and documentation of cultural resources on American Indian–controlled lands in the United States. The Navajo CRM program also initiated one of the earliest efforts to integrate consideration of "sacred places" into the CRM process as mandated by federal law.

To address the problem of adequate separation of cultural resource research and CRM, the Navajo Nation established its Historic Preservation Department (NNHPD) in 1986 to assume the Navajo Nation's responsibilities for management and preservation of cultural resources. It is interesting to note the interaction among the NNHPD, professional archaeologists, and traditional Navajo individuals, but the question is whether the NNHPD preserves the Navajo Nation's cultural resources as the traditionalists would. Traditional people are often uncomfortable with the testing and excavation of archaeological or historical properties on Navajo lands, but, because most of the programs within the NNHPD receive federal funds, the nation is required to comply with federal regulations that often conflict with tribal traditions. Therefore, while the Navajo Nation has taken great strides to integrate the federal system with protection of cultural resources on and within the reservation, it is still mostly a foreign system. Traditional Navajo individuals still view archaeologists with suspicion, including Navajo archaeologists employed to ensure compliance with federal laws and regulations.

It is important for archaeologists to realize that American Indian groups *may* someday control cultural resources on all federal lands and not just on tribal lands. It is possible that if American Indians were provided a more open opportunity to implement the spirit of cultural preservation regulations rather than the letter of such regulations, they might someday develop programs that would do away with the testing and excavation of threatened archaeological sites in favor of a program of recording that preserves the information and spirit of the site while allowing the physical "body" of the site to be destroyed.

Today, more tribal groups are adapting archaeological practices and methodology to protect cultural resources on their reservations. As a result of the 1992 amendments to the National Historic Preservation Act, twelve American Indian tribes took over a portion of the historic preservation duties from State Historic Preservation Officers in July 1996 (NPS Press Release, July 31, 1996). As of February 1999, seventeen tribes had Tribal Historic Preservation Officers in place to formally participate in the National Historic Preservation program, but the relationship between the American Indian and the field of historic preservation remains tenuous at best. There have been successes, but, as a rule, American Indians tend to equate archaeologists with pothunters, grave looters, or, even worse, animals who feast off of the dead (i.e., the "Vulture Culture"). Most do not trust the system supposedly designed to protect their heritage. The future of archaeological and anthropological research on American Indian or federal property may soon be in the hands of the group that can organize most efficiently or exert the greatest influence on federal legislators.

American Indians and the Excavation and Reburial of Human Remains

Even prior to the passage of the National Museum of the American Indian Act (NMAIA) in 1989 and the Native American Graves Protection and Repatriation Act (NAGPRA) in 1990, the idea of repatriation led some archaeologists to believe that all excavations would be controlled by radical American Indians claiming infringement of their religious rights. Physical anthropologists decried the potential loss of a large and necessary (in their view) database, and ethnologists and museum professionals were afraid of losing a large body of cultural material from museum collections. In short, the scientific community rose against the perceived threat to "its" databases—material culture and human remains alike—from those whose ancestors formed the information within the databases.

The NMAIA required the various museums of the Smithsonian Institution to go through their collections and identify human remains and associated grave objects, sacred objects, and objects of cultural patrimony that could be identified with a specific American Indian tribe (or general group of American Indian tribes) and to return those items if the tribe so desired. NAGPRA required agencies and museums that received federal funds to do the same. While scientists argued that the repatriation acts jeopardized their research, American Indians claimed that science could no longer operate within the cultural and social vacuum it had since the investigations of burial mounds in the 1790s; it had to deal with the living ancestors of the individuals represented by the human skeletal materials.

The passage of NAGPRA gave American Indians some of the tools necessary to implement the changes for which they had protested in the 1970s regarding the perceived desecration of American Indian human remains. While NAGPRA is thought to be human rights legislation aimed at providing equal treatment to all human remains under the law, without consideration of "race" or cultural background, American Indians and archaeologists alike realize there are inadequacies and ambiguities to the law. In general, American Indian opinion is that NAGPRA has failed to prevent the continuing desecration of American Indian human remains through further scientific study, to protect human remains on private land, to protect "culturally unidentifiable human remains," and to address the needs of nonfederally recognized American Indian tribes.

American Indian religious views about the handling and treatment of human remains and associated materials vary widely, as do the views of non–American Indian religions, and to speak of a "universal American Indian view of religion" is as impossible as trying to condense all world religions into a single statement. However, most tribal groups do not wish graves to be excavated and are generally united in their views to have human remains that have been excavated returned to the tribes for reburial or reconsecration. But NAGPRA, while allowing for the ultimate return of human remains that can be identified to a specific tribe, does allow scientific study of human remains in certain circumstances. Perhaps, the most concise statement of these issues and justification for the continued study of human remains is presented in Douglas Ubelaker and Lauryn Guttenplan Grant's 1989 article "Human Skeletal Remains: Preservation or Reburial?" In this article, the authors present reasons for the scientific analysis and long-term curation of skeletal remains, an overview of American Indian concerns, a discussion of organizational responses to the call for reburial, and an assessment of American Indian sentiment.

Instead of impinging on rights and repatriation legislation, such as the NMAIA and NAGPRA, it has opened up opportunities for everyone involved. It has given many American Indians the opportunity to regain control over the skeletal remains of their ancestors and over objects that formed the core of their tribal being and has provided tribal groups with a means of gaining information about their past. It has provided archaeologists and museum professionals with opportunities to learn more about contemporary tribal politics and belief systems and has given them the opportunity to understand tribal viewpoints about what archaeologists do and the reports they produce. The NMAIA and NAGPRA have lessened the gulf between archaeologists and American Indians in some areas while widening it in others. This legislation has not only helped solidify the tribes' requests for control over their heritage, but also threatened the fragile alliance between scientists and American Indians.

But perhaps the greatest opportunity repatriation legislation has presented is the opening of communication between archaeologists and tribal people. While legislation provided minimal levels of consultation and communication, many archaeologists and tribal groups have stepped beyond those minimum requirements and have developed strong programs that are beneficial to all parties involved, with tribal involvement in the development of research designs and project design as well as during archaeological investigation and testing programs.

American Indians and "Kennewick Man"

Archaeologists generally have acceded to the return of human remains to ethnic groups who can demonstrate "cultural affiliation" with the remains, even while biological anthropologists argue that returning these materials removes a large portion of information concerning past cultures and civilizations. The dilemma over material that cannot be assigned to existing ethnic groups remains a philosophical sticking point with many anthropologists, especially the issue of returning human remains to groups who can demonstrate only a generalized descent from those populations.

The four-and-half-year protracted legal and media battle over "Kennewick Man" is a perfect example of some of the ethical issues involved in the practice of archaeology (see also Claire Smith and Heather Burke, chapter 14). The 1996 discovery of the skeleton in Washington State exposed to the public once again the conflict between archaeologists and native groups concerning cultural material representing the earliest inhabitants of the Western Hemisphere. First, several anthropologists alleged that the Army Corps of Engineers determined the remains were culturally affiliated to a local tribe, the Umatilla, without sufficient evidence by assuming that the skeleton's age automatically meant the individual was "Native American." Second, while NAGPRA allows the study of remains when the outcome of the study would be "of major benefit to the United States," the anthropologists asserted that the corps' intent to repatriate would prevent such a study. Third, scientists asserted that their civil rights were denied by the corps' action, claiming they were denied the right to study the remains simply because they were not "Native American."

At present, the disposition of the human skeletal remains known as "Kennewick Man" is uncertain. If truly ancient remains such as these are excluded from protection or disposition under NAGPRA, the U.S. District Court for the District of Oregon will need to provide guidance on the minimum antiquity for human remains to be considered "ancient," the roles of science and tribal oral history in defining that threshold, and the extent that scientific values are balanced with cultural values of indigenous populations.

Archaeology, American Indians, and Ethics

Most writers present the conflict between archaeologists and American Indians as grounded in the excavation and study of human remains, but to do so is to oversimplify. The conflict is not one of science versus religion, as some of the popular press has surmised, but more a conflict between the philosophy of American science and that of American Indians. The philosophy of American science—that the world is to be analyzed and explained through a series of hypotheses that impose human order and logic on nature—serves to segregate humans from nature. American Indian philosophy, on the other hand, does not attempt to impose such external limitations on the natural world and serves to integrate humans with the natural world through a philosophical understanding of the interrelationship of human and nature. It is within these philosophical structures that archaeology has developed. The idea that the American past is a heritage to be shared by the entire world—one that scientists are most qualified to understand and present to the public—removes American Indians from the stage. It also effectively removes American Indians from the present by denying them their past as the foundation on which their current cultures are based.

The study of human skeletal material, it has been argued, is vital to the scientific understanding of the past through the information it provides on disease, nutrition, population stress, and so forth. However, American Indians argue that the excavation and study of American Indian human remains, regardless of age, should be treated equally to those of non–American Indians, so that the disturbance of American Indian human remains without court permission should be prosecuted in the same manner as the disturbance of non–American Indian burials. They argue that the excavation of American Indian human remains by scientists is tantamount to grave robbing and that archaeologists, pothunters, and grave robbers are only different subspecies of the same animal.

How important are ethics to the practicing archaeologist? Federal laws and regulations such as the National Historic Preservation Act, the National Environmental Policy Act, and the Archeological Resources Protection Act spell out the duties of archaeologists in certain circumstances in a rather straightforward way. When federal funding is involved, when excavations are undertaken on federal or tribal land, or when a federal permit is required, the archaeologist must protect the cultural environment during the planning, construction, and completion stages of a project. The archaeologist must contact tribal groups and federal or state agencies involved in the land on (or within) which the cultural material is located. Other laws such as the NMAIA and NAGPRA spell out the duties of federal agencies and museums regarding the cultural material recovered during archaeological excavations and collections. These laws establish the minimum legal standards to which archaeologists must adhere in order to practice archaeology on federal or tribal lands.

Each of these laws also requires consultation between the archaeologist and the affected tribal group. At a minimum, consultation establishes the roles of the parties involved, the rules of communication, the scope and limits of research, and the expectations of all groups involved. But should archaeologists be satisfied to meet the minimum requirements for consultation set forth through legislation, or should we be reaching to do more? Personal and professional choices shape consultation programs more than is commonly acknowledged. Those choices—such as the tribes with which we choose to consult, the individuals within those tribes we choose to contact, and the negotiation stances we adopt—play major roles in consultation. Consultation requires work, and from that work all affected parties can benefit through programs of collaboration (where archaeologists and American Indian groups are involved equally throughout the initiation, conduct, completion, and publication of an archaeological project), training, and education. Ethical choices require us to communicate more fully and more honestly in order to be certain that multiple groups are invited to participate in the archaeological enterprise where power is shared by all parties involved rather than wielded by a single party.

Why should we be concerned with stepping beyond the minimum requirements of consultation set forth in legislation? Perhaps, if we don't we will no longer be welcome to conduct archaeological research on federal lands. No longer are American Indians satisfied with being viewed as laboratory or museum specimens to be manipulated for scientific study or as outsiders with little control over the cultural materials on their lands. The 1992 amendments to the National Historic Preservation Act give federally recognized tribes more authority regarding cultural properties located on tribal and aboriginal lands. This was an initial step toward cultural resource autonomy. The Archeological Resources Protection Act of 1979 gave congressional recognition to the right of American Indian tribes to regulate the excavation or removal of archaeological resources from tribal lands and also required the consideration of provisions of the American Indian Religious Freedom Act of 1978. Finally, NAGPRA gives ownership to archaeological resources from federal or tribal lands to those tribes that can prove cultural affiliation, as well as those materials that eventually come under control of a federal agency regardless of the status of the lands from which they are excavated. Is this a bad thing? I don't think so. Archaeologists must be aware that we must do all we can to involve local populations in our research, or else archaeology will dwindle until it becomes no more than a footnote in history. In order to involve populations such as American Indian groups, it will be necessary for archaeology to share the power involved in making decisions that affect the cultural world. The worldview portrayed in legislation has evolved from that of a Euro-American one to a more multifaceted perspective on the value and control of the physical and spiritual manifestations of the past.

Scientists have been forced to reexamine their own ethical positions by defining the extent that they will alter their scientific programs to include or preclude the wishes of the people they study. Archaeologists who feel that cultural material within the United States belongs to all of the people of the United States can excavate archaeological sites and curate the material from those sites providing they do not choose to excavate on federal or tribal lands, do not need a federal permit, or do not place the materials within a museum that receives federal funds. Archaeologists who believe that cultural resources belong to the ancestors of those who produced them are free to consult closely with American Indian tribes likely to be related to "archaeological groups," and, if there are competing claims of ancestry, archaeologists are free to choose the group with which to work. The positions of both groups of archaeologists are ethically sound, but revolve around different ethical precepts.

The principles of the SAA Code of Ethics (Lynott and Wylie 1995b) recognize that there are interests in the archaeological record other than those of archaeologists, but the orientation of the code is toward protection of the material that forms the foundation of archaeology's databases and the archaeologist's livelihood. These principles provide a starting point for the ethical practice of archaeology, but should not be considered to be the ultimate authority in such a practice. Archaeologists should be free to exercise their choices concerning communication, consultation, and cooperation with American Indian groups throughout the United States and should not feel constrained by minimum standards set out by various organizations. More realistically, archaeologists should feel obligated to share the field with those who show an interest in the past and to recognize that the many publics involved in archaeology (archaeologists, government agencies, American Indians, and other descendant communities) have a stake in the presentation and preservation of the past.

Discussion Questions

1. How can we rationalize the ethics of American Indians with those of archaeologists? Should the wishes and concerns of American Indians receive special treatment or consideration by archaeologists or museums? Why or why not, and if so, in what ways?

2. When people or groups with conflicting values are faced with decisions about how to act, what is an ethical approach? How can compromises be worked out to the satisfaction of all interested parties?

3. Would it help if American Indian nations developed protocols for archaeological research? What would happen in the event that, as an archaeologist, you felt you could not ethically agree to the terms set forth in the research protocol?

4. What do I mean when I state that the future of archaeological and anthropological research on American Indian or federal property may soon be in the hands of the group that can organize most efficiently or exert the greatest influence on federal legislators?

5. South Africans have generally chosen not to repatriate human remains to a specific descendant group on the grounds that doing so simply repeats the ethnic distinctions that created the abuse, and apartheid, in the first place. Instead, in some cases they rebury human remains on specially consecrated ground, unaffiliated with any one ethnic group. How does this compare with NAGPRA? Might this be another solution for repatriation?

Recommended Readings

Advisory Council on Historic Preservation
    2002   Tribal Historic Preservation Officers, at www.achp.gov/thpo.html (accessed April 2002).

Bray, Tamara
    2001   *The Future of the Past.* Garland, New York.

Bray, Tamara L., and Thomas W. Killian (editors)
    1994   *Reckoning with the Dead: The Larsen Bay Repatriation and the Smithsonian Institution.* Smithsonian Institution Press, Washington, DC.

Dongoske, Kurt E. et al.
    1997   Archaeological Cultures and Cultural Affiliation: Hopi and Zuni Perspectives in the American Southwest. *American Antiquity* 62(4):600–8.

Downey, Roger
    2000   *The Riddle of the Bones: Politics, Science, Race and the Story of Kennewick Man.* Copernicus, New York.

Ferguson, T. J.
    1996   Native Americans and the Practice of Archaeology. *Annual Review of Anthropology* 25:63–79.

Klesert, Anthony L., and Alan S. Downer (editors)
    1990   *Preservation on the Reservation: Native Americans, Native American Lands, and Archaeology.* Navajo Nation Papers in Anthropology no. 26. Navajo Nation Archaeology Department and the Navajo Nation Historic Preservation Department, Window Rock, AZ.

Landau, Patricia M., and D. Gentry Steele
    1996   Why Anthropologists Study Human Remains. *American Indian Quarterly* 20(2):209–28.

Magistrate John Jelderks
    1997   Opinion, *Bonnichsen v. United States,* USDC CV no. 96-1481-JE, at www.goonline.com/science/kennewic/court/opinion.htm (accessed April 2002).

McGuire, Randall
    1992   Archaeology and the First Americans. *American Anthropologist* 94(4):816–36.

Mihesuah, Devon
    2000   *Repatriation Reader: Who Owns American Indian Human Remains?* University of Nebraska Press, Lincoln.

National Museum of the American Indian
    2002   at www.nmai.si.edu/ (accessed April 2002).

National Park Service
  2002   What's New in National NAGPRA? at www.cr.nps.gov/nagpra/index.htm
          (accessed April 2002).
  2002   Tribal Historic Preservation Offices, at www2.cr.nps.gov/tribal/thpo.htm
          (accessed April 2002).

Nicholas, George P., and Thomas D. Andrews (editors)
  1997   *At a Crossroads: Archaeology and First Peoples in Canada.* Archaeology
          Press, Department of Archaeology, Simon Frazier University, Burnaby, BC.

Oregon Live
  2002   News: Kennewick Man, at oregonlive.com/special/kman (accessed April
          2002).

Rose, Jerome C., Thomas J. Green, and Victoria D. Green
  1996   NAGPRA Is Forever: The Future of Osteology and the Repatriation of
          Skeletons. *Annual Review of Anthropology* 25:81–103.

Smithsonian Office of Repatriation
  2002   Anthropology: Kennewick Man, at www.nmnh.si.edu/anthro/repatriation/
          (accessed April 2002).

Swidler, Nina, Kurt Dongoske, Roger Anyon, and Alan Downer (editors)
  1997   *Native Americans and Archaeologists: Stepping Stones to Common Ground.*
          AltaMira, Walnut Creek, CA.

Thomas, David Hurst
  2000   *Skull Wars: Kennewick Man, Archaeology, and the Battle for Native American
          Identity.* Basic, New York.

Tri-City Herald
  2002   Kennewick Man Virtual Interpretive Center, at www.kennewick-man.com
          (accessed April 2002).

Trope, Jack F., and Walter R. Echo-Hawk
  1992   The Native American Graves Protection and Repatriation Act: Background
          and Legislative History. *Arizona State Law Journal* 24(1):35–78.

Zimmerman, Larry J.
  1996   Epilogue: A New and Different Archaeology? *American Indian Quarterly*
          20(2):297–307.

THERESA A. SINGLETON
CHARLES E. ORSER JR.

Chapter Eleven

Descendant Communities: Linking People in the Present to the Past

Descendant communities are, broadly speaking, present-day groups of people whose heritage is under investigation at an archaeological site or who have some other historical, cultural, or symbolic link to the site. As archaeologist Randall McGuire puts it, some descendant communities see the site being studied as a shrine (2000:767). Whether or not they think of the site as a shrine, they believe they have some claim to the site. Descendant communities, therefore, may be diverse groups of people with varying interests in the archaeological project. Consequently, several descendant communities may exist for any one archaeological project. The differing interests of these communities at times may be at odds with each other as well as with an archaeologist's interests and goals. Thus, working with descendant communities presents challenges for archaeologists that cannot simply be resolved by consulting a generic list of ethical principles presumably applicable to every situation. While most, if not all, sites have a descendant community, the unique circumstances of every research project require archaeologists to consider each group's claim carefully and to exercise good judgment in addressing the concerns of descendant communities.

There are, however, some issues and practical concerns common to working with all descendant communities. In this chapter, we focus on issues emanating primarily from our own work with descendant communities to examine several questions: Who constitutes a descendant community? How can the archaeologist locate and identify such communities? When a community appears disinterested, what should be the course of action? Can or should conflicting site narratives or research interests between the community and the archaeologists be resolved?

Identifying Descendant Communities

Many kinds of descendant communities exist. Too many archaeologists imagine descendant communities simply as biological descendants of the people who once occupied the site. Consequently, they tend to overlook present-day communities as either potential research resources or as constituencies of their research. Descendant communities are defined by their relationship to a site. As previously stated, that relationship can be historical, cultural, symbolic, or may hinge on some other significant factor. While our goal is not to develop a typology, we distinguish here between two primary groups of descendant communities: *local* or *resident* communities are those that live in the general vicinity of the archaeological project, and *diasporic* communities are groups that are linked to a site, but that live in another location, potentially hundreds or even thousands of miles away.

Local Communities

Most archaeologists work with local or resident communities, and the vast majority of literature on descendant communities is concerned with these groups. Today, archaeologists are encouraged to seek out local descendant communities prior to beginning research; some archaeologists have developed partnerships with local communities and involve them in various aspects of the project. Many archaeologists, however, come to know local communities by chance, as a result of living and working in the project area. Theresa A. Singleton's early experience with descendant communities falls within this serendipitous approach. While undertaking fieldwork for her dissertation in the late 1970s, she worked with two distinct descendant communities: 1) descendants of the former enslaved populations in the area, many of whom were impoverished laborers working in agriculture or fisheries and 2) an urban-based, middle-class African American community living in cities and towns throughout the State of Georgia.

Singleton initially contacted local descendants of the former enslaved population to gain more information on the twentieth-century history of a rice plantation she was investigating. She was particularly intrigued by a map dated 1889 she had found in the state archives. It showed the plantation in question divided into small plots, each plot marked with the initials of what she assumed were renters or tenants. Unfortunately, there was no key to the map to identify the renters or tenants to clarify the meaning of the initials or any other information. Archaeological testing, particularly in the slave villages, yielded very few late nineteenth- and twentieth-century artifacts. Singleton turned to local residents who might have known about the last days of rice cultivation in the area and whether or not rice farmers had lived on the plantation in the 1900s. Her entry to the local black community was through a self-trained, local, Euro-American historian who knew people who had once cultivated rice in the area. Singleton interviewed several of those farmers; three of them confirmed that rice cultivation had continued on the plantation well into the 1900s, but said that the rice farmers had not resided on the former plantation. They preferred living elsewhere and commuting daily in their small boats to and from the rice fields.

All of the interviewees, with one notable exception, gave Singleton the impression that they were not eager to recount this history even to her, even though she is African American. They also were not particularly interested in her project, but they were curious about why she was doing the research. She told them she had become fascinated with the history and archaeology of the area after spending a summer working on a prehistoric site some three years prior to this project. She also had worked on another archaeological project on a former cotton plantation in the area before beginning her dissertation research on the rice plantation. While they seemed satisfied with her answer, they showed no further interest in the project. Singleton did not consult with them afterwards. This would have been the end of the story, but another descendant community and other interest groups soon emerged.

Several months after the initial interviews, an African American museum director contacted Singleton for assistance with a temporary exhibition project. The museum director was organizing a statewide exhibition on African American family life that would have a small section on slavery. The director wanted to use archaeological data from Singleton's excavations to develop display cases of artifacts and to construct an interior of a slave dwelling. Singleton eagerly embraced this project, and in the process met numerous African Americans from around the state. These individuals—unlike the local residents she had previously interviewed—were very interested in her work. Over the next few years, she interacted with people she met through the exhibition project and gave talks to a variety of African American organizations. The exhibition opened in 1981, showcasing data from Singleton's investigations.

Coincident with the planning of the temporary exhibition, another museum project was developing in the county directly south of Singleton's field site. The State Department of Historic Sites acquired a former rice plantation and began planning to develop a historic site devoted to the interpretation of both the agricultural and social history associated with rice culture. This time, Singleton initiated contact with the manager of the property. He was very enthusiastic to have her work with his volunteer advisory board, which included many African Americans from the area. To Singleton's surprise, one of the persons she had interviewed, the one person who enjoyed talking about working on rice plantations, was among the members of this group.

Considerable time elapsed between Singleton's initial contact with the property manager and the launching of activities for the advisory board. By the time she received a call about attending a two-day planning meeting and participating in a public program, Singleton had returned to her university, located several hours away. She was busy writing her dissertation and hunting for a job, and lacked the time and financial resources to attend the meeting. Singleton later withdrew from the advisory board because she was unable to participate, but agreed to make available resources from her dissertation research for use in developing the interpretive center. The state historic site opened in the mid-1980s.

Although Singleton's early experience predated most archaeologists' ethical concerns about descendant communities, she learned valuable lessons that set the stage for her more recent involvement: local historians, museum professionals, and community organizers are excellent resource people for gaining access to the community. One should not, however, rely on a single contact person. Make contacts with diverse members of the community. Do not be discouraged by initial disinterest. Some members of the community may just not be interested in what you are doing, but they do not necessarily reflect the entire community's attitude. The idea of using archaeology to study the history of people in the recent past is still a foreign concept to many laypeople who associate archaeology with the study of the ancient world. It may take a while for some people to fully comprehend the project's significance and its relevance. If some individuals are not interested, do not push. Accept and respect their opinions. Be realistic in the commitments you make to descendant communities, and be realistic about what you are capable of doing. Singleton realized belatedly that she had made too many commitments and could not attend meetings or participate in public programs on a regular basis once she moved from the area, and, as a graduate student, she simply lacked the personal resources and institutional support to be actively engaged with these groups. Today, however, it might be possible to maintain an ongoing long-distance dialog with descendant communities through a Web page, chat room, or other virtual resources.

Diasporic Communities

Our concept of a diasporic descendant community is taken from definitions of "diaspora," as a group whose collective identity is defined by a history of dispersal and by myths and memories of the homeland (Clifford 1997:227). Archaeological investigations taking place in the homeland may involve a diasporic descendant community.

Charles E. Orser Jr. discovered the importance of acknowledging the diasporic community during his research in the Republic of Ireland. Scholars who have examined traveling and migration admit that unique social identities can be created during the journey itself (see Leed 1991). A sense of ritual death may occur at the departure from one's ancestral home, especially among those individuals who have been forcibly removed or who are fleeing racial, ethnic, or religious persecution. At the same time, migrants can also experience distress when entering a new environment composed of unfamiliar natural and social landscapes. Belonging to a diaspora provides an almost spiritual mechanism for individuals to connect the "home" with the "homeland," and in this manner can help to create a collective memory and a shared identity (see Brah 1996:183; Cornwell and Stoddard 2001:7).

Ireland has an indisputable place within the history of the world's great diasporas. Thousands of emigrants left Ireland, both voluntarily and involuntarily, and traveled to various locations around the globe. In the United States alone, about 44 million people today acknowledge Irish ancestry, and the term "Irish American" is an accepted identity. The widespread location of people claiming Irish descent means that historical archaeologists face potential pitfalls that may not be readily apparent at the outset of the research.

Orser's research in Ireland to date has focused on the nature of rural life during the early nineteenth century, more specifically, the decades just preceding the Great Famine of the 1840s. That statement, though seemingly innocuous, is actually, within the context of the Irish Diaspora, fraught with political implications. By itself, it demonstrates the complexities posed by the presence of the diasporic descendant community and provides an excellent, illustrative example.

Many individuals who self-identify as having Irish ancestry perceive the events in Ireland during the early 1840s as profoundly meaningful. At the very least, the outcome of those events caused the death of thousands and the emigration of thousands more. The terms individuals use to identify the period express the importance they attach to it as well as provide possible information about their stance on present-day politics. For instance, individuals unengaged or disinterested in the famine generally refer to it as the "Great Potato Famine" or the "Irish Potato Famine." These individuals may be not of Irish ancestry or only nominally Irish, with no knowledge of or interest in history. During the 1840s, those men and women who experienced the events often referred to it as "The Great Hunger," and people wishing to commemorate the dead frequently use this term today. Others use the term "The Great Starvation," and still others employ the more strident, and politically explosive term "The Irish Holocaust." Anyone who speaks of the early 1840s must necessarily abandon neutrality because of the terms they must employ, and at the same time, they must understand the seriousness of the politics involved. The field of public education provides a superb example.

Attempts to require the teaching of the Irish famine in the public schools of New York, Illinois, and California—alongside the mid-twentieth-century Holocaust in Europe—have been hotly contested, ideologically based battles. Opponents to the teaching of the Irish famine as a holocaust argue that the famine began with a naturally occurring crop fungus, whereas the Nazis consciously created, organized, and perpetuated the mass murder of millions. Where one was a true holocaust, the other was a series of extremely unfortunate circumstances. Proponents of teaching the Irish famine as a holocaust counter that the events of the 1840s were not all caused by nature. They argue that the British did little or nothing to prevent the human tragedy and in fact exported food crops grown in Ireland during the height of the devastation. For these interpreters, the British government is culpable through its callous administration.

Archaeologists who attempt to engage in dialogs about the famine with individuals who self-identify as "Irish"—regardless of where they may actually live—must realize the present-day politics of the past. Some men and women may believe that biology caused the famine through simple crop failure, and that Irish farmers were ultimately to blame for the human toll because of their reliance on a single food crop and their overlarge families. Others may fervently maintain that while the fungus was indeed naturally caused, the British administration did too little to assist the starving Irish population and that crass politics were to blame for the human devastation. The way an archaeologist is received can be a reflection of how the audience perceives the events of the early 1840s.

The controversy that exists over the terms used to identify the horrific events of the early 1840s impacts the way in which members of a descendant, diasporic community may perceive an archaeologist's interpretations of a particular site. Orser discovered these differences in perception during his research at Ballykilcline, in north County Roscommon. The terminal history of Ballykilcline included a rent strike that began in 1834 and ended in 1847–1848 with the mass eviction of the over 500 tenants who lived on the property. After the removal, the tenants traveled to Liverpool and then to New York and elsewhere.

In the mid-1990s, historian Robert Scally (1995) published an account of Ballykilcline, in which he detailed the eviction and the resettlement of the tenant families in North America. As a result of this book, a number of descendants living in North America created the Ballykilcline Society. The first reunion of the society was held on the lands of the former Ballykilcline in 1999; over 100 North Americans attended. Reunions have been held every year in the United States since, with the second reunion in Ireland occurring in 2002.

Orser has learned through the course of many discussions and much correspondence that the descendants of the Ballykilcline tenants care deeply about the archaeological findings, as well as the manner in which the interpretations will be offered. In fact, members of the diasporic community—living thousands of miles from Ballykilcline and generally from each other—tend to have more reverence for the artifacts than do local Irish men and women, many of whom may care little about the area's history. It is a simple historical fact that the individuals who are most emotionally connected to Ballykilcline live far away from it. Thus, men and women living thousands of miles away may, in fact, express the feelings that an archaeologist might be more inclined to expect from a descendant community still living in the vicinity of a site. The Ballykilcline situation is undoubtedly unique in many respects, but archaeologists conducting research on sites that can be associated with a diasporic descendant community should remember the potential geographical diversity of that community. North Americans with clear descent lines to past residents of Ballykilcline view themselves as emotionally connected to the site and to other members of the community, even though, as individuals, they may never actually have visited it or even traveled to Ireland. This characteristic is perhaps widely indicative of the diasporic descendant community.

Conflicting Site Interests and Narratives

One of the greatest challenges of working with descendant communities occurs when the archaeologists' interests and interpretations collide with those of the descendant communities. In many cases, the communities see archaeologists as the experts, so this problem may never arise in some projects. In situations where it does, archaeologists need to be sensitive to the communities' viewpoints. Often, the communities' ideas are derived from cherished myths or legends that are in themselves worthy of further analysis. Such narratives may yield insights into the sociopolitical construction of the past, and may ultimately be valuable to the overall project. In other cases, it may be impossible to reconcile archaeological interpretations with those of the community. It is important, however, not simply to dismiss alternative interpretations, but to point out their weaknesses in noncondescending ways. At the same time, archaeologists should support their archaeological interpretations with good evidence.

A recurrent concern encountered in the archaeological study of another diaspora, the African one, is the extremist position of Afrocentrists whose ideas go against well-grounded scholarship on Africa and the African experience in the Americas. Certain factions of African American descendant communities will want to have the site interpreted from this perspective. Our approach to this prospect is to be honest in the beginning and point out to the community that we are not adherents of Afrocentrism and will not interpret the site from that point of view. This will certainly anger some members of the community, but it is not possible to give all voices equal time, particularly those representing extremist positions based on questionable scholarship.

Sometimes, local traditions can neither be confirmed nor denied. In Singleton's current research on a Cuban coffee plantation, she has been unable to validate the local tradition of who founded the plantation, his ethnicity, and the number of slaves he owned. Archival sources suggest that the local tradition is false; however, there are gaps in the documentary records, and the archival research is ongoing. An additional consideration is that the local tradition of the plantation has made its way into the official history of the area. Therefore, she feels that she must have strong documentation before she can effectively support or refute the local tradition. In the meantime, she presents the site by pointing out the competing narratives. The same is true of Orser's work in Ireland, where different views of history compete for dominance. It is important to convey to descendant communities that several interpretations are possible, and that two archaeologists looking at the same information will not necessarily reach the same conclusions.

Conclusion

Archaeologists who work at sites associated with descendant communities, regardless of the historical composition and diversity of those communities, should be prepared to exercise flexibility in their research methods, outlooks, and interpretations. Archaeologists should not anticipate that the dialog with members of the community will be either straightforward or necessarily easy. Nor should scholars pretend to have all the answers or to project the attitude that they are the owners of history. In the final analysis, archaeologists should be willing to acknowledge that what they perceive as their job is someone else's tradition and history, and the way in which both are presented can have a highly personal and profoundly lasting impact on members of the descendant community.

Discussion Questions

1. How can archaeologists successfully integrate the interests of descendant communities with those of host countries/governmental agencies or other constituencies, particularly when these interests may be at odds with each other?
2. How does an archaeologist determine whether there is a diasporic descendant community with potential interests in the archaeology of a site, and if there is, who is a legitimate member of such a group, particularly when it may be composed of individuals currently residing in very distant and scattered places?
3. To what extent, if at all, should an archaeologist mold his or her interpretations to conform to the wishes/beliefs of representatives of a descendant community? Explain your response, including how you would chose among those beliefs if there were conflicting ones.
4. How should archaeologists address fanciful claims to the ownership of site?
5. When working in a diasporic community, should an archaeologist try to mediate between the views of those individuals from outside the region of the site and those individuals who still live in the vicinity of the site? How could such mediation affect the archaeological interpretations?
6. Some archaeologists seem to have difficulty working with descendant communities; some even seem to resent that they have to. Why do you think

this might be the case? What are the possible ramifications of ignoring the concerns of descendant community members?

7. Have archaeologists in your geographic area of archaeological interest generally made an effort to contact descendant communities, whether local or diasporic? If not, do you think they should? If so, ask them about their experiences. Explore the possibilities and implications of making such consultations standard practice.

8. In the mobile world of the twenty-first century, most archaeological sites are likely to have some version of a diasporic descendant community. Think of the possibilities in your geographic area of interest, how you might contact such groups, and what impact doing so might have on your archaeological work and understanding. What impact would *not* contacting them have?

9. You're in the middle of one of the busiest semesters of your life, with major committee obligations, deadlines for several articles, new courses to organize, and a proposal for funding to keep your project in the field next summer, among other things. You receive an urgent e-mail message from the mayor of the (overseas) village in which your project is based, asking you to answer some "simple" questions: What did the ancient people do for entertainment? What kinds of clothes did men and women wear for special occasions? For everyday? How about the young boys and girls? Were they all farmers? And so on. He needs this information right away because the local school children are writing a play about life at your site and the play is going to be featured at the village festival next month. What do you do?

10. Imagine a (realistic) situation or context in which you think it would *not* be advisable to seek out and consult with descendant communities (a class or group might find it useful to form teams to debate the pros and cons, ideally, with a specific project in mind).

11. What do you imagine the positive aspects of working with a descendant community are for the individual archaeologist?

Recommended Readings

Epperson, T.
  1999   The Contested Commons: Archaeologies of Race, Repression, and Resistance in New York City. In *Historical Archaeologies of Capitalism,* edited by M. P. Leone and P. B. Potter, 81–110. Kluwer Academic, New York.

Logan, G. C.
  1998   Archaeologists, Residents, and Visitors: Creating a Community-Based Program in African-American Archaeology. In *Annapolis Pasts: Historical*

Archaeology in Annapolis, Maryland, edited by P. A. Shackel, P. R. Mullins, and Mark S. Warner, 69–96. University Press of Tennessee, Knoxville.

McDavid, C., and D. W. Babson (editors)
  1997   In the Realm of Politics: Prospects for Public Participation in African-American and Plantation Archaeology. *Historical Archaeology* 31(3).

Watkins, Joe
  2000   *Indigenous Archaeology: American Indian Values and Scientific Practice.* AltaMira, Walnut Creek, CA.

Watkins, Joe, K. A. Pyburn, and P. Cressey
  2000   Community Relations: What Practicing Archaeologists Need to Know to Work Effectively with Local and/or Descendant Communities. In *Teaching Archaeology in the Twenty-First Century,* edited by S. J. Bender and George S. Smith, 73–86. Society for American Archaeology, Washington, DC.

JOHN H. JAMESON JR.

Chapter Twelve

Purveyors of the Past: Education and Outreach as Ethical Imperatives in Archaeology

Throughout my career as a public agency archaeologist, I have always been in-trigued by what appears to be a natural fascination people have with things histori-cal and archaeological. I have wondered whether this is simply a human response to self-interest and cultural identity. Indeed, why was *I* attracted to the subjects of an-thropology and archaeology to the point of making a living at it? It was the holistic approach of anthropological studies and the attempted objectivity of archaeological methods and inquiry, plus the challenging and interesting people and places associ-ated with archaeology, that attracted me to the field.

When I came to the National Park Service (NPS) in late 1988, I looked around and wondered why more attention was not given to helping people know and ap-preciate the archaeological gems that the agency was charged to preserve and pro-tect for posterity. For over a decade, I have been privileged to work with archaeologists, interpreters, and educators of the highest caliber in promoting the public interpretation of archaeology in the national parks and other public lands. I have worked with archaeologists who recognize the role of public interpretation in explaining the relevancy and value of archaeology in everyday lives of people. I have worked with national park rangers to explore the conceptual relationships and emotional connections that stimulate public access to, appreciation for, and inspira-tion from archaeology and cultural history. These colleagues are firmly committed to finding engaging and innovative ways to reach out to national and local commu-nities and involve them in the rich diversity of human experience.

Professional archaeologists are positioned to be the experts and purveyors of archaeologically derived information that fills in missing pieces of history and places flesh on the skeleton of historical events. For the most part, we deal with a nonrenewable and fragile resource whose physical integrity can easily be com-promised. As archaeologists and anthropologists, we have been trained to study, manipulate, interpret, and, yes, selectively destroy the artifacts and physical residue of the past. Because archaeology can provide techniques for identifying and explaining cultural events and patterns that are outside of written accounts, it provides unique and otherwise unobtainable insights into cultural history and behavior. Notwithstanding alternative interpretations, such as indigenous oral histories, what archaeology offers is an interpretation of material remains and contexts not often accounted for in other versions of the past.

Because the archaeological record represents the heritage of all people, archaeologists have a responsibility to communicate with the public about the nature of archaeological research and explain the importance and relevance of archaeological resources. Archaeologists also have responsibilities to be sensitive to local and indigenous communities and to respect local cultural systems and attitudes. We do these things in the name of science and education and under the auspices of cultural resource protection mandates. As professionals, we cannot take these public responsibilities lightly.

The conservation movement began in the late nineteenth century and continued to grow in the twentieth century. In conjunction with the rise in historic preservation sentiments and a post–World War II economic boom, it produced a bevy of protection laws in the 1960s and 1970s. These cultural resource laws in turn produced a flood of archeological information with which we are just beginning to deal. Public archaeology has evolved from a definition synonymous with cultural resource management (CRM) to a broader scope that includes educational archeology, public interpretation of archaeology, and what has been called the new era of Native American archaeology—which brings us closer to our anthropological roots. In working with and involving local communities and Native American groups, we are, in the tradition of cultural anthropology, establishing a rapport with these groups that enables us to form partnerships in making more meaningful and accurate observations about cultural systems and lifeways.

We do not talk enough in archaeological circles about the anthropological perspectives of our work. As anthropologists, we use concepts of culture and material culture to explain who and what we have been as humans. The essence of the relevance of archaeology is that the whole of what we have been is who we are.

We use archaeology to teach concepts of culture and to learn important things about ourselves, about who we have been, who we are, and where we are going. Archaeologists deal with three-dimensional artifacts that people can feel, smell, touch, dream about, and care about. We should strive to build bridges between anthropological studies and the realities of what is important to people. Although our professorial categories and strategies are, by definition, abstractions, they nevertheless communicate important concepts about culture and human behavior. All archaeologists should strive to be good anthropologists. In turn, all anthropologists should recognize the power of archaeology to reach and inspire people.

The Rising Importance of Educational Archaeology

The development and expansion of educational archaeology in the 1980s and 1990s speaks directly to the relevance of anthropological and archaeological inquiry in modern multicultural societies. Although notable efforts had occurred previously (South 1997), the last quarter of the twentieth century was a time when many in the archaeology profession came to the realization that they could no longer afford to be detached from mechanisms and programs that conveyed archaeological information to the lay public.

Many private and public universities, archaeology and anthropology departments, and museums have placed a high priority on establishing and promoting effective education and outreach programs. One example is Sonoma State University's Anthropological Studies Center, which places special emphasis on education and outreach in the production of publications and activities for teachers, local civic organizations, archaeology groups, and continuing education programs.

A large number of private CRM contracting firms expend considerable resources in promoting educational opportunities for volunteers and students. An example is the establishment of a full-time public programs division by Statistical Research, Inc. (SRI) in Tucson, Arizona. At SRI, public programs are structured into applicant-sponsored compliance projects as well as by "stand alone" contracts for public outreach activities by companies and institutions not tied to regulatory compliance. SRI produces the U.S. Forest Service's Passport in Time *PIT Traveler* publication that advertises nationwide programs and volunteer opportunities.

In the United States, professional organizations, most notably the Society for American Archaeology (SAA), the Archaeological Institute of America (AIA), and the Society for Historical Archaeology (SHA), plus state and local groups, have played important roles in promoting education in archaeology. The first item in the AIA Code of Professional Standards states that "professional archaeologists should be actively engaged in public outreach through lecturing, popular writing, school programs, and other educational initiatives" (1994). One example of this is SHA's Unlocking the Past: Historical Archaeology in North America project, a multiyear public outreach and education effort. This project, composed of a well-illustrated book and a companion website, explains how historical archaeological sites and research offer new perspectives on the history of Americans' encounters with the land and each other. It explains how preserving archaeological sites and collections protects America's heritage for the future. The project demonstrates that historical archaeology is a shared venture with all peoples of North America and that the past belongs to us all. The Unlocking the Past material is designed to appeal to a wide general audience of young readers as well as adults interested in archaeology, North American history, and historic preservation (De Cunzo and Jameson 2000).

The U.S. Bureau of Land Management's Heritage Education Program has made important contributions to archaeology education at the federal level. Project

Archaeology is a multidimensional program that includes quality educational materials and teacher workshops. *Intrigue of the Past: A Teacher's Activity Guide for Fourth through Seventh Grades* is a teaching guide containing twenty-eight classroom-tested lesson plans that use history and archaeology to teach science, math, history, social studies, art, language arts, and higher-level thinking skills, such as problem solving, synthesis, and evaluation (Bureau of Land Management 2002).

Passport in Time is a volunteer archaeology and historic preservation program of the U.S. Forest Service. Volunteer participants work with professional archaeologists and historians on projects including archaeological excavation, rock art restoration, survey, archival research, historic structure restoration, gathering oral histories, and writing interpretive brochures (U.S. Forest Service 2000).

Among government-sponsored programs, the NPS, the traditional leader in promoting education and outreach activities at the federal level, emphasizes the importance of developing educational partnerships and initiatives both within and outside the government. These activities and programs reflect the leadership role assigned by the U.S. Congress to the secretary of the interior and delegated largely to the NPS. The NPS distributes *Common Ground,* a quarterly magazine, to more than 12,000 members of the public as well as archaeologists, land managers, preservation officers, museum professionals, Native Americans, law enforcement agents, and educators. The NPS Southeast Archeological Center (SEAC) in Tallahassee, Florida, provides leadership in educational archaeology by helping to develop archaeology-related curricula, both in formal school settings and at more informal settings such as national parks and museums. SEAC's activities have included the organization and coordination of public-oriented publications, academic symposia, workshops, and training sessions presented in a variety of professional venues (Jameson 1999, 2000).

NPS has also been a leader in developing performance standards for archaeologists that emphasize competency in developing and implementing education and outreach activities. The Essential Competencies for archaeologists include proficiencies in writing and communication. They also require knowledge and understanding of public interpretation philosophy and techniques, outside consultations, and cultivating partnerships and contacts with the professional community. According to the standards, even at entry levels, archaeologists should have 1) basic knowledge of techniques of conveying technical archeological information to the lay public; 2) the ability to work as team members in the design and implementation of effective public interpretation programs, such as popular histories, brochures, pamphlets, videos, exhibits, posters, lesson plans, and other public interpretation devices; and 3) knowledge of public speaking techniques (National Park Service [NPS] 1996).

In 2000, NPS finalized the Effective Interpretation of Archaeological Resources "shared-competency" training module (NPS Interpretive Skills Module 440). An interagency, interdisciplinary work group developed the module over the course of three years. It outlines a unique, interdisciplinary course of study that can be used in cross-training employees in the three career fields of archaeology, interpretation, and education. Specialists in these fields are trained together in the skills and abilities (shared competencies) needed to carry out a successful public interpretation program. Among the main precepts of the curriculum are the needs for interdisciplinary communication and for interpretation sensitive to multicultural audiences (Jameson 2000; NPS 2001).

Archaeology as Inspiration: Reaching Out to Our Communication Partners

Archaeologists are increasingly concerned with how the past is presented to, and consumed by, nonspecialists. We want to examine new ways of communicating archaeological information in educational venues such as national parks, museums, popular literature, film and television, music, and various multimedia formats. Many are not content to rely solely on traditional methodologies and analytical techniques in their attempts to reconstruct human history and bring it to life for the public. We realize the value and power of artistic expression in helping to convey archaeological information to the public (Jameson, Ehrenhard, and Finn, in press). We want to venture beyond utilitarian explanations and explore the interpretive potential of cognitive imagery that archaeological information and objects can inspire a wide variety of artistic expressions ranging from straightforward computer-generated reconstructions and traditional artists' conceptions to other art forms such as poetry and opera. Although some level of conjecture will always be present in these works, they are often no less conjectural than technical interpretations and have the benefit of providing visual and conceptual imagery that can communicate contexts and settings in compelling ways. Two such interpretive formats, two-dimensional paintings and popular history writing, are regularly used by the NPS as public interpretation and education tools (Jameson 2000, 2001; Jameson, Ehrenhard, and Finn, in press).

Some modern practitioners in educational archaeology express ethical concerns that certain "artistic" expressions, such as in multimedia presentations and motion pictures, present archaeology in negative and "noneducational" ways. Modern debates on the merits and deficiencies inherent in archaeotourism and consumer archaeology hinge on the appropriateness of sensationalized depictions evoking a treasure hunt versus seeing fictional values as opportunities and tools for education. The 1996 movie *The English Patient,* for example, draws on archaeological themes and imagery that imposes an indirect and unconscious connection by the audience to the value and relevance of the resource. Popular historical movies such as *Gladiator* should not be summarily dismissed as misleading and inaccurate. Instead, we should strive to understand their entertainment values and learn how to use them and other popular media to control the process of communicating mainstream messages about history and archaeology (Jameson, Ehrenhard, and Finn, in press).

If we want more effective public participation and appreciation, we need to reach out to our communication partners and arm them with the knowledge and understanding of how archaeology can contribute to people's sense of identity and ultimately improve their lives. We as individual archaeologists cannot hope to do it all ourselves; we are too few in number and often lack the training and skills needed to be good public communicators. In essence, we can no longer afford to be detached from the mechanisms that convey archeological information to the public. This means working with teachers, tour guides, museum educators, park rangers, artisans, members of the media, government officials, and community leaders (see also Brian Fagan and Mark Rose, chapter 13).

Ethnicity Issues

In the 1990s, a new era of Native American archaeology emerged in the aftermath of the passage and implementation of the Native American Graves and Repatriation Act (NAGPRA). Many archaeologists, historians, and cultural resource managers have been forced to rethink fundamental assumptions that traditionally guided the development of research designs and the interpretation of findings. Archaeologists find that they are no longer the sole proprietors and interpreters of pre-European history. In fact, the definition of "cultural resources" in the archaeological sense has broadened from a focus on objects, features, and architectural elements to less tangible items such as place, setting, or traditional cultural property. This is due primarily to the effects of new federal mandates that make Native Americans integral players in CRM, a redefinition of what constitutes "data," and a reconsideration of who owns or controls the data (Edgar 2000). Archaeologists and cultural resource managers can no longer rely on material culture alone to identify or describe historic and archaeological properties. This change from the traditional definition also means that cultural resources, especially archaeological resources, cannot be identified through traditional investigation procedures (Banks, Giesen, and Pearson 2000).

Just as the concept and context of cultural landscape have been added to the evaluation criteria for National Register of Historic Places eligibility, so has traditional cultural property. Both terms were outside the boundaries of items traditionally considered by archaeologists until the CRM developments of the late twentieth century. The era of Native American archaeology with its different concepts of cultural resources is here. Many archaeologists as well as Native Americans are looking to these new definitions and concepts to help mend past animosities and provide a bridge for communication and cooperation in their common passion for Native American cultural history (Banks, Giesen, and Pearson 2000).

A recent NAGPRA-related controversy involves the human skeletal remains associated with the "Kennewick Man." A nearly complete skeleton was found in July 1996 below the surface of Lake Wallula, a pooled part of the Columbia River behind McNary Dam in Kennewick, Washington. Based on the preliminary 1996 study, the remains were determined to be approximately 9,000 years old, thus qualifying them as "of, or relating to, a tribe, people, or culture that is indigenous to the United States, including Alaska and Hawaii" and therefore "Native American" as defined by NAGPRA (McManamon 2000). The original scientist on the scene retrieved a nearly complete human skeleton, with a long, narrow face suggestive, he thought, of a person of European descent. Following subsequent study and debate, in September 2000, the secretary of the interior concluded that, based on the radiocarbon dates, geographic data, and oral history accounts, the remains were affiliated with Native American tribes of the region and should be returned to those tribes as required by NAGPRA (Babbitt 2000). To date, laboratory studies have failed to obtain DNA from tiny bone samples taken from the Kennewick Man remains.

The Kennewick Man controversy has heightened the post-NAGPRA debate among archaeologists and Native Americans about who owns, controls, and interprets the artifacts and data. In the new era of Native American archaeology, many American archaeologists are questioning the appropriateness of the privileged access that professionals, especially prehistorians, have long enjoyed. The challenge will be in moving toward a greater reconciliation among divergent cultural perspectives in ways that enhance both the archaeologists' and the public's knowledge and appreciation for the past (Edgar 2000). No doubt, the controversy and litigation surrounding the Kennewick Man issue will be with us for some time to come.

Another recent focus in the "archaeology of ethnicity" has been in African American studies. An impressive collection of data has accumulated from rural plantation sites as well as urban settings. One assumption has been that slave populations thought about and used objects differently than the object manufacturers had originally intended, adapting these new forms of material culture for use within African American cultural systems (Samford 1994). Work has resulted in new insights to the lives of enslaved African Americans. Most importantly, these insights are beginning to make their way into public interpretation programs and exhibits.

Our Continuing Challenge

Public interpretation of archaeological research is essential if we are to provide increased access and input about the past. In the 1990s, I joined a number of colleagues in pointing out that opening archaeological research to public view and critique adds multiple voices to archaeological interpretation. Effectively executed public interpretation initiates a variety of dialog simultaneously informing the present as well as the past. This dialog can help make archaeological research a more democratic process. While only a relatively small percentage of practicing archaeologists are involved in researching the past, there is no reason why the public cannot participate in this process through a critical evaluation of the interpretations that are presented. To do this, we must provide the public with participation opportunities, as well as evaluation skills. As we enter the twenty-first century, we must summon ourselves to reach out to people and involve them in the rich diversity of their national and ethnic experiences. Our unabated challenge is to effectively bring the fascinating subject of archaeology into public focus (Jameson 1994; Jameson and Ehrenhard 1997).

Successful efforts in archaeology education and outreach have overcome political and social obstacles in promoting a more informed and involved public, a public whose lives have been improved and made more meaningful. Is this charge for public inspiration not the ultimate goal of archaeological inquiry? Innovative approaches encourage dialog, establish communication partnerships, and work toward a more inclusive or participatory archaeology.

All trained archaeologists may not have the skills or resources to personally deliver a public educational message or program (Roberts 1995), but all archaeologists are obliged to take actions that foster or facilitate the educational goals of archaeology and an ethical imperative that ensures that the information generated by archaeological investigations reaches the public in a form that the public can readily understand. This occurs most often and most effectively with hands-on involvement. We need to continue the noteworthy educational efforts of the last decades and recharge our efforts in the realization and implementation of our legal and ethical mandates, through programs of public interpretation, education, and outreach, to provide archaeological information "for the inspiration and benefit of the people" (Jameson 1994:4).

Conclusion

As professional archaeologists, we deal with a public resource. We deal with public monies, policies, and laws that often drive preservation and protection efforts. We deal with a resource that has a natural human attraction. Professional archaeologists are the experts and purveyors of the rich diversity of a shared cultural heritage. For the most part, we deal with a nonrenewable and fragile resource whose physical integrity can easily be compromised. As cultural resource professionals, we have specialized knowledge that equips us to study and interpret archaeological information and objects. Increasingly, we do this in partnership with communities and ethnic groups that have an equal stake in interpretation. We do these things in the name of science and education and under the auspices of cultural resource protection mandates. As professionals, we cannot take these public responsibilities lightly.

What are the ultimate goals of archaeological inquiry? To improve people's lives by helping them to enjoy and appreciate their cultural heritage, that is, to educate them. When we know that our work affects this knowledge and appreciation, how can we see ourselves as detached from the public arena? We cannot.

We commonly measure our success by how well we earn the public trust as intellectual proprietors and curators of cultural resources and the unwritten record. Posterity will judge us, however, on how effectively archaeologically derived insights contribute to the education and enjoyment of present and future generations.

Discussion Questions

1. How are archaeologists uniquely equipped to interpret the past? Are public agency archaeologists specially positioned or mandated to undertake this task? Why or why not?

2. What assumptions and dilemmas about the "ownership of the past" are inherent in the statement "the archaeological record represents the heritage of all people"?

3. In the context of responding to looting, Julie Hollowell-Zimmer (chapter 4) says that "in many cases it may not be what you do, but how you do it that matters most." Give examples of how this might also apply to educational outreach efforts (or try role-playing several examples).

4. How can archaeologists avoid appearing paternalistic, or worse, when attempting to "educate" people about their heritage?

5. Design an educational, interactive half-hour presentation on some aspect of archaeology for a specific age group of precollege students. Have another group of colleagues critique the presentation for unintended messages, effectiveness, and ethical concerns.

6. "Successful efforts in archaeology education and outreach have overcome political and social obstacles in promoting a more informed and involved public, a public whose lives have been improved and made more meaningful. Is this charge for public inspiration not the ultimate goal of archaeological inquiry?" Do you agree with this statement? Why or why not?

7. I state that some modern practitioners in educational archaeology have ethical concerns that some "artistic" presentations, such as in multimedia presentations and movies, present archaeology in negative or "noneducational" ways. The debate centers on whether "consumer archaeology" and sensationalized depictions evoke a treasure hunt, or whether their fictional values should be viewed as opportunities and tools for education (see also Brian Fagan and Mark Rose, chapter 13).

What are your thoughts on this debate? Other than those mentioned in this chapter, what in this sense are some examples of "good" versus "bad" movies and television shows? Do you agree that a line should be drawn in how far a presentation goes in its sensationalized and fictionalized depictions? If so, how and where should this line be defined (and by whom)?

8. How has the "archaeology of ethnicity" as it is discussed here affected the development of archaeological practice? What issues are raised for archaeological ethics? Is it unethical for archaeologists and historians to interpret the past without consultation and collaboration with local communities and ethnic groups?

Recommended Readings

Bender, Susan J., and George S. Smith (editors)
    2000   *Teaching Archaeology in the Twenty-First Century.* Society for American Archaeology, Washington, DC.

MacManamon, Francis P., and Alf Hatton (editors)
    2000   *Cultural Resource Management in Contemporary Society.* One World Archaeology no. 33. Routledge, London.

Smardz, Karolyn, and Shelley J. Smith (editors)
    2000   *The Archaeology Evolution Handbook: Sharing the Past with Kids.* AltaMira, Walnut Creek, CA.

Smith, George S., and John E. Ehrenhard (editors)
    1991   *Protecting the Past.* CRC Press, Boca Raton, FL.

Stone, Peter G., and R. Mackenzie (editors)
    1990   *The Excluded Past: Archaeology in Education.* One World Archaeology no. 17. Routledge, London.

Stone, Peter G., and Brian L. Molyneaux (editors)
    1994   *The Presented Past: Heritage, Museums, and Education.* One World Archaeology no. 25. Routledge, London.

U.S. Forest Service
    2000   Welcome to Passport in Time! At www.passportintime.com/ (accessed 29 May 2002).

BRIAN FAGAN
MARK ROSE

Chapter Thirteen

Ethics and the Media

Television, Radio, and the Web

I have gotten to the point where I am reluctant to answer the phone. During the past three months, I have been contacted by three independent TV producers wanting to pick my brain about potential series, four researchers for other producers wanting information on topics ranging from the first Americans to ancient cannibalism, and several requests for interviews on topics on which I am supposed to be an expert (but usually am not). This is over and above the lady from England, who called wanting to make a series out of a book of mine.

Almost all these callers have one thing in common: They have no funding for their program or series, or if they do, they want my services, and, indeed my travel, for nothing. From long experience, I have found that a willingness to help involves long hours taken away from other work, usually without any outcome on the air. I am now at the point where I face an ethical dilemma that pits the need for public outreach against a harsh reality that I am usually wasting my time. The solution is to be highly selective, which means I say "no" most of the time. When making a decision, I ask searching questions about production credits, try to view some of the films he or she has made, and ask to see a treatment of the program, if there is one. And if it transpires that the producer has an obsession with gold or buried treasure, I am especially careful and usually run away. As with all forms of public outreach, it is the quality of the experience that is most important, not the fact that one just does it.

All this is a product of a massive expansion in visual entertainment. TV archaeology has exploded in recent years, away from the select and often tweedy world of the BBC and WGBH, into a multitude of cable programs and low-budget programming. Archaeology is popular with cable, especially if it involves ancient civilizations, large extinct animals, or mysteries of any sort. Gone are the days of

Kenneth Clark and Jacob Bronowski, when genial hosts conducted galactic series with serene authority, leading the viewer through the world of art, of human diversity, or whatever subject was at hand. I suppose many of us have images of instant celebrity and hosting roles, but, in reality, today's programmers, except for the British, seem to want celebrities to pronounce the word and bless the programming. Archaeologists, like other scientists, have become interview subjects, advisors, or background players on an excavation. Sometimes, too, we commentate in the field, standing at the entrance to a tomb or on a windy rampart. When the producers listen to you and take your advice seriously, allowing input into the script, the experience can be profoundly rewarding. But, on all too many occasions, we have almost no control over the content, even over what is being said. There is little we, as scientists, can do to change the situation, so our best tactic is to choose the project carefully and demand full involvement from treatment to finished product. It is easy to become jaded from a series of negative experiences, but I have found that they are more than compensated for by a few marvelous ones.

Cable TV today lives in a world of unsolved conundra and docudramas, often aimed at young, testosterone-filled audiences, the meat and drink of so much television programming. Many popular archaeological programs target people who buy pickup trucks, love hunting, and have been brought up since birth on a diet of visual action and violence. Much of today's archaeological programming for television is produced for a very broad audience indeed; it has to be to sell advertising. All of this poses some interesting ethical dilemmas for the archaeologist caught between a rock, the findings of science, and a hard place, the demands of the television marketplace.

Please understand that I am not talking about higher-end archaeological programming, which still often delights, ever rarer as it is. I am talking about more general programs and series, aimed at the widest possible audience. The archaeologist sucked into this world faces challenging ethical problems surrounding the thorny issue of scientific accuracy and credibility. Some of the time, you can decline to participate on the grounds that the subject matter is obviously pseudoarchaeology, or, quite simply, nonsense. No thinking archaeologist is going to be sucked into a debate over the viability of theories about ancient astronauts, or associate their expertise with a program based on one of Graham Hancock's archaeological fictions, or genres involving "unsolved quests" or their ilk.

On the other hand, one has a considerable obligation to be interviewed for a program on pyramids or some other subject where you have a serious and legitimate expertise. Here, professional ethics demand that you participate if you can. The problem arises when dramatizations and reconstructions come into play. Here, the scientist provides detailed expertise, only to have this turned into a living scene by treatment and scriptwriters, many of whom live in the lush and passionate world of Hollywood. Then you are asked to read the script, which is when the fun starts. You end up navigating delicately between scientific verisimilitude and the need for vivid engaging drama. Invariably, the science gives a bit, sometimes a lot, challenging your scientific integrity. All this happens before a foot of film is shot or before the network functionaries make change after change to the script, many of which impinge directly on the science. In a recent script in which I was involved, the network vacillated between more drama and less narrative, then the reverse, then coming down halfway in between, driving both the script writer and the scientists to distraction. And after these issues were resolved, both filming, and, above all, editing produced new problems, compromises, and permutations. The end product, while quite good, bore little resemblance to the original story.

With TV programs involving dramatization or reconstructions, you are usually not going to win. All you can do is ensure that the science is compromised as little as possible, realizing that some loss of integrity, some overstatement, is inevitable. Your ethics will be least challenged when you deal with producers who are truly concerned with accuracy. Most of them try, but the truly committed are a joy to work with.

A new and potentially sinister twist on the entertainment versus science controversy has manifested itself in recent years, with cable networks like Discovery Channel and National Geographic investing large sums of money in excavations where spectacular discoveries are likely, thereby creating an instant TV program. The recent discovery of an arrowhead in the shoulder of the Bronze Age Ice Man from the Alps was funded by the Discovery Channel. Such funding is rationalized as a way of giving people a science education, or as a form of reality TV. No question, some projects, like the Ice Man, have been beneficial all round. But the line between responsible science and mere gold digging in shipwrecks, or the "let me give you some money; what can you dig up for us" syndrome is fine indeed.

The ethics of accepting research money for such enterprises are convoluted. Does one accept the money on the grounds that you will do good science anyhow, regardless of the movie? Does the television program guide and inform the excavation rather than the other way round? What compromises will be made to create a visually exciting film? You certainly cannot rationalize the money by saying, as some people have, that what appears on TV does not matter; it is what is published in the journals that is important. If you have that indefensible attitude, you should never be let near an archaeological site, or any kind of science for that matter.

The ethics of working with TV are complex; they involve scientific integrity and your willingness to stick your neck out. Such activity can be frustrating, intensely time-consuming, but, at its best, fascinating and intellectually rewarding. I urge you to engage in it, avoiding at all costs producers who do not care about accuracy and programs that masquerade as archaeology and are not. And please do not take money for research if there is the slightest doubt that the end product is damaging to science.

Radio is the great, unexploited avenue for public outreach in archaeology. It is a transitory medium, but one where you reach enormous numbers of people with virtually no feedback from the audience. Most people listen to the radio in their cars. Thus, much programming lasts two to five minutes, which makes it even more fleeting. With radio, you are dealing with journalists who are looking for a straightforward, engaging story line. Again, the ethics of scientific integrity are involved, for even the briefest radio spot involves a story and accurate facts. I have found that radio producers are more willing to share their script drafts with you, which makes the task of fact checking easier. Also, the script does not pass through complex filming and editing processes, which can change the content beyond recognition without your being aware of it.

Successful radio involves a partnership among producer, scriptwriter, and archaeologist, which can work very well indeed, provided the spirit of cooperation translates into practice. I once worked on a three-year archaeology program called *Patterns of the Past* with Western Public Radio in San Francisco. The process involved a producer and me and was a sheer joy because scientific accuracy married well with interesting stories. Ethical judgments were never a problem; they controlled the programs. I believe that radio is a rewarding way of reaching a broad audience, especially at the local level, with minimal ethical conflicts. But, of course, the same, general constraints apply as those with television.

The World Wide Web is the potential Goliath of public outreach, with tentacles that already extend into every corner of the archaeological world. This is the ultimate, simple way to carry a message out to a broad audience, as well as an avenue to propagate any idea about the past one wishes. Increasingly, too, the Web is becoming a vehicle for digital publishing of archaeological data. Some archaeologists even maintain their own domains, while many excavations and other research projects publicize themselves, even recruit excavators, through their Web pages. But ethically, the Web represents a new challenge for anyone concerned with professional standards and ethical practice.

With TV and radio, one deals with third parties—producers, scriptwriters, network officials, and so on. With the Web, you may put together a Web page alone, or work with others, depending on the project, but the process tends to be much more informal. The Web is far more than a vehicle for communication; it is a marketplace, among other things, for antiquities. eBay's antiquities auction site offers coins, Egyptian vases, pottery, figurines, and other artifacts on the open market. Enter "Antiquities dealers" into Google.com and a host of outlets selling the past are before your eyes. The Web is rapidly blurring the frontier between the legitimate and the illegitimate, between the licensed sale of duplicates (if we accept that as a legitimate proposition) and the clandestine disposal of artifacts looted from undisturbed contexts. Science is almost powerless in the face of such an onslaught, for the endless boundaries of cyberspace make local antiquities regulations much harder to enforce. The ethics of the situation are absolutely uncompromising. No professional archaeologist can ethically associate him- or herself with such activity. All we can do at this stage is to study the phenomenon and devise strategies for restricting it.

The Web also promises a revolution in publication, a freedom and flexibility in reporting on discoveries, publishing reports, and displaying raw data that will probably transform both archaeology and public outreach about the past beyond recognition within a generation. There will always be a place for the written word, probably a more important role than many cyber enthusiasts will allow. But the Web offers open-ended opportunities for all manner of digital publishing, including on-line debates and interactive site reports. The prospects are intoxicating, but fraught with important ethical issues.

We live in an era of transition from a world where print publication ruled the universe to a new one that provides many appropriate and highly credible alternatives. Inevitably, there are those among us, often Web-illiterate, who rant about academic standards and the illegitimacy of such publication. There are even some who refuse to call Web-based monographs or CD-ROMs legitimate publications, arguing that they are not peer reviewed as rigorously as print publications. This is arrogant nonsense. Many of the best archaeological reports on the Web have been rigorously scrutinized. I am irresistibly reminded of the common perception among more conservative academic archaeologists that cultural resource management (CRM) literature is useless because it is not peer reviewed or subject to quality control. In fact, many CRM reports are heavily peer reviewed, often more than work that appears in academic journals. Furthermore, such reports often appear in both print and electronic versions. The credibility of the Web as a means of publishing archaeological data is beyond question. Among other things, it provides a wonderful place to access enormous quantities of raw data that would otherwise be inaccessible to all but a few, either in excavation archives or in a small number of libraries, even when it is published. For example, the Pylos Regional Archaeological Project in Greece has put much of its survey work on the Web, at least four or five years in advance of publication.

Anyone can publish on the Web and achieve wide distribution, which is certainly not the case with print media, even in these days of desktop publishing. There is a huge and proliferating archaeological literature on the Web—papers, reports, even entire monographs in cyberspace, to say nothing of site-specific websites and numerous informational domains. Much of this literature is of high quality, sometimes peer reviewed. There are several academic journals on the Internet, even entire doctoral dissertations. Unfortunately, however, the quality of Web-based publication, just like that of conventional books and journals, sometimes leaves much to be desired, accentuated by the ease with which one can publish in cyberspace. Some people have found it easy to build an impressive-looking, potentially career-enhancing bibliography from Web-based titles. They place undigested, often somewhat casual preliminary reports or cursory site descriptions in cyberspace. This is not an appropriate or ethical form of publication.

The unrelenting ferocity of the "publish-or-perish" culture is in considerable part responsible for this proliferation, since the Web offers a cheap and unrestricted way of publishing your work, good or bad. Multiple entries of Web-based publications look good on someone's bibliography, especially when no one on a review committee has time to read them. This particular ethical problem can be laid, in part, at the feet of the contemporary academic culture, which worships publication (but not always in cyberspace) above all else. Ethically, undigested, too rapid publication is indefensible, however benign the intent; it undermines the quality of the entire enterprise and opens up archaeologists to accusations of freewheeling speculation and irresponsible science by those with axes to grind, such as pseudoarchaeologists. And, it must be admitted that they are sometimes right. The same uncompromising ethics of quality and accuracy must also surround any efforts at public outreach on the Web.

The world of the Web is still in its boisterous frontier days, where almost anything goes, but these will not last forever. The archaeological ethics of the future will have to accommodate the realities of a world where cyber and visual communication are the norm rather than the exception. So far, we have done little to formulate these ethics.

Ethical archaeological behavior is largely a matter of common sense and sound intellectual judgment. These same qualities apply with equal force to the printed word, TV, radio, and the Web. The proof of the pudding is in the way we actually perform when we walk in the tempting Garden of Eden of popular entertainment.

—BF

Archaeology and Publishing

During my fourteen years as an editor at *Archaeology* magazine, I've seen many situations where archaeologists, indigenous and descendant communities, and the media have had conflicting priorities. As an archaeologist, I've seen scholars and the media both use our subject matter in ways that mislead the general public. Although this chapter is in part a recollection of my time at *Archaeology,* it does not represent the views of the magazine or of its publisher, the Archaeological Institute of America. Nor is it intended to be a definitive account of the events; others may recall them differently.

Descendant Communities and the Publication of Human Remains

Who should determine what can and cannot be shown is a difficult problem when it comes to human remains and the beliefs of descendant groups. There is no set policy on this at *Archaeology,* but we try to be sensitive to the wishes of descendant communities. On our March–April 1993 cover, we did show an in situ skeleton from Lower Manhattan's African Burial Ground. Two years later, in our May–June 1995 issue, we published an article about a Maya cave site in Honduras and featured a dramatic photograph of a calcite-encrusted skull from the site on the cover. We heard no complaints, directly or indirectly, from descendant groups in either case, though a Mayanist on our editorial advisory board objected to the latter cover. We would not have used either photograph on the cover if the bones had come from a Native American site in North America. Inside the magazine, we sometimes show human bones, depending on the importance of showing the remains and the sensibility of descendant groups. For example, our January–February 2002 issue included an article on Celtic Gordion. Showing photographs of human bones in situ was important and no descendant group was likely to raise objections, so we ran several of them.

A Diverse Past and a Diverse Audience

Archaeologists have a responsibility to reach out to as broad an audience as possible, but have we brought the diversity of the North American past to the public effectively? One simple gauge is looking at the number of stories. Over the past twelve years, *Archaeology* has had about 134 features, departments, and news items relating to Native Americans, 18 with African Americans (including important articles on New York's African Burial Ground, Brooklyn's Lott House, and Fort Mose in Florida), 9 with Spanish Americans, 7 with French colonials, and 2 with Asian Americans. There's room for improvement, but our mandate is to report on archaeology worldwide, so it isn't too bad. Have we reached a broad audience with that information? We don't have figures on the magazine, but 88 percent of viewers of our website identify themselves as white, 4 percent as Hispanic, 3 percent as Native American, 2 percent as Asian, and 1 percent as African American. For comparison, in the 1994 Society for American Archaeology survey *The American Archaeologist: A Profile,* only 2 percent of all respondents identified themselves in the latter four categories. Clearly, the discipline as a whole needs to do more here if it hopes to have support in all communities.

Media in between Archaeologists

High-profile, personal disagreements over the interpretation of artifacts, sites, and hominid fossils occur time and again in archaeology and paleoanthropology. Should these debates be behind closed doors or in public? I think it is good for the public to see how scientific consensus is, or is not, achieved, especially if the research is publicly funded. We have published such debates, in articles about the book

Black Athena on Africa and Egypt's impact on classical culture (September–October 1992), the Getty Museum's *kouros* (May–June 1994), and the Native American Graves Protection and Repatriation Act (November–December 1994). In each case, the opposing viewpoints appeared within a single issue and the discussion was civilized.

The Miami Circle is another case in which *Archaeology* was involved. The discovery of this circle of holes cut into limestone at a downtown Miami building site made headlines in January 1999. That summer, as a multimillion-dollar acquisition of the site was in the works, one of our contributing editors approached us with his doubts about the site's legitimacy. He felt strongly that more work should be done before public funds were committed (Miami-Dade eventually paid $26.7 million for the site). We aired his doubts in an article titled "Much Ado about a Circle" under the rubric "American Scene" (September–October 1999).

Responses to the article came quickly. The Miami Circle project director and field director submitted long letters that appeared in our November–December 1999 and January–February 2000 issues. Reactions to the article and events surrounding the circle soon outpaced our bimonthly publication schedule, so we covered it on our website (www.archaeology.org/online/features/miami/index). But this was all after the question about the site's validity was raised. Were we wrong to raise that question in a public forum? No, because it involved serious archaeological questions and a large amount of public money. A title emphasizing the call for further investigations would have been more appropriate, and using the "viewpoint" rubric as we had in previous debates would have alerted readers that it was an opinion piece. Inviting a single rejoinder, to appear in the same issue as the original article, would have been better than the extensive, though after-the-fact coverage we gave them, and would have made the debate more valuable to our readers.

Media, Archaeologists, and the Big Find

Is what we publish a reflection of archaeology or Indiana Jones? Most work today is in the realm of CRM, but does the public really want to read about bridge abutments or, for that matter, the detailed analysis of fish bones or potsherds? I don't want to argue the merits of CRM work in general or of particular projects—that's not the point, though I agree we (and most other media outlets) don't cover the topic adequately. It is not what will grab the attention of readers who may know little or nothing of the field. If somebody looks at our magazine on the newsstand, we have about seven to eight seconds for the cover to get his or her attention and for him or her to decide whether or not to buy it. If he or she doesn't pick up the magazine, we've lost a potential supporter of archaeology and historic preservation. If he or she reads nothing but claims about the oldest, biggest, and so on, he or she will not know what archaeology is.

This question goes beyond *Archaeology*, however, and includes archaeologists hyping discoveries in the media, media hyping discoveries to the public, and media funding of projects for controlling the publicizing of them. It can be argued that any publicity for archaeology is good, but how far can we push something before we do a disservice to the public, making claims that get headlines but might mislead people about what we have accomplished or what the field of archaeology is all about?

Over the Top Underwater?

At times, the quest for media glory becomes an exercise in verbal gymnastics. One institute's website, for example, touts two shipwrecks found in the eastern Mediterranean in 1999 as "the oldest vessels ever discovered in the deep sea." Sounds impressive, no? The claim is correct because the vessels, dated circa 750 BC, are in 1,000 feet of water while the Uluburun shipwreck, which is from 1300 BC, is on Turkey's southern coast. Then there's a much older Early Bronze Age (2600–2150 BC) wreck, but it is on the Greek coast at Dokos. So the 1999 discovery stands on the basis of its depth. Now, there are ancient shipwrecks in the eastern Mediterranean that are 9,000 feet deeper, but they aren't quite as old as the 1999 ones. And of course, there's no need to mention the intact 142-foot-long boat of the pharaoh Khufu from circa 2550 BC that was dug out of a pit near the Great Pyramid at Giza back in 1954. Given all this, the 1999 discovery was carried widely in the media; after all, they are "the oldest vessels ever discovered in the deep sea."

An Astonishing Excavation?

Probably the most successful archaeological public relations campaign of the twentieth century was the promotion of the "discovery" of Tomb 5 in Egypt's Valley of the Kings (KV 5) in 1995, but what actually happened that made this story appear on the May 23 cover of *Time*? It wasn't the discovery of the tomb, despite *Time*'s website ("An astonishing excavation last week uncovered a burial place") or the complex title of a 1998 book about it (*In 1995, an American Egyptologist Discovered the Burial Site of the Sons of Ramesses II. The Lost Tomb. This Is His Incredible Story of KV 5 and Its Excavation*). The tomb had been noted on a map made by scholars who accompanied Napoléon Bonaparte to Egypt and the Englishman James Burton explored its outer chambers in 1825. Kent Weeks relocated the tomb's entrance in 1987, and on February 2, 1995, he and two others opened up a crawl space leading into a corridor that had not been entered before and realized the tomb was much larger than previously known, indeed possibly the largest in the Valley of the Kings.

Whose tomb was it? In a preliminary report titled "The Berkeley Map of the Theban Necropolis: Report of the Sixth, Seventh, and Eighth Seasons," the Egyptologist Elizabeth Thomas's 1966 *Royal Necropoleis of Thebes* is quoted: "[I]t is likely that the tomb, with offshoots in three directions at minimum and removed only a few meters from his own in a similar site, was meant for more than one member of his family. His numerous sons suggest themselves most readily, for vague indications may point in this direction and provision for several wives and daughters was definitely made in the Queens' Valley." In later accounts of the "discovery," Thomas's role seems to be downplayed (as does Burton's). Both Burton and the German egyptologist Karl Lepsius noted a partial cartouche with Rameses' name near the tomb's doorway. Thomas knew that, and she also knew that in Turin there was a papyrus suggesting there was a tomb of Rameses' children near their father's tomb and possibly opposite it. Did Thomas have proof of the tomb's identity? No. Did she have more than a guess? Absolutely. So, back in 1966, she knew about where the tomb was and likely who had been buried there.

KV 5 is huge and unique in layout, but a May 18, 1995, press release from the American University in Cairo reads, "Ancient Egyptian Tomb of Ramesses II Children Discovered in Egypt's Valley of the Kings. Experts Consider Tomb to Be More Significant Than the Discovery of King Tutankhamun." Who were the experts? The press release doesn't identify them. KV 5, despite its complexity and large number of rooms, rather obviously is not the most important find of the century. If you want my pick, it is the tomb of Tutankhamen (1922), but there are, barring some new find in KV 5, many discoveries from the past 100 years that are more important than it. *Ancient Egypt: The Great Discoveries* (Reeves 2000) lists some of them. Of course, this type of listing, and the type of publicity garnered by KV 5, has a fundamental problem. It reduces archaeology to the "big find" and reinforces a public conception of archaeology and archaeologists that may belong more properly to the nineteenth century and the opening decades of the twentieth than to today.

Lost Cities, Mummies, and Ratings

The National Geographic Society (NGS) has the ability to publicize and promote archaeology across the full range of media: print, film, Web, and news outlets (newspaper and broadcast). Its most recent application of this saturation approach raises questions that go beyond the immediate case—that of Inca discoveries at Cerro Victoria in the Vilcabamba region of Peru and in Lima. The NGS presented these discoveries to the public in March and April 2002 via news releases in advance of a May television documentary (*Inca Mummies: Secrets of a Lost World*) and a cover story in *National Geographic*. Both news releases mentioned the May broadcast, so at some level there was coordination of the announcements with the broadcast and, likely, the publication. The NGS publicized the Cerro Victoria site—found in 1999 and surveyed in 2001—as a major discovery. The NGS news release quoted a National Geographic explorer in residence as saying it "is one of the most important sites to be located in the Vilcabamba region since the Inca abandoned it over 400 years ago."

Soon afterwards, however, this assessment was challenged by Peruvian archaeologists. The director of the National Cultural Institute in Cuzco labeled the claims as "very, very exaggerated." A report by one of the NGS expedition leaders describes the site as "a temporary or hastily built settlement of low-status workers." That description is not in the news release. A tape of the documentary can be purchased on the NGS website and there the site is dubbed "a vast and previously unknown citadel." Did promotion of the television documentary affect how the discovery of the site and its importance were presented to the public? In Lima, the NGS provided partial funding for the excavation of thousands of mummies, but more than 70 percent of the excavation dollars came from the residents of a shantytown on the site. The benefits to the NGS, in terms of yielding film and photographs for its documentary and cover story, were tangible and possibly revenue generating (through new memberships, video sales, and so on). Did the shantytown residents share in those benefits? If archaeologists and media benefit from cooperation, are they obligated to extend benefits to local communities and descendant groups?

The overarching concern here, and I am not singling out the NGS, is that marketing archaeology to the public may produce ethical conflicts between, for example, accurate reporting and hyping. Cross-marketing increases the potential gains—and therefore the danger—exponentially.

Conclusion

Archaeologists and the media both have expectations and goals in dealing with one another. Archaeologists may use the media to communicate with a broad audience for the good of the field and for the benefit of the public. They may also use the media to promote themselves and their research, advance their own career, make their university look good, or help drum up funding. There's nothing wrong with any of that provided archaeologists don't venture into self-aggrandizement or purposefully distort their research. Media have a simple motivation: They want something that will capture eyes for newspapers, magazines, websites, and televisions and ears for radio. The profit motive and an ignorance about archaeology can easily lead media astray. But there's much on the line: for archaeologists it is public support for research and protection of sites; for media it is credibility. Both sides need to be on guard in their interactions. Also at risk is the public, in terms of what archaeologists and media tell them about the field. Perhaps most vulnerable are the local and descendant communities that archaeologists must reach out to when they use the media and that the media must treat fairly if they intend to profit by them.

—MR

Discussion Questions

1. You are asked to contribute as an archaeologist to a television program. What questions would you want to ask before saying "yes"?
2. What might be some useful criteria for evaluating Web-based publications? What do you see as the ethical issues of archaeological cyberspace today and what, if any, additions or modifications to our codes of ethics would you suggest to address them?
3. Should an archaeologist insist on being paid for consulting and other work with the media or should the importance of public outreach supercede all other considerations?
4. Your research project includes elements with the potential for high drama, of the sort that might well interest the popular media. Would it be ethical to adjust your grant proposal and research plan to highlight that aspect and send it to potential media sponsors? Is it ever ethical to adjust one's research plan and proposal to better suit the interests of a funding agency, regardless of media interest?
5. Mr. TV Producer has heard about your field project and is offering you big bucks, but you have to sign a contract giving him exclusive first rights to any discoveries so he can broadcast them on his "Biggest Mysteries of the Ancients" series. Is there a conflict between this exclusivity and your responsibility to those who have backed you in the past—taxpayers whose money was funneled to you through federal agencies?
6. You're a paleoanthropologist on an international expedition to the fossil-rich prewash area of Riftopia, an east African nation. While walking to the latrine, you stumble on a 4-million-year-old cranium eroding out of a rocky slope. If you can set up a press conference featuring yourself and the cranium, but not the Riftopians or your expedition colleagues, you can claim the discovery as your own. This will guarantee you tenure, a popular book or two, and a television documentary in which you'll appear in footage recreating the moment of the great find. This will foster a simplistic public perception of paleoanthropology as a field dominated by individual fossil hunters rather than a multidisciplinary one in which teamwork and sophisticated analyses of multiple lines of evidence produce meaningful results, but so what?

7. What would the possible reasons be for treating South American human remains differently from North American human remains in the mass media?
8. How would you approach and present CRM work and findings to make them interesting to the general public? Design (or write!) an article for the popular media that presents a CRM project in a way that has popular appeal.

Recommended Readings

Asheshov, Nicholas
2002 Inca Trail of Hype? *The Times* (London), 8 April:10, at www.newsint-archive.co.uk/pages/welcome-post.asp (accessed April 2002).

Atwood, Roger
2002 Squeezing the Squatters. *Archaeology* (July–August):16.

Braun, D.
2002 Thousands of Inca Mummies Raised from Their Graves. *National Geographic,* 22 April, at www.nationalgeographic.com/news/2002/04/0410_020417_incamummies.html (accessed April 2002).

Çatalhöyük Archaeology Project
2002 Excavations of a Neolithic Anatolian Höyük, at catal.arch.cam.ac.uk/catal/catal.html (accessed April 2002).

DeCicco, Gabriel
1988 Forum: A Public Relations Primer. *American Antiquity* 54(4):840–56.

Mysteries of Çatalhöyük
2001 at www.smm.org/catal/home.html (accessed April 2002).

Parsell, D. L.
2002 City Occupied by Inca Discovered on Andean Peak in Peru. *National Geographic,* 21 March, at www.nationalgeographic.com/news/2002/03/0314_0318_vilcabamba.html (accessed April 2002).

Potter, Peter
1990 The "What" and "Why" of Public Relations for Archaeology: A Postscript to DeCicco's Public Relations Primer. *American Antiquity* 55(3):608–13.

Powell, Eric
2000 Mammoth Distortion. *Archaeology* (March–April):58–59.

Pylos Regional Archaeological Project Internet Edition
2001 at river.blg.uc.edu/prap/PRAP.html (accessed April 2002).

Roberts, Mark B.
1994 Picking a Bone with the Media. *Times Higher Education Supplement,* 27 May (1125):5ff.

Silverman, Helaine
   1997   Anthropologist As Filmstar: Projecting Points. *Anthropology Newsletter* (September):40–41.

Stevens, Kristen L., Elizabeth Anderson Comer, and Roger E. Kelly
   1987   *Captivating the Public through the Media While Digging the Past.* Technical Series no. 1. Baltimore Center for Urban Archaeology, Baltimore, MD.

Wiseman, James
   2001   Camelot in Kentucky. *Archaeology* (January–February):10–14.

CLAIRE SMITH
HEATHER BURKE

Chapter Fourteen

In the Spirit of the Code

An Archaeological Impact Statement

One of us came to understand the significance of indigenous[1] Australians controlling their cultural heritage the evening she discovered she had learned a secret Aboriginal men's word—and that she should have been killed for knowing that word. Claire Smith had been reading aloud to Aboriginal elders some 1940s articles she had located as part of her background research that contained the secret word. Inadvertently, she posed a dilemma for the Aboriginal elders. If they didn't kill her, they were transgressing cultural rules that were critical to their control of indigenous knowledge and the maintenance of their traditional systems of authority. If they did kill her, there were other problems. At the time, she was mostly worried about the other problems.

This incident highlights the fact that doing archaeology often involves working with cultural material in which other people have rights and responsibilities. That these interest groups will have their own values and notions of priority immediately creates a working situation of complex interactions and potentially competing agendas. "Who has a right to control the past?" is not just an academic question, but a practical reality that must be faced in the many day-to-day interactions between archaeologists and the material remains of other peoples' pasts. No archaeology is conducted within a social vacuum and, at some point in their careers, virtually every archaeologist will experience the ethical dilemma of making choices among a range of potentially conflicting values. Everyone, it seems, has an interest in his or her past—especially once archaeologists start messing with it.

An Ethical Dilemma: Indigenous versus Scientific Stewardship

The increased professionalization of archaeology has resulted in the relatively recent development of ethical codes. The American Anthropological Association (AAA) developed one of the first in the United States. Since then, the Society for American Archaeology (SAA) and a number of other national bodies in First World countries have also developed codes of conduct to assist their members in the recognition and resolution of ethical dilemmas. Each body has produced a formal document that distills the beliefs of its members, articulates the underlying assumptions and guiding principles of the association, and provides a fundamental framework for conducting research in an ethical and responsible way. While each of these codes in some way expresses the common core of group wisdom that originally created them, each was also created within its own social "bubble," resulting in widely differing core values. These vary enormously from code to code: from promoting the greater understanding of archaeology (Archaeological Institute of America) and the stewardship of cultural heritage (SAA and New Zealand Archaeological Association) to recognizing a paramount professional responsibility to those who are being studied (AAA), or acknowledging the importance of indigenous cultural heritage to the survival of indigenous cultures (Canadian Archaeological Association, World Archaeological Congress [WAC], and Australian Archaeological Association). While all of these aspects are undoubtedly a part of professional archaeological responsibility across the discipline, there is one very clear difference: As a first principle, stewardship of the archaeological resource privileges a completely different ethical standpoint than a principle that privileges the survival of indigenous cultures. This is not to say that one set of core values is more acceptable or "correct" than any another, simply that each code has been developed from the needs of a particular group at a particular time and place to deal with local situations in different parts of the world.

The existence of alternative ethical starting points, however, does mean that archaeological responses to ethical dilemmas in different parts of the world can have vastly different outcomes. Two relatively recent cases involving the custody of ancient human skeletal remains clearly demonstrate this divergence. The ongoing furor over the significance and ultimate future of the 9,800-year-old skeleton of the "Kennewick Man" excavated in 1996 near Kennewick, Washington, has become a symbol of a wider debate between scientific rights to knowledge and indigenous rights to control their cultural heritage. A similar controversy took place in Australia in the late 1980s and early 1990s in response to indigenous requests to rebury Pleistocene skeletal remains excavated at Kow Swamp, in Victoria, and in Lake Mungo, in New South Wales (see Bowdler 1992; Davidson 1991; McBryde 1986; Mulvaney 1991). While the final disposition of the Kennewick remains has yet to be determined, both the Kow Swamp and Lake Mungo remains were returned to the indigenous populations who have contemporary cultural affiliation to the places where the remains were found. In each case, there was a struggle between local indigenous groups, who wanted to have the remains returned to them, and a group of scientists, who argued for conserving the remains for future generations by keeping them in the custody of a museum. In each case, the local archaeological communities had to come to grips with alternative opinions on the ultimate meaning of these long-dead individuals and thus on the most appropriate solution for their future. Neither side was "wrong" in the position it adopted; rather, each was guided by its respective codes of ethics to argue from opposing first principles.

It can be argued that the most important attribute of ethical codes is that they provide a spirit within which to work through ethical dilemmas. But how do you work out the spirit of an ethical code? This is not straightforward, especially if, like most of us, you were not privy to the debates that were undertaken when that code was established. In this chapter, our approach is to assume that the first principle is the most important priority, with the second being the second most important, and so forth. This hierarchy presumably reflects the hierarchy of core values that the association considered important. Our conclusions in this regard are cross-referenced to the internal wording of each principle and, where appropriate, considered in the light of other ethical statements or codes put out by that association.

The Kennewick Man

The skeletal remains of what American Indians refer to as the "Ancient One" were discovered inadvertently in 1996 at Columbia Park, near the city of Kennewick, Washington. A series of radiocarbon dates from these remains indicated that the man had lived between 9,500 and 8,500 years ago. These remains have become the center of an ongoing debate between a small group of forensic anthropologists and archaeologists and a coalition of five American Indian tribes in the region. The groups involved are the Confederated Tribes of the Colville Reservation, the Nez Perce Tribe, the Confederated Tribes of the Umatilla Indian Reservation, the Confederated Tribes and Bands of the Yakima Nation, and the Wanapum Band. They have taken a united stand, seeking repatriation and reburial of this ancient material (Confederated Tribes of the Umatilla Indian Reservation 2001).

The group of eight scientists presented two arguments to prevent the remains from being returned to the American Indian tribes who claimed them under the Native American Graves Protection and Repatriation Act (NAGPRA). First, they argued that the remains were not necessarily those of American Indians. Some of them argued that the remains had Caucasoid features, perhaps indicating the previous colonization of North America by a non–American Indian group of people. This argument was refuted by the Department of Interior (DOI) in January 2000, but an appeal was still being assessed in the middle of 2001, five years after the remains had been found.

The length of time it took to establish and substantiate this determination makes it clear that this was not a simple process. Once the remains were determined to be "American Indian," the DOI had to decide their disposition under the requirements of NAGPRA (see National Park Service 2002). An important step here is that of assessing whether there is a cultural affiliation between the skeletal remains and one or more contemporary American Indian tribes. "Cultural affiliation" is defined by the statute as "a relationship of shared group identity which can be reasonably traced historically or prehistorically between a present day Indian tribe or Native Hawaiian organization and an identifiable earlier group." NAGPRA identifies a range of evidence that may be used in evaluating cultural affiliation, including geographical, kinship, biological, archaeological, anthropological, linguistic, folklore, oral tradition, historical, or other relevant information or expert opinion (Native American Graves Protection and Repatriation Act 1990).

The second argument presented by the scientists was that the remains were not culturally affiliated to the contemporary American Indian groups who were claiming them. The scientists argued against cultural affiliation on the grounds that there is archaeological evidence of movement among American Indian groups in this region over the last 10,000 years, and that in their opinion it is likely that contemporary American Indian populations in the region are not descended from that particular individual (Hackenberger 2000; National Park Service 2002; Thomas 2000; Watkins, chapter 10). This perspective, in which skeletal material from the distant past is viewed as quite separate from the present, contrasts with an indigenous perspective, in which the past is thought of as somehow part of the present (see Zimmerman 1995; Smith and Burke, in press).

On August 30, 2002, Magistrate John Jelderks, of the U.S. District Court for the District of Oregon, issued a decision in favor of the scientists, finding that the secretary of the interior "erred in defining 'Native American' to automatically include all remains predating 1492 that are found in the United States." Jelderks's decision is based on the assumption that if remains are identified as "Native American" they will not be open to scientific study: "*All* pre-Columbian people, no matter what group they belonged to, where they came from, how long they or their group survived, or how greatly they differed from the ancestors of present-day American Indians, would be arbitrarily classified as 'Native American,' and their remains and artifacts could be placed totally off-limits to scientific study" (Jelderks 2002:29). This decision leaves the Kennewick Man in the custody of scientists. The finding challenges the long-standing assumption that human remains predating 1492 in the United States necessarily are those of the ancestors of contemporary Native Americans. It means that human remains that are found without associated cultural materials may no longer be assumed to be Native American. The decision also asserted that the parties joint agreement (no. 170) "shall remain in effect pending development of a study protocol" (73). However, collaborative research is unlikely to emerge from such a combative and contentious situation and currently the matter is under appeal.

In terms of ethical codes, an important point to draw from the Kennewick debate is that most of the arguments relating to the deposition of these remains have been framed in terms of the legal positioning in relation to NAGPRA. In this chapter, we shall seek guidance by assessing this example against the most relevant ethical codes, those of the AAA, SAA, and WAC. This keys into a long-standing ethical debate over the rights of scientists versus those of indigenous peoples (Anderson 1996; Ferguson 1984; Janke 1999; McBryde 1986; Messenger 1999; Mulvaney 1991; Smith 1999; Zimmerman 1989, 1996).

AAA

The AAA showed a relatively early willingness to grapple with the difficulties involved in developing ethical codes. After a period of substantial debate in May 1971, the council adopted a number of Principles of Professional Responsibility, which acted essentially as an ethics code. These principles were subject to ongoing discussion, and the first statement in the principles about the paramount responsibility of the anthropologist being to those studied was often quoted during the early years of the reburial debates in the United States. These principles were revised in the mid-1990s and incorporated into a formal Code of Ethics that was approved in June 1998. This code identifies the first responsibility of members as "responsibility to people and animals with whom anthropological researchers work and whose lives and cultures they study," stating that: "Anthropological researchers have primary ethical obligations to the people, species, and materials they study and to the people with whom they work. These obligations can supersede the goal of seeking new knowledge, and can lead to decisions not to undertake or to discontinue a research project when the primary obligation conflicts with other responsibilities, such as those owed to sponsors or clients." This addresses the conflict that is inherent in anthropological research, giving researchers what appears at first to be a clear directive on how to act when faced by conflicting obligations to different groups. It states clearly that responsibility to those studied takes precedence over seeking new knowledge or obligations to other interest groups or sponsors. Thus, the spirit of the code places obligations to those studied above the second responsibility of the association, which is to "scholarship and science."

The complexity of practice becomes clear when you try to apply this to the situation of the Kennewick Man. At first glance, it might appear that archaeologists would be guided to return the remains to the local indigenous populations, since their primary ethical responsibility is to the people and materials they study and to the people with whom they work. How do you determine your ethical obligations to materials if the materials are the remains of a dead person? Do you try to figure out what the dead person would have wanted? This is an impossible line to follow. Do you think about what you would do in terms of archaeological "materials" generally and then apply those rules to the dead person's remains? In this case, you would be thinking along the lines of long-term conservation and protection. Or do you subjugate this obligation to the more knowable part of the ethical equation, responsibility to the people with whom you work, in which case you would return the remains to the local indigenous populations? But if you feel that the remains should be kept available for scientific study, you might choose not to contact, or work with, these populations. This could lead to a situation in which you were conducting "ethical research" according to the letter of the code, but possibly against the spirit of the code.

SAA

The SAA was formed as "an international organization dedicated to the research, interpretation, and protection of the archaeological heritage of the Americas." Although formed in the 1930s, the SAA had only a simple ethics code until the 1990s. The first ethical statements were oriented almost entirely to the protection of the archaeological record and professional approaches to the past. In the 1990s, demands on the organization had changed to the point where additional ethical concerns had to be addressed. Adopted in April 1996, the SAA Principles of Archaeological Ethics focus on the professional standards and responsibilities of archaeologists, with little explicit consideration of how archaeological work impacts ethnic or indigenous groups. The first two principles of the SAA code are stewardship and accountability:

> Principle no. 1: Stewardship
> The archaeological record—that is, in situ archaeological material and sites, archaeological collections, records and reports—is irreplaceable. It is the responsibility of all archaeologists to work for the long-term conservation and protection of the archaeological record by practicing and promoting stewardship of the archaeological record.
> Stewards are both caretakers of and advocates for the archaeological record for the benefit of all people. As they investigate and interpret the record, they should use the specialized knowledge they gain to promote public understanding and support for its long-term preservation.

> Principle no. 2: Accountability
> Responsible archaeological research, including all levels of professional activity, requires an acknowledgment of public accountability and commitment to make every reasonable effort to consult actively and in good faith with affected group(s), with the goal of establishing a working relationship that can be beneficial to all parties involved.

The SAA code identifies the primary ethical responsibility of archaeologists as stewardship, aimed toward the long-term conservation of archaeological materials for the benefit of all people. The core concern is with the materials, rather than the living groups that are affiliated to those materials, and with the general good, rather than the good of individuals or particular groups. Unlike the AAA Code of Ethics, there is no explicit recognition of the contested nature of archaeological practice and no clear directive on how to act when faced with conflicting obligations to different groups. What is clear, however, is that the spirit of the code places stewardship for future generations above responsibility to individual groups in the present.

Again, the complexities of practice are highlighted by using this code to guide you in terms of the disposition of the remains of the Kennewick Man. In this case, you will be guided to privilege the notion of stewardship and the associated notion of world heritage, above responsibility to the people who are being studied and the associated notion of the rights of indigenous people to control their cultural heritage.

On closer examination, the situation becomes more complicated. How do you determine what is of "benefit to all people"? If you take this to mean that all sectors of the population should have equal benefit, how do you deal with dissonance among these sectors? Do you choose to support the sector that is most directly affected, in this case, local indigenous populations? Or do you decide to support the largest number of people, in which case you will always be arguing for the interests of the dominant population? What happens when the composition of that dominant population changes, as with the influx of Spanish-speaking people in California? What is a dominant population, anyway? Is it the most numerous group or the people who are in power?

We can seek clarification through reference to the second principle of the SAA Code of Ethics, that of public accountability and commitment to consult actively with affected groups, but this is not a simple matter either. How do you work out what constitutes being affected? How do you judge an effect? Physically? Emotionally? Spiritually? How do you identify "affected group(s)"? In this example, are they the genetic descendants of the Kennewick Man? Or are they the people who are the traditional owners of the land on which he was found, irrespective of genetic relationships? Even the very notion of "cultural descent" is problematic, given that the very system that seeks to evaluate indigenous claims in this respect is part of a long trajectory of deliberately erasing that descent. Apart from this, what does it mean to "consult actively"? Does this mean asking people questions and then doing whatever you planned to do anyway, irrespective of their views? Or does it mean that you take these views into account and modify your actions to accommodate them? In the case of the Kennewick Man, the tribes involved have taken a consolidated position, but what do you do in cases where there is more than one indigenous view?

WAC

In any ethical dilemma in which one side argues for the importance of world heritage, it is logical to seek guidance at an international level. Here, we shall consider the ethical codes of WAC, which was founded in 1987 as an international organization with elected representation from all regions of the world. The WAC Executive Committee includes eight representatives of peoples appointed by indigenous organizations. WAC has a series of ethical codes that are specific to indigenous cultural heritage. These include the First Code of Ethics, the Vermillion Accord on Human Remains, and the Draft Code of Ethics for the Amazon Forest Peoples. WAC's interest in this area is apparent in even a cursory glance at the principles of its First Code of Ethics:

1. To acknowledge the importance of indigenous cultural heritage, including sites, places, objects, artefacts, and human remains, to the survival of indigenous cultures
2. To acknowledge the importance of protecting indigenous cultural heritage to the well-being of indigenous peoples
3. To acknowledge the special importance of indigenous ancestral human remains, and sites containing and/or associated with such remains, to indigenous peoples
4. To acknowledge that the important relationship between indigenous peoples and their cultural heritage exists irrespective of legal ownership
5. To acknowledge that the indigenous cultural heritage rightfully belongs to the indigenous descendants of that heritage

All of these provisions are based on the primacy of indigenous interests over indigenous cultural heritage. From this viewpoint, the primary responsibility of archaeologists is to acknowledge the importance of indigenous cultural heritage to the survival of indigenous cultures. This is a very different standpoint to the one that holds that the primary responsibility is stewardship for all people. The WAC code not only identifies and privileges the interests of one particular group in society, but it is also based on the premise that indigenous cultural heritage is part of a living culture and that the primary responsibility of archaeologists is to the survival of that culture. This is in contrast to the position taken by the SAA, which fails to make explicit recognition of the link between indigenous cultural heritage and indigenous cultures in the present.

WAC adopted the Vermillion Accord on Human Remains in 1989. This code places the scientific value of skeletal material as only the fourth governing principle, subordinate to respect for the remains of the dead; their wishes, if known or can be reasonably inferred; and the wishes of the local community and of relatives or guardians of the dead. If you were to abide by this ethical code, you would be guided to act according to the wishes of the local community and relatives of the dead. Again, this raises the question of determining genetic relationships to a person who has been dead 9,800 years. Does this involve expensive and widespread DNA testing? What if such testing is against the wishes of the local indigenous population, as in the case of the Kennewick Man? In this case, the tribes vehemently opposed DNA testing on the grounds that it would establish a precedent in NAGPRA that looking at DNA was reasonable to show cultural affiliation, because of the destructive nature of the testing and because it was being conducted without their consent (Confederated Tribes of the Umatilla Indian Reservation 2001). Even the question of who constitutes the "local community" is not straightforward. Does this mean the local indigenous community? Or does it mean the "locals," the general public, irrespective of ethnic affiliation?

The ethical position of WAC is supported by that of other international bodies. For example, the UN Draft Declaration on the Rights of Indigenous Peoples affirms

> Indigenous Peoples have the right to manifest, practice, develop and teach their spiritual and religious traditions, customs and ceremonies; the right to maintain, protect, and have access in privacy to their religious and cultural sites; the right to the use and control of ceremonial objects; and the right to the repatriation of human remains. States shall take effective measures, in conjunction with the indigenous peoples concerned, to ensure that indigenous sacred places, including burial sites, be preserved, respected and protected. (Part III, article 13)

This view would support the return of the Kennewick Man to local indigenous populations. However, other international bodies, such as the UN Educational, Scientific, and Cultural Organization, are likely to support the notion of world heritage. Clearly, these matters are not straightforward, at either a national or an international level. In our view, the differing ethical approaches to the issue of repatriating ancient human remains are based on fundamentally different conceptions of the material under dispute. The scientific perspective, exemplified by the SAA Code of Ethics, views skeletal material as part of the cultural heritage of all peoples, with archaeologists as the designated stewards. In contrast, the indigenous perspective that informs the WAC Code of Ethics views this material as a part of a living heritage, with indigenous stewardship an integral part of the identity and well-being of both contemporary and future indigenous populations. Fundamentally, this distinction between scientific and indigenous philosophy, and the ethical codes that they inform, turns on whether you consider a skeleton to be an object or an ancestor.

The Lake Mungo Remains

The Willandra Lakes region in far western New South Wales, Australia, is a semiarid landscape of dried saline lake beds fringed by sand dunes. It has been granted a World Heritage Listing for its outstanding cultural and natural values and contains some of Australia's oldest archaeological sites. Among these is a site excavated from the core of a lunette sand dune, which was found to contain hearths, stone artifacts, and faunal remains, as well as the burial of a young woman. A young adult female, known as Lake Mungo 1 (LM1), had been cremated and her bones smashed after burning before being carefully buried in a shallow pit. Radiocarbon dates initially placed this event at 24,710 BP (give or take 1,270 years) (Thorne 1976), but radiocarbon redating of both LM1 and a male found in the same stratigraphic level in the Mungo dune, known as Lake Mungo 3 (LM3), gave revised age estimates of around 35,000 BP (Bowler et al. 1970), to "more than 40,000" BP (Bowler and Thorne 1976), and later to probably "at least 45,000" (Bowler 1998). The recent redating of LM3, using ESR (electron spin resonance), OSL (optically stimulated luminescence), and Uranium Series approaches, gave a result that places both LM1 and LM3 at "about 60,000" BP (Grün et al. 2000). Excavated in 1969, the skeleton was stored at the Australian National University for over twenty years. The remains of what local Aboriginal people called the Lake Mungo Lady provided archaeologists with some of the earliest incontrovertible evidence for deliberate human burial anywhere in the world, and gave Australian archaeologists valuable insight into the lives of the country's earliest indigenous inhabitants. The two burials, LM1 and LM3, are still the oldest cremation disposal and oldest burial with red ochre that are known for humans.

Following several years of debate over the return of human remains excavated at Kow Swamp (see Bowdler 1992; Mulvaney 1991), the question arose about the possible return of the Mungo Lady to the local Aboriginal community. The decision to return the remains to the community was made quickly:

> Sharon Sullivan convened a meeting at the Australian Heritage Commission where four Aboriginal people from the Willandra Community met with Commission staff and myself. After about 10 minutes of talking about the fact that some of the younger people were getting itchy about why something like the Kow Swamp return was not being applied to the Willandra remains and that they thought "something needs to be done" I thought for about 10 minutes and suggested that I return the Mungo Lady's remains. The reaction from the leading Willandra person was to say "You'd do that??!!" in a tone of incredulity. I said yes. (personal communication, Alan Thorne 2002)

In March 1992, a group of Aboriginal people met Alan Thorne on his journey from Canberra with the remains of the Mungo Lady and provided an escort back to Lake Mungo. After a private ceremony in the ranger station involving the elders and three non-Aboriginal people who had been involved, the remains were handed over to the community on the spot where they had been buried originally. They were placed into a velvet-lined wooden box and now reside in a decorated safe on the Lake Mungo site. The placing of the skeleton in a specially made safe—a locked Keeping Place— returned Lady Mungo to her original burial site, but did not make the skeleton completely unavailable for potential investigation by future generations. This safe has two keys—one held by the archaeological community and one by the Aboriginal community—and both are required to unlock it (Sullivan 1999).

Jointly approved research between archaeologists and the Willandra community continues and is producing scientific results of global significance, such as redating of the remains of LM3, outlined earlier, and the analysis of mitochondrial DNA recovered from the LM3 burial, along with nine other recoveries from remains from Kow Swamp and the Willandra (Adcock et al. 2001). Perhaps, the lesson to be learned from this is that sharing the past can provide a foundation for working together in the future.

The return of LM1 came at a time in Australian archaeology's development that had already witnessed the reburial of several important collections of skeletal material, largely in response to an increased politicization on this issue by Australian Aboriginal people. In February 1990, the Murray Black Aboriginal skeletal collection of around 800 individuals was reburied at Deniliquin, New South Wales (see Pardoe 1991), and in August of the same year the Museum of Victoria returned the Kow Swamp Collection of human remains and associated grave goods to the Echuca Aboriginal Cooperative, Victoria. The Kow Swamp material, dated to between 9,500 and 13,000 BP, was the largest population from the Pleistocene excavated from a single locality anywhere in the world (Thorne 1976). The decisions to rebury these collections did not come easily to the archaeological community, however, and prior to reburial Australian archaeologists became galvanized over the issue of who holds the right to control the past. Throughout the debate, several archaeologists and paleoanthropologists made it clear they could not condone what they saw to be the destruction of ancient remains. Their arguments were based firmly on the notion of custodianship and privileged a universal human culture, stressing that humanity could only suffer from the loss of such precious material (Mulvaney 1991). Other archaeologists took the position that this was not a decision for Western culture to make and that consultation with Aboriginal people "does not mean giving them the opportunity to sanction what has already been done or decided. It means engaging in a dialogue which allows them the genuine possibility of saying 'no,' and preferably before any research has commenced" (Bowdler 1992:104). This debate was fueled by an increased politicization on the part of Australian Aboriginal people and their determination to obtain the return of the remains of their ancestors (e.g., Langford 1983). From this perspective, indigenous stewardship of these remains is essential to the health and well-being of future generations of indigenous peoples, and this outweighs their scientific value: "Aborigines see human remains within their country as their ancestors. The relationship they have with these remains is to me more important than whether, scientifically, that person is directly related" (Francesca Cubillo quoted in Jones 2002).

That indigenous people see this as an issue of respect is shown in the statement by Chris Wilson that "they were buried with respect. Why can't we just leave them in respect?" (personal communication 2002). Largely as a result of this debate, the Australian Archaeological Association formalized its code of ethics; in this sense, then, this code of ethics was an outcome of the reburial debate, rather than a guide used during the debate.

Australian Archaeological Association

The need for a code of ethics for Australian archaeologists was first mooted at the annual Australian Archaeological Association conference in December 1990. Based largely on the code of ethics adopted by WAC, it was amended and ratified by the association in 1992. Most of its Principles to Abide By are identical to those contained in the WAC Code of Ethics; its Rules to Adhere To vary only slightly. The timing for this was crucial: the Australian Archaeological Association Code of Ethics was formulated at a time when a huge shift had already occurred in the ways in which indigenous people could influence the disposition of items of their cultural heritage. As a result, the code was shaped by a commonly held view that indigenous people should have the primary right to control their own cultural heritage.

When applied to the case of the LM1, the first principles of the Australian Archaeological Association Code of Ethics are quite clear in privileging the importance of indigenous cultural heritage to the survival of indigenous cultures and the special importance of ancestral human remains to indigenous peoples. Both its and the WAC Code of Ethics establish a platform from which indigenous peoples' right to dispose of items of their own cultural heritage takes precedence over the claims of science. Furthermore, one of the key amendments made by the Australian Archaeological Association to the WAC Code of Ethics relates directly to aspects of the reburial debate, particularly the arguments against present-day peoples having any connection to peoples in the archaeological past. A rider attached to the first Rule to Abide By ("Prior to conducting any investigation and/or examination, members shall define the indigenous peoples whose cultural heritage is the subject of investigation") states: "We do not recognize that there are any circumstances where there is no community of concern" (Australian Archaeological Association 1994).

Australian Association of Consulting Archaeologists Inc.

The other primary professional association for Australian archaeologists is the Australian Association of Consulting Archaeologists Inc. (AACAI). As its name implies, the AACAI is more concerned with the practice of archaeology in the public sphere and its Code of Ethics with the proper conduct of the business of archaeology. Similar in content to the Code of Conduct of the Register of Professional Archaeologists (RPA) in the United States, the AACAI Code of Ethics focuses on the promotion and maintenance of professional standards in archaeology and requirements for professional competence.

The AACAI Code of Ethics outlines members' duties to the various interest groups with whom archaeologists intersect in practice: the public, "certain groups" (the people whose "cultural background is the subject of investigations"), informants, the profession, and employers or clients. While there are no core "principles to abide by" in the same mold as the WAC Code of Ethics, the first duty of archaeologists represented in the code is to the public: "2.1 A Member should take a responsible attitude to the archaeological resource base and to the best of her/his understanding ensure that this, as well as information derived from it, are used wisely and in the best interest of the public."

As befits a document that primarily seeks to provide guidelines for the conduct of archaeological consultancies (e.g., standards of work, appropriate remuneration, and training of potential archaeologists), there is little reference to the relationship of archaeology to the rights and responsibilities of indigenous peoples. Principle 3.1 comes closest to dealing with this when it states that "[a] Member shall be sensitive to, and respect the legitimate concerns of groups whose cultural background is the subject of investigations." To deal with this, the AACAI has formulated a separate policy document dealing explicitly with the process of consultation with Aboriginal communities, the first three principles of which are:

1. The Association recognizes that Aboriginal sites are of significance to Aboriginal people as part of their heritage and as part of their continuing culture and identity.
2. The Association recognizes that Aboriginal communities should be involved in decision-making concerning Aboriginal sites. Aboriginal opinions, concerns and management recommendations should be presented alongside those of the archaeological consultant.
3. The Association recognizes that Aboriginal people have a right to be consulted about the intention to undertake archaeological work, to be consulted about the progress and findings of this work, and to be consulted about any recommendations arising from this work.

To apply this Code of Ethics to the case of Lake Mungo provides a less clear-cut answer. While the AACAI would certainly recognize indigenous rights to control aspects of their cultural heritage, this is not formally set out in its Code of Ethics in the same way as it is for WAC or the Australian Archaeological Association. For one thing, the principles of a policy document are more open to interpretation and in a sense less tightly binding than the values espoused in a code of ethics.

For example, a recognition that "Aboriginal people have a right to be consulted about the intention to undertake archaeological work" (see the appendix) is not the same as an admission that "Members shall ensure that . . . indigenous peoples . . . are kept informed during all stages of the investigation and are able to renegotiate or terminate the archaeological work being conducted at that site" (Australian Archaeological Association 1994:Rule to Adhere To no. 3). We could seek clarification through policies 1 and 2, which recognize the importance of sites (and presumably their contents) to the continuing culture and identity of indigenous peoples and their right, as a result, to be consulted about the decision-making process. If the archaeologist decided to follow only the AACAI Code of Ethics, however, an entirely different accommodation could be reached, guided by the first principle, which implies that a member's primary responsibility is to the archaeological resource base and the use of the information derived from this as being "in the best interest of the public." The problems are similar to those encountered in interpreting the SAA Code of Ethics and may privilege arguments for the ongoing stewardship of archaeological remains by the scientific community.

Who is "the public"? Presumably, it is not solely indigenous groups, although they may be included, but if so, then is it a dominant culture that by and large subscribes to the centrality of science for understanding the past? What is the public's "best interest"? If it is a public enmeshed in science, then its best interests may well be served by preserving material for the benefit of future generations. This is a powerful assumption, one that underlies the view that archaeologists should be the primary stewards of the past, but which fails to consider how diffuse the "public" is in terms of attitudes to cultural heritage and the exigencies of particular situations. Developers, for example, may care about preserving a site in an abstract sense but may change their view if this site is in the way of a project. Similarly, taxpayers in hard economic times become increasingly reluctant to fund museums or other curatorial facilities, or even basic research (see fig.14.1).

Figure 14.1. Anthropologist Alan Thorne (left) returning remains of the Mungo Lady to Aboriginal elders at Willandra Lakes. (Photo courtesy of Dragi Markovic and Alan Thorne and with the approval of the Willandra Lakes Region World Heritage Area Three Traditional Tribal Elders Council.)

The Ethics of Archaeological Practice

The very existence of an ethical code can present certain dangers. Ironically, the very codification of behavioral standards can provide a means for escaping ethical requirements as well as enforcing them. Some people will act on the basis that it is legitimate to do anything that isn't specifically prohibited by a code. The counterargument is that simply because a behavior hasn't been proscribed doesn't make it ethical. The point here is that ethical codes are to be studied, not as strict principles of legal interpretation, but in terms of the spirit in which they were made and the principles that they were intended to further. Ethical behavior requires that individuals articulate their ethical values in practice. It means having a standard against which to assess the choices that archaeologists are continually required to make. It can be argued that the most important attribute of any ethical code is the provision of a spirit within which to work through ethical dilemmas. Such a spirit can only be defined in practice, however, as new situations develop and ethical challenges arise. Moreover, because each code of ethics only reflects the professional needs of archaeologists in that region at the time the code was developed, then codes of ethics must always be in flux. Professional debate is one of the most important aspects in this process of ongoing revision. Without it, the disjunctions between general codes and the specifics of daily archaeological practice have no forum for resolution.

Once entered into, any debate over the ethics of practice will raise significant, and potentially unanswerable, questions. What happens if you are a member of WAC, the SAA, and the AAA? Do you pick the most appropriate code of ethics to suit either yourself or the situation? How do you determine what is "most appropriate"? At a more general level: What use is archaeology? Who does archaeology serve and whom does it disempower? Do archaeologists have a right to create and control the past of others? As archaeologists, we assume the answers to these kinds of questions. We take it as self-evident that archaeology is useful, and that we have a responsibility, as well as a right, to create the pasts of others. It seems clear to us that this needs to be done and that it needs to be done in the scientific, rigorous manner that is archaeology. Rarely do we question the agendas that are furthered by our work and what groups are disempowered as a result. While archaeology is a powerful tool in the creation of cultural identities in the past, and we know that evidence is chosen selectively and interpreted according to our own biases and inclinations in the present, we still work on the assumption that our work should be considered as being beyond politics.

Looking to the future of ethics in archaeology, it is clear that we need a more systematic evaluation of the consequences of what we propose as "ethics" before we assume that our strategies are effective. One real problem is that few organizations have established procedures for evaluation of their ethical codes. Though WAC, for example, has had a profound impact on the development of other codes,

192 CLAIRE SMITH AND HEATHER BURKE

it is difficult to assess what "real" impact these codes have had in terms of implementation. In fact, most codes are deficient when it comes to operationalizing them, enforcing them, or adjudicating purported violations. This raises the question of how much these codes actually inform the behavior of archaeologists. Do we have ethical codes only for moral authority? What do we do when there is a violation, either obvious or more ambiguous? The SAA Ethics Committee, for example, has no authority or mechanism to investigate complaints, even though there have been charges of ethics violations brought to its attention. Neither do other organizations, such as WAC, the Canadian Archaeological Association, or the New Zealand Archaeological Association. The RPA (2002) and the Archaeological Institute of America are better positioned here, as each has a tribunal system that confidentially deals with ethical violations, but these are exceptions rather than the rule (see Hester A. Davis, chapter 19).

The existence of so many potentially conflicting ethical codes also brings into question the possibility of ever having common international ethical standards. While we may hold certain moral tenets in common (e.g., respect for others and for archaeological material), if our ethical codes provide such widely divergent starting points, will it ever be possible to reconcile our different approaches to ethics in practice? This is an important issue not only in theory, but also in practice. American Indians may never have the control that is currently held by the Aboriginal and Torres Strait Islander peoples of Australia, but if American archaeologists wish to work in Australia, they had best be prepared to deal with local expectations of ethical behavior. This means they would have to be prepared for a level of indigenous control over their work, especially if the work receives support from Australian funding agencies. For Americans, who are accustomed to the notion of free speech, this can create a serious ethical dilemma. Should they submit to Aboriginal approval of their results, simply because they want to conduct research in Australia? From an American point of view, this could seem like "censorship" but Australians are more likely to consider it as being "edited for content." Moreover, many Australian archaeologists would consider the obtaining of indigenous approval of publications, especially photos, as exemplary ethical behavior on the part of the researcher.

While this chapter has used the dilemma between indigenous and scientific stewardship as an example of the ways in which different ethical codes provide different forms of guidance for archaeological practice, this is only one of a wide range of ethical dilemmas. Another example is the use of archaeological research to privilege some pasts over others. The social impact of this kind of question is clear in the case of Ayodhya, India, where hundreds of people have died in conflicts between Hindu and Muslim people over the existence of a Rama Temple at the site of the Babri Masjid mosque and the possible replacement of that mosque with new temple architecture. In this case, the Ayodhya site has become an emotive emblem that has been both a catalyst for, and a reflection of, long-standing enmities. Archaeological interpretations of this material have become central to a debate that is not only heated but life threatening (Golson 1996; Hassan 1995).

Finally, we would like to return to the disparate fates of the Kennewick Man and the LM1. Currently, one is located in a laboratory, far removed from where he was found, the other on her traditional lands in a custom-made chest with two locks. One is the subject of a bitter dispute; the other is in joint stewardship. Each of these ancient individuals is a powerful symbol of the state of contemporary relations between indigenous peoples and archaeologists. Lake Mungo, however, demonstrates that the outcome of such struggles need not be an either/or scenario, and that an acceptable accommodation can emerge from meaningful communication rather than polarized disputes. In such circumstances, ethical codes are not only guidance for archaeological practice, but also outcomes of the wider social and political matrices in which they are embedded

Discussion Questions

1. What are the researcher's responsibilities to the people with whom he or she works? Who benefits from archaeological research?
2. Do archaeologists have a right to control the pasts of others?
3. What problems are raised for physical anthropologists trained to study archaeological remains when our codes privilege indigenous rights? What options do such specialists have?
4. Is the development of ethical codes a response to the need for formal guidelines to assist in the resolution of ethical dilemmas or simply due to a professionalization that attempts to draw a line between who has the power and license to do archaeology and who doesn't?
5. What are the repercussions of working in a situation where more than one code of ethics applies? How do you choose?
6. Is it reasonable for archaeologists to impose the ethical codes of their home country when working in another country?
7. What procedures would you recommend to evaluate ethical codes more systematically?
8. What revisions to the SAA principles, created in the early 1990s, seem needed now, and why? (Send your responses to the chair of the Ethics Committee!)
9. Various ethical codes include a directive that they will respect the "legitimate" concerns of indigenous peoples. Who determines what is legitimate? How can this be assessed?
10. How is it that priorities in ethics codes are established? Do you think that authors of codes really think in these terms or just reflect their organization's desires?

11. Is there a potential conflict between the spirit of the code and the practice of the code? If the spirit of the code is so important, should there ever be an effort to enforce codes?

12. If one disagrees with an organizational code of ethics, should one not participate in that organization?

Note

Karen D. Vitelli, Julie Hollowell-Zimmer, Amy Roberts, Audie Huber, and, especially, Larry J. Zimmerman gave us detailed, thoughtful, and insightful comments. We are grateful to Martin Wobst, who is always encouraging and generously found the time to read a draft of this chapter. Above all, we thank the indigenous people with whom we work for making us think about who we are as archaeologists.

1. Following the increasing practice of indigenous authors, we use the term "indigenous peoples" (see Smith 1999:114–15).

Recommended Readings

Adcock, G. J., E. S. Dennis, S. Easteal, G. A. Huttley, L. S. Jermin, W. J. Peacock, and A. G. Thorne
    2001   Mitochondrial DNA Sequences in Ancient Australians: Implications for Modern Human Origins. *Proceedings of the National Academy of Sciences of the USA* 98:537–42.

American Anthropological Association
    1998   Code of Ethics of the American Anthropological Association, at www.aaanet.org/committees/ethics/ethcode.htm (accessed April 2002).

Anderson, Duane
    1996   Reburial: Is It Reasonable? In *Archaeological Ethics,* edited by Karen D. Vitelli, 200–8. AltaMira, Walnut Creek, CA.

Australian Archaeological Association Code of Ethics
    1994   Code of Ethics. *Australian Archaeology* 39:129.

Australian Association of Consulting Archaeologists
    1980   Code of Ethics, at www.archaeology.usyd.edu.au/aacai/ethics/index.html (accessed April 2002).

Bowler, J. M.
    1998   Willandra Lakes Revisited: Environmental Framework for Human Occupation. *Archaeology in Oceania* 33:120–55.

Bowler, J. M., and A. G. Thorne
    1976   Human Remains from Lake Mungo: Discovery and Excavation of Mungo 3.
           In *The Origin of the Australians,* edited by R. L. Kirk and A. G. Thorne,
           127–38. Canberra: Australian Institute of Aboriginal Studies.

Bowler, J. M., R. Jones, H. Allen, and A. G. Thorne
    1970   Pleistocene Human Remains from Australia: A Living Site and Human
           Cremation from Lake Mungo, Western New South Wales. *World Archaeology*
           2:30–60.

Bowdler, S.
    1992   Unquiet Slumbers: The Return of the Kow Swamp Burials. *Antiquity* 66:103–6.

Canadian Archaeological Association
    1999   Statement of Principles for Ethical Conduct Pertaining to Aboriginal Peoples,
           at www.canadianarchaeology.com/ethicseng.html (accessed April 2002).

Confederated Tribes of the Umatilla Indian Reservation
    2001   Ancient One Determined to Be Culturally Affiliated with Five Tribes. Press
           release. September 25, at www.umatilla.nsn.us/kennman6.html (accessed
           December 2002).

Davidson, Ian
    1991   Notes for a Code of Ethics for Australian Archaeologists Working with
           Aboriginal and Torres Strait Islander Heritage. *Australian Archaeology*
           32:61–64.

Ferguson, T. J.
    1984   Archaeological Ethics and Values in a Tribal Cultural Resource Management
           Program at the Pueblo of Zuni. In *Ethics and Values in Archaeology,* edited by
           Ernestine L. Green, 224–35. The Free Press: London.

Golson, J.
    1996   What Went Wrong with WAC3 and an Attempt to Understand Why.
           Australian Archaeology 41:48–54.

Hackenberger, S.
    2000   Cultural Affiliation Study of the Kennewick Human Remains: Review of Bio-
           Archaeological Information. Report by National Park Service, at
           www.cr.nps.gov/aad/Kennewick/hackenberger.htm (accessed April 2002).

Hassan, F.
    1995   The World Archaeological Congress in India: Politicizing the Past. *Antiquity*
           69(266):874–77.

Janke, Terri
    1999   *Our Culture, Our Future: Proposals for the Recognition of Indigenous
           Cultural and Intellectual Property.* Monograph prepared for Australian
           Institute of Aboriginal Studies and the Aboriginal and Torres Strait Islander
           Commission, Canberra.

Jelderks, John
    2002   Opinion and Order, Civil no. 96-1481-JE, in the U.S. District Court for the
            District of Oregon, at www.Tri-CityHerald.com/kennewick (accessed March
            2002).

Jones, C.
    2002   Bones of Contention. *The Bulletin* (Australia) (April):37–39.

Langford, Ross
    1983   Our Heritage—Your Playground. *Australian Archaeology* 16:1–6.

Lewis, D., and D. Rose
    1985   Some Ethical Issues in Archaeology: A Methodology of Consultation in
            Northern Australia. *Australian Aboriginal Studies* 1:37–44.

McBryde, Isabel
    1986   *Who Owns the Past?* Oxford University Press, Melbourne.

Messenger, Phyllis Mauch (editor)
    1999   *The Ethics of Collecting Cultural Property: Whose Culture, Whose Property?*
            2nd ed. University of New Mexico Press, Albuquerque.

Mulvaney, D. J.
    1991   Past Regained, Future Lost: The Kow Swamp Pleistocene Burials. *Antiquity*
            65(246):12–21.

Native American Graves Protection and Repatriation Act
    1990   at www.cast.uark.edu/other/nps/nagpra/nagpra.dat/lgm003.html (accessed
            April 2002).

National Park Service
    2002   Kennewick Man, at www.cr.nps.gov/aad/Kennewick/index.htm (accessed
            April 2002).

Nicholas, George P., and Thomas D. Andrews (editors)
    1997   *At a Crossroads: Archaeology and First Peoples in Canada.* Archaeology
            Press, Department of Archaeology, Simon Fraser University, Burnaby, BC.

Pardoe, Colin
    1991   Farewell to the Murray Black Australian Aboriginal Skeletal Collection.
            World Archaeology Bulletin 5:119–21.

Register of Professional Archaeologists
    2002   at www.rpanet.org/about.htm (accessed April 2002).

Smith, Claire, and Heather Burke
    In press. Joining the Dots . . . Managing the Land and Seascapes of Indigenous Aus-
tralia. In *Northern Ethnographic Landscapes: Perspectives from the Circumpolar Nations*, edited by I. Krupnik and R. Mason. Smithsonian Institution Press, Washington, DC.

Smith, Linda Tuhiwai
    1999   *Decolonizing Methodologies: Research and Indigenous Peoples.* 2nd ed. Zed,
            London.

Society of American Archaeology
    1996   Principles of Archaeological Ethics, at
    www.saa.org/Aboutsaa/Ethics/prethic.html (accessed April 2002).

Sullivan, Sharon
    1999   Repatriation. *Conservation, The Getty Conservation Institute Newsletter*
    14(3), at www.getty.edu/conservation/resources/newsletter/14_3/ (accessed 14
    April 2002).

Thomas, David Hurst
    2000   *Skull Wars: Kennewick Man, Archaeology and the Battle for Native American
    Identity.* Basic, New York.

Thorne, A. G.
    1976   *Origins of the Australians.* Australian Institute of Aboriginal Studies,
    Canberra.

Vitelli, Karen D. (editor)
    1996   *Archaeological Ethics.* AltaMira, Walnut Creek, CA.

Watkins, Joe
    1999   *Indigenous Archaeology: American Indian Values and Scientific Practice.*
    AltaMira, Walnut Creek, CA.

World Archaeological Congress
    1989   Vermillion Accord on Human Remains, at
    www.wac.uct.ac.za/archive/content/vermillion.accord.html (accessed April
    2002).
    1990   First Code of Ethics, at www.wac.uct.ac.za/archive/content/ethics.html
    (accessed April 2002).

Zimmerman, Larry J.
    1989   Made Radical by My Own: An Archaeologist Learns to Understand Reburial.
    In *Conflict in the Archaeology of Living Traditions,* edited by R. Layton,
    60–67. Unwin Hyman, London.

PART IV

Responsibilities to Colleagues, Employees, and Students

DONALD L. HARDESTY ☙

Chapter Fifteen

Safety and the Ethics of Archaeological Fieldwork

The movie *Indiana Jones* conjures up a popular image of what archaeologists do in the field. Jumping into pits filled with writhing snakes and barely escaping a host of other threats to life and limb are commonplace for this fictional character. Exciting, yes, but is Indiana Jones a good role model for the safe conduct of fieldwork by the professional archaeologist? What are the ethical obligations of an archaeologist to do fieldwork safely?

The Ethics of Safety

The ethical basis of safety lies in the Hippocratic Oath, which underlies the Code of Conduct of medical practitioners. In part, the oath states, "I will follow that system of regimen which, according to my ability and judgment, I consider for the benefit of my patients, and abstain from whatever is deleterious and mischievous." This part of the oath is often restated as "do no harm" and is the fundamental tenet of the ethics of safety to oneself and to other people in the field. It follows that a related ethical principle is "do not encourage others to do harm" by establishing "risky" policies, plans, and methods that guide the conduct of archaeologists in the field.

Fieldwork Safety and the Archaeological Profession

What does the archaeological profession say about an archaeologist's obligation to do fieldwork safely? The codes of conduct of several archaeological organizations include a statement about safety. The Archaeological Institute of America, for example, states in its Code of Professional Standards: "The principal investigator(s) of archaeological projects should maintain acceptable standards of safety and ascertain that staff members are adequately insured" (Archaeological Institute of America 1994:section III, part II). Likewise, the Code of Practice of the European Association of Archaeologists states: "The management of all projects must respect national standards relating to conditions of employment and safety" (European Association of Archaeologists 1997:2.10).

Business-oriented archaeological organizations have the strongest statements. The reason for this lies, at least in part, in their association with large engineering and environmental companies that have a long record of experience with the Occupational Safety and Health Administration and other governmental safety agencies. The Code of Ethics and Professional Conduct of the American Cultural Resources Association (ACRA) is typical. It states in part: "As an employer, an ACRA member firm has certain responsibilities to its employees, and shall strive to: . . . provide a safe work environment in compliance with all applicable laws and regulations" (American Cultural Resources Association 1996).

Another example is the Code of Conduct of the United Kingdom's Institute of Field Archaeologists (IFA), which is an organization of archaeologists and companies that, like the Register of Professional Archaeologists (RPA) in the United States, agree to abide by a code of conduct and a set of performance standards. The code contains the statement that "an archaeologist shall give due regard to the requirements of health and safety legislation relating to employees or to other persons potentially affected by his or her archaeological activities" (Institute of Field Archaeologists [IFA] 1985:principle 5). Even more specific, however, is the IFA's Standard Guidance for Archaeological Excavation, which contains the following statement:

> Health and Safety regulations and requirements cannot be ignored no matter how imperative the need to record archaeological information; hence Health and Safety will take priority over archaeological matters. All archaeologists undertaking fieldwork must do so under a defined Health and Safety Policy. Archaeologists undertaking fieldwork must observe safe working practices; the Health and Safety arrangements must be agreed and understood by all relevant parties before work commences. Risk assessments must be carried out and documented for every field project, in accordance with Management of Health and Safety at Work Regulations 1992. Archaeologists should determine whether field projects are covered by Construction (Design and Management) Regulations 1994, and ensure that they meet all requirements under the regulations. In addition they must liaise closely with the principal contractor and comply with specified site rules. Archaeologists are advised to note the onerous responsibilities of the role of a planning supervisor. (IFA 1985:3.3.11)

Whether or not these guidance principles are encouraging safe behavior in the archaeological workplace is unclear. None of the professional organizations promulgating the principles discussed earlier have mechanisms for enforcing appropriate behavior, neither carrots nor sticks. The RPA has a grievance process that can lead to expulsion from the register, but its Code of Conduct and Standards of Research Performance do not include any clear statement on safety. Arguably, the most successful statements have been by business-oriented archaeological organizations (e.g., ACRA and IFA) in the area of legally mandated workplace behavior, what has been described as "legislated ethics" (Watkins 2000:43ff). The following section considers legislated safety ethics in the archaeological workplace in more detail.

Fieldwork Safety and the Law

Archaeological fieldwork is a "workplace" that is subject to government laws and regulations. In the United States, for example, perhaps the most important of these is the 1970 Occupational Safety and Health Act (OSHA), which regulates safety in the workplace with a set of regulations or standards administered by the Occupational Safety and Health Administration. OSHA regulations affect archaeological fieldwork most often when it involves hazards and temporary field camps.

Hazard Assessment and Characterization

OSHA requires ongoing site assessment to identify hazards as a critical first step to the safe management of any archaeological project. Hazards at an archaeological site are varied and may include toxic materials contained in the sediments, excavation machines such as backhoes, power tools, atmospheric contaminants such as dust, ladders or photographic towers, and underwater sites.

Awareness and Communication

The Hazard Communication Standard or "Employee-Right-to-Know" regulation (29 Code of Federal Regulations 1910.1000, 1200) requires that field-workers be informed of whatever hazards are found and what to do about them.

Heath and Safety Plans

Developing a health and safety plan (HASP) to cope with the hazard or hazards is another key OSHA requirement. The HASP should have a provision for informing field-workers of the safety conditions to be expected and what to do about the hazardous conditions. A fieldwork HASP should also provide for necessary training, protective devices, site safety engineering, and emergency procedures. The law requires the use of "personal protective equipment" under hazardous conditions.

Protective equipment, including personal protective equipment for eyes, face, head, and extremities; protective clothing; respiratory devices; and protective shields and barriers, shall be provided, used, and maintained in a sanitary and reliable condition wherever it is necessary by reason of hazards of processes or environment, chemical hazards, radiological hazards, or mechanical irritants encountered in a manner capable of causing injury or impairment in the function of any part of the body through absorption, inhalation, or physical contact (29 Code of Federal Regulations 1910.132).

What actually goes into a HASP is very much determined by the characteristics of the hazard and often is stipulated by other OSHA regulations. Hazardous Waste Operations and Emergency Response (HAZWOPER) (29 Code of Federal Regulations 1910.120), for example, is a regulation that applies to workers exposed to hazardous chemicals or materials in uncontrolled hazardous waste sites. Finally, it is worth noting that OSHA regulations include general environmental controls in temporary labor camps, of which archaeological field camps are a part (29 Code of Federal Regulations 1910.142). Examples of environmental controls are camp placement, toilets and sanitation, architecture, cooking facilities, water supply, first aid facilities, insect and rodent control, and disease control.

Certainly, an ethic of archaeological safety must include an awareness of governmental mandates, but a more vexing ethical issue is safe behavior that is not specifically legislated. Adherence to the ethical code of "do no harm" means that a professional archaeologist is obligated to ensure workplace safety both within and outside the legal context of laws and regulations. What can be done? Certainly, the development of a safety plan that anticipates hazards before going into the field is essential. The following section considers some of the common and not so common threats to safety that might be considered in such a plan.

Not-So-Strange Encounters of the Hazardous Kind

The *Indiana Jones* image is not entirely wrong in conveying the idea that the "real world" of field archaeology is filled with hazards that threaten physical or mental health and, therefore, place archaeologists at risk. Some of the most common risks are personal health, environmental hazards (e.g., wildlife, endemic diseases, and toxic materials), hazardous field methods and technologies, logistical hazards (e.g., transportation), and social and psychological hazards.

Personal Health as a Safety Hazard

The first encounter a project director has with hazards surrounding fieldwork safety is the preexisting medical conditions of field-workers. Archaeological fieldwork often takes place in an environment that could place an individual with a unique medical condition at risk. Risky conditions range from severe allergic reactions to bee stings to plant pollen or to claustrophobia in enclosed places like caves or well shafts or under the floor of a standing building. Fieldwork activities such as excavation, pedestrian survey in rugged terrain, or other strenuous work can place individuals with heart defects or other medical problems at risk. What is the appropriate ethical behavior?

Remember the underlying principle: "Do no harm." Field-workers must be made aware of potential hazards for idiosyncratic medical conditions. This means that communication between the field-worker and the project manager about the expected field conditions and the medical condition is necessary. Communication often begins with questionnaires or other requests for disclosure of preexisting medical conditions as a part of an application for a field school, volunteer service, or employment. If the applicant identifies the condition, what should be the response of the project director? In some cases, the most ethical behavior is avoidance—the field-worker does not go into the field. In other cases, it is entirely ethical for the field-worker to go after planning for a predictable emergency, for example, by carrying antihistamines or other drugs for use in the event of a severe allergic reaction. In addition, it is common practice to require that all field-workers sign a blanket liability waiver. Whether such waivers absolve legal risk, however, is debatable. The other side of the coin offers another ethical issue. What if the applicant doesn't identify a preexisting medical condition (e.g., diabetes)? Certainly, this is unethical behavior on the part of the applicant, but what about the project director? Above and beyond legal liability, is there an ethical obligation to inquire further about the potential medical problems of the applicants?

Robert Miller (1984) describes the risks to personal health of doing archaeological fieldwork in rural Egypt where dehydration, fleas, flies, and dysentery are common hazards. Ground surface temperatures there frequently reach 144 to 146 degrees Fahrenheit. House plaster tempered with dung is a medium for the transmission of tetanus throughout East Africa. Flies, the principal vector for dysentery and other gastrointestinal diseases, thrive in the mud and dung floors of the indigenous houses occupied temporarily by archaeological field-workers. Contaminated river and well water carry a variety of similar hazards to personal health. What could be done to minimize the personal health risks of doing archaeological fieldwork on this project?

Awareness is the key. Miller observes that "not all expeditions have health-care specialists; not all medical specialists would be prepared to learn from local public health traditions first hand where there are linguistic and cultural barriers"

(1984:438). Much of the information needed to greatly reduce the risk to personal health is available in existing sources in the ethnography of public health, which once again points to the need for the archaeologist to do adequate background research on safety risks and hazards before going into the field. Miller suggests the development of an "archaeo-epidemiological" clearinghouse for better awareness of the risk to personal health posed by archaeological field projects around the world and recommends a health and safety plan (HASP) that combines medical technology with the adoption of traditional practices of environmental adaptation. Tetanus shots greatly reduce the risk of living in houses with dung-tempered plaster. Covering mud and dung floors with concrete minimizes the risk of dysentery from flies. Frequently sweeping the floors, a traditional Egyptian practice, reduces fleas. Wearing loose clothing, another traditional practice, greatly reduces the environmental heat load, as does sprinkling water on floors and courtyards (439).

Environmental Hazards

Once in the field, archaeologists encounter a variety of environmental hazards that threaten life and limb. Archaeological sites typically occur in local "microenvironments" that have unique safety conditions in addition to those of a general regional or continental environment. The site at which fieldwork takes place, for example, may be in the Mojave Desert of the American West and, therefore, be subject to all of this region's wildlife, climate, and weather. But the site may also contain unexploded ordnance from a twentieth-century military training facility. Environmental hazards fall into three general categories: biological hazards, such as wildlife (e.g., bears, poisonous snakes, killer bees, and poisonous plants) and microorganisms (e.g., hantavirus, Valley Fever, and privy pit bacteria); chemical hazards, such as toxic wastes (e.g., mercury) and unexploded ordnance; and landscape and atmospheric hazards, such as abandoned mine shafts and underground workings, caves, rivers and lakes, extreme weather events (e.g., tornadoes, flash floods, earthquakes, and hurricanes), and extreme climates (e.g., cold, heat, high altitude, and underwater).

In light of the previous information, consider the fieldwork safety situation and what the appropriate ethical behavior might be for an archaeological field project in the eastern interior of Alaska in a boreal forest region on a tributary of the Yukon River. The fieldwork sites are associated with the early twentieth-century Washington-Alaska Military Cable and Telegraph System, the first military and civilian communications system linking Alaska to the continental United States. Preliminary assessment and characterization of the sites identified a range of biological (bears), landscape (wild rivers and unpredictable weather), chemical (lead battery plates in refuse dumps), and logistical (remoteness) hazards. What is an appropriate ethical plan of action?

Consider first the biological hazards. Black bears, especially juvenile males, are aggressive and not easily frightened away. What is an appropriate black bear safety plan that is consistent with ethical behavior? All field-workers should attend a class on bear safety from wildlife specialists before going into the field. But even before this, field-workers need to be informed of the potential hazard from bears so that they can decide whether or not to continue with the project. The plan also requires some of the field staff to complete field certification in rifle or shotgun use and safety at a firing range. Once in the field, field-workers are required to travel in groups of no fewer than three people and each group has to have at least one person with a rifle or shotgun capable of dispatching bears and who has been field certified in firearms use and safety, even when traveling to a toilet. The plan also requires a twenty-four-hour bear watch that rotates field crew members in shifts. In the past, the field staff of one archaeological project in the area had to shoot a bear that could not be stopped from invading food and lab tents in search of food.

In addition to wildlife, the site landscape is marked by potential hazards that include extreme arctic climate conditions and periodic flooding from the river that flows by the site. A colleague conveyed to me her past experience working in such extreme climates for the first time. Her principal investigator (PI) failed to make the field crew aware of the equipment or the behavior needed to cope with very cold temperatures. Nor was the field crew informed of the symptoms of hypothermia or chilblains experienced by some of the crew members. In general, the most effective planning to cope with local landscape hazards draws on the traditional ecological knowledge of local people.

What about the lead battery plates in some of the trash dumps? The plan calls for making field-workers aware of lead as a toxic substance and for developing a HASP to cope with the lead plates before going into the field. Field-workers are required to wear appropriate protective equipment such as latex gloves when working in the dumps or handling the plates and contaminated deposits.

In another toxic waste situation, Ronald L. Reno, Stephen R. Bloyd, and Donald L. Hardesty (2001) describe fieldwork conditions at a nineteenth-century silver ore processing mill on the Carson River in northwestern Nevada, a site that is on the Environmental Protection Agency Superfund list. The Birdsall Mill, which operated from 1865 to 1900, used the Washoe process of pan amalgamation to recover silver from the ore mined on the Comstock Lode during much of this time. In this process, ore is crushed and ground, then put in steam-heated pans where it is mixed with water, mercury, and various chemicals. Mercury played the key role in the Washoe process, first combining with silver in the ore to form an amalgam, after which it was vaporized. Mill operators attempted to recover the expensive and toxic mercury; nevertheless, the Washoe process mills lost an enormous amount of mercury. The loss of mercury for each ton of ore mined on the Comstock was about 1 pound, or a total of around 14 million pounds (Smith 1943:257). What was done to minimize the risk to personal safety of doing archaeological fieldwork on this project?

The safety program began with prefieldwork documentary research and interviews, as mentioned earlier, and with site assessment and characterization. Mercury can be inhaled or passed through the skin and is toxic at levels ranging from two to fourteen milligrams per cubic meter of air. The toxic effects can include tremors or shaking, memory loss, bronchial pneumonia, skin rashes, weakness, and chest pain. On-site testing of soils at the Birdsall Mill site showed that mercury levels were not exceptionally high, but that the risk to personal safety still required the implementation of a HASP. The HASP procedures began with all field-workers taking a forty-hour HAZWOPER course given by the Occupational and Safety Hazards Administration and reviewing the HASP for the site. Field-workers used personal protective equipment such as Tyvek suits and latex or nitrile gloves for contaminated dirt and dust, Saranex coveralls for visible mercury, and respirator masks with mercury filters for areas with poor ventilation. Water sprays reduced dust in the workplace. Personal dosimeter badges in the field and blood tests before and after fieldwork monitored mercury levels.

Hazardous Field Methods and Technologies

Archaeological methods and technologies often create hazardous conditions in the field. The most obvious are deep excavations that leave high sidewalls capable of collapsing, the excavation of deep wells or privy pits, and excavations inside large structures such as pyramids or temple mounds. Open excavations left unprotected after work hours or that have not been backfilled after the excavation is completed create hazards. Protective fencing and backfilling are essential, not only to reduce risk to people and animals that come into the area, but also to help preserve the remaining archaeological record. Other field hazards that must be taken into account when developing a project-specific HASP include heavy equipment such as backhoes and graders as excavation tools at archaeological sites and electronic technologies such as total station transits that use lasers.

Logistical Hazards

Yet another set of hazards arises from the logistics of fieldwork. Transportation to and from the field is a significant source of hazards, with automobile accidents as the most common peril. Over approximately thirty years, for example, my field crews have had some kind of automobile accident every five or six years, none of which, luckily, caused any injuries to field crew members or students. A couple of these involved running into cattle on rural roads in open rangeland. Another originated from the common problem of becoming "mesmerized" while driving on the "loneliest road in America" through northcentral Nevada, drifting off the berm, and overturning. Yet another resulted from burning out brakes while driving down a steep mountain road. Clearly, the dangers of the road are many.

Other forms of transportation may be even more perilous. A colleague told me that in one year alone he used four-wheelers, helicopters, small single-engine planes, river rafts, and canoes to do archaeological fieldwork in the eastern interior of Alaska (see also George F. Bass, chapter 5).

Consider the following example of another logistical hazard encountered during archaeological fieldwork. Just outside of Lake City in the San Juan Mountains of southwestern Colorado lies "Little Rome," an early twentieth-century mining settlement once occupied by Italian immigrants. The site lies on a steep bank of Henson Creek, a tributary of the Lake Fork of the Gunnison River, and can be reached only by crossing a deep gorge. The only access is by walking over a narrow, 100-foot-high concrete dam that was constructed in the early part of the twentieth century and partially demolished later on to allow the creek to flow through. The journey across the dam is hazardous, with few guardrails or other barriers to protect pedestrians. What would be an appropriate and ethical safety plan for gaining access to the site? The government agency that sponsored the archaeological project first considered having the Colorado National Guard build a new footbridge across the gorge, but this plan didn't work out. The alternative plan was to use safety ropes and harnesses. Agency employees strung safety ropes along the top of the dam and secured them at each end. Field supervisors required archaeological field-workers crossing the dam to wear rock climbers' safety harnesses attached to the ropes, which provided a handrail for support. In the worst-case scenario, if a field-worker fell off the dam he or she would be suspended in the air by the safety harness until rescue. A psychological fear of heights still bothered some field-workers, but the plan minimized the risk of physical danger.

In addition to problems during travel, hazardous conditions occur in field camps. Common hazards, for example, include the propane tanks used to power stoves and refrigerators in the field. Another hazard comes from the geographical remoteness of many field camps, which makes it difficult to provide rapid medical attention in the case of emergencies. What about logistical emergencies in field camps? First and foremost, it is absolutely essential for the PI and field staff to ask questions about and discuss emergency issues before going into the field. An emergency plan should be developed and made available to all field-workers so that they will know what to do. Emergency equipment and contacts should be available at the field camp, which in remote sites might include a body bag for airlifts, a satellite phone or ground/air radio for rapid communication, and access to a helicopter to evacuate emergency cases rapidly.

Social and Psychological Hazards

The social and psychological environment of fieldwork is another source of hazards that must be considered. Hazardous social conditions that sometimes exist in and around archaeological field projects include warfare or terrorism, local communities that are suspicious of outsiders, urban archaeology in high-crime neighborhoods, *huaqueros* (vandals), illegal drug producers, and antigovernment zealots. My own fieldwork history illustrates the types of social hazards that can be encountered. As a student, my fieldwork in the mountains of eastern Kentucky brought me in contact with "moonshiners" operating illegal whiskey stills and with the gunfire of labor unrest at a nearby dam construction site. Years later, one of my first archaeological field schools took place in the western highlands of Guatemala accompanied by a military escort because of antigovernment guerillas operating in the region. More recently, fieldwork under a federal contract in a national forest in northeastern Nevada encountered antifederal zealots protesting the closure of a rural road in the forest for environmental reasons. Unquestionably, the first ethical issue to be raised about these and other situations of war and political unrest is whether or not archaeological fieldwork should take place at all. Assessing the risk of field-workers in individual cases requires, first and foremost, accurate information about the situation, which is often difficult to obtain beforehand. A decision to go ahead with the project demands that field-workers be made aware of the social situation and its potential risk. In many cases, of course, war and political unrest are totally unexpected, either because of bad information before going into the field or because of a new event. What is the ethical response? Abandoning the fieldwork and leaving immediately is one option, but the dictum of "do no harm" should be behind whatever action is taken.

Other sources of social and psychological hazards include the social dynamics of the field-workers themselves. Archaeological field camps in particular are often isolated in remote places. The idiosyncratic behavior and personalities of individuals sometimes lead to interpersonal conflicts that are magnified under field conditions. In extreme cases, such conflicts can create a perception of unsafe or insecure conditions in the field camp. As in situations of war and political unrest, risk assessment requires accurate information about the history and personalities of field-workers before going into the field.

Finally, archaeologists have an ethical obligation to protect the safety of people and animals living in localities where fieldwork is done. Sometimes, this involves building protective fences or other devices around excavations to be sure that local visitors, domestic animals, or wildlife do not fall in and injure themselves. At other times, the risk to local residents comes from the potential introduction of diseases carried by archaeological field-workers, a particularly important problem during the conduct of international fieldwork when historically long-separated populations come into contact. Yet, other safety risks come from social liaisons between field-workers and local residents that may lead to pregnancies or violent acts. What might seem harmless mating behavior such as dating of local residents can have quite harmful consequences, especially in socially and culturally remote places. Archaeological fieldwork does not take place in a social and cultural vacuum.

Conclusion

Archaeological fieldwork often takes place under hazardous conditions that put at risk the personal health and safety of field-workers. The ethical premise of "do no harm," reflected both in the codes of conduct of professional archaeological organizations and in governmental laws and regulations, demands that these risks to personal safety be minimized by overt actions. What should those actions be? The details obviously depend on the specific archaeological project, but there are several general guidelines. Site assessment and characterization, which includes gathering information ahead of time about hazards and how to respond to them from historical and legal documents, governmental agencies and nongovernmental organizations, local residents, and direct field observation (e.g., soil testing), are necessary actions. Traditional ecological knowledge from local people is an especially useful source of information. Develop HASPs for field projects. Awareness before going into the field is the key to safe conduct. Be aware of the physical, social, and cultural environment in which fieldwork is to be done. Make sure that field-workers are aware of potential problems and know how to respond to them before going into the field. Acquire and communicate information about the preexisting medical conditions of field-workers. Conduct prefieldwork training classes in field safety procedures (e.g., first aid and CPR, firearms use and safety). Use personal protective equipment in the field. Consult medical specialists and safety engineers for appropriate methods and tools when needed. Now, what advice would you give Indiana Jones on his next archaeological project?

Discussion Questions

1. Are the ethics of safety different for commercial (culture resources management) archaeology and academic archaeology? Should they be?
2. What are the ethical implications concerning safety when conducting fieldwork outside of the United States? Should U.S.-sponsored projects outside the United States abide by OSHA guidelines? Are they legally required to?
3. Is it ethical to ask archaeological field-workers to sign a blanket liability waiver? What are some of the possible consequences of doing so? Of not doing so?
4. What are the ethical implications concerning safety of doing archaeology at the site of the World Trade Center disaster? Should OSHA regulations have been rigorously followed in a case like this?
5. What are some of the ethical concerns for a project located in an area of political unrest?

6. What hazards have you encountered on field projects and how were they dealt with? Were you informed of them before going into the field? Could they have been avoided if you had been informed of them?

7. If a project is located in an area prone to earthquakes (or other potential natural or social threat), what precautions can be taken to ensure the safety of both personnel and the archaeological record—without making everyone paranoid? What additional costs are involved?

8. Your fieldwork at a large, well-known prehistoric site is completed. Although the site is located rather off the beaten track, substantial numbers of tourists come to visit it each year, contributing to the local economy—at least at the restaurants, where all stop for at least one meal. Typically, there are no monumental remains. In fact, the only excavated "features" visible are the three- to four-meter-deep trenches with their excellent stratigraphy. Left open, these trenches are dangerous—to people, wild and domestic animals, and the unexcavated archaeological remains. But if you backfill the trenches for safety, there will be nothing for the tourists to see. What should you do?

Recommended Readings

American Cultural Resources Association
  1996   Code of Ethics and Professional Conduct of the American Cultural Resources Association, at www.acra-crm.org/Ethics.html (accessed December 2002).

Archaeological Institute of America
  1994   Code of Professional Standards, at www.archaeological.org/About_the_AIA/CodePS.html (accessed April 2002).

European Association of Archaeologists
  1997   European Association of Archaeologists Code of Practice, at www.e-a-a.org/Codeprac.htm (accessed April 2002).

Institute of Field Archaeologists
  1985   Code of Conduct, at www.archaeologists.net/code.html (accessed April 2002).

Miller, Robert
  1984   Health Care on Field Projects. *Journal of Field Archaeology* 11(4):438–40.

Poirier, David A., and Kenneth L. Feder (editors)
  2001   *Dangerous Places: Health, Safety, and Archaeology.* Bergin and Garvey, Westport, CT.

K. ANNE PYBURN

Chapter Sixteen

What Are We Really Teaching in Archaeological Field Schools?

The Society for American Archaeology (SAA) has identified stewardship as the first priority of the professional archaeologist. This decision was based on the fact that although local and descendant communities may not always be in agreement with archaeologists about the need to excavate a site, they almost invariably agree on the need for site protection (Lynott and Wylie 1995b). The result is that the focus is on the greater good; even though some research may be curtailed, the resources themselves will continue to exist.

To most people, stewardship means "the wise use of resources [that] can include stabilizing an archaeological site, preserving it in place, excavation, or promoting public understanding of the information content of the resources through site development and interpretation" (Bender 2000:34). This priority has a number of ethical implications for field schools. In a pragmatic sense, it means that not all sites are available for excavation and fewer may be appropriate for training, since professional archaeologists may regard deposits as too complex or local and descendant groups may feel student behavior and naiveté are incompatible with some culturally important contexts. Even in situations where interested groups cannot prevent excavation or disallow the use of a site for training, the principle of stewardship makes it incumbent on the archaeologist to consider whether disregarding negative sentiments might lead to vandalism or the loss of access in the future. This principle also affects the teaching priorities of the field school, since students must be trained to place stewardship above their own personal priorities, and the instructor must prioritize it above the quality of the instruction and place teaching stewardship above teaching research technique. In other words, it is not acceptable to disturb ancient deposits simply because Janey needs to learn how to recognize and record stratigraphy. Janey's training must be a subsidiary part of a broader research design that ensures both the importance of the research questions pursued and the preservation and stewardship of the data that are recovered, as well as the data that remain unrecovered. The main thing that students learn must be stewardship.

What Do Students Really Need to Learn?

Striking a balance among stewardship, academic freedom, and teaching responsibilities is a complex ethical puzzle with no simple remedial formula. The practice of using paying students to provide the physical labor for archaeological research is a time-honored strategy for the chronically underfunded discipline of archaeology. But since my first field school experience with an excavator who referred to students as "warm bodies," the world has changed. A few archaeologists still take students to provide labor and money without much intention of teaching them anything, but this is increasingly rare, and it is really the tip of a much bigger and more dangerous iceberg. At least as important as the methodological training we give field school students is the example we set of how social scientists behave and how science is done that will leave them with a sense of respect for the field and for the archaeological record. Gone are the days when I was told "what you do in the field doesn't count," meaning that my personal behavior was irrelevant. Teaching stewardship means teaching students and showing them that, in the field, all their behavior counts.

Training students that stewardship comes first is not a trivial issue. The only way to teach this priority is to obey it ourselves in our every act, in and out of the field, in and out of our professional skins. In a recent SAA symposium on field schools, several of my colleagues surprised me by suggesting that although field schools cannot do professional-quality data recovery, this issue is alleviated if the sites chosen for excavation are endangered. Endangered sites are good for student excavations, they argued, because the data that will be lost in the interest of providing students with a positive experience and complete training would be lost anyway. I disagree with this on several levels; let me address them one at a time.

Are Some Sites More Equal Than Others?

First and foremost, *all* archaeological sites are endangered. There are no sites at which archaeologists can afford to work without haste; there is not enough money or time anywhere to support such a luxury. No one should cut corners and sacrifice data for expediency, but to say that some sites are less valuable because they are in danger creates a problematic dichotomy. If it is acceptable to lose data because a site is in danger, then we are accepting the same argument made by looters and collectors, who claim to be rescuing the artifacts they recover. This is a variation on what has come to be known as the "Elgin Excuse" (Elkins 1999), in reference to the claim of the collector that under her care artifacts were protected that might otherwise have been lost. Most collectors make this sort of argument; if we employ it, we reduce archaeology's priority to collecting and indulge in a sort of "we have to get it before they do" attitude that amounts to looting. This is the last sort of behavior we need to display to students.

To Teach Science, You Have to Do Science

The second issue to be considered here is the issue of research design. Even in the postmodern climate, archaeologists recognize the importance of being open and frank about the goals of their work, and of inviting criticism and improvement to their methods and interpretations. The traditional way of doing this is with a hypothesis that clearly lays out the archaeologist's intent and makes it available for discussion. The principle of stewardship seems to me to require archaeologists to be clear about their intentions, so the interested groups of both scientists and the public can consider whether the questions posed merit site destruction through excavation and promote the collection and stewardship of important data. Data are not the artifacts that appear in the screen, they are an intellectual construction that results from a research design that determines what information will be identified as relevant and therefore collected. Usually, this will include what appears in the screen. "The site is endangered" is not a research design; using this as a reason to excavate promotes the idea that the artifacts, rather than the generation of knowledge, are the focus. Again, this is not a lesson we want to teach students.

A South African colleague once told me that in contract work it was not possible to have the luxury of a research design. All we have time to ask is: What is there? I think this line of thinking is entirely wrong. In places where a great deal of contract research has been carried out from the perspective that data identify themselves to the archaeologist, companies required to pay for the research are beginning to ask why so many sites require investigation, all for exactly the same reasons. "This is the largest, best-preserved example that is known" is not a good research design, and implies that smaller, less well-preserved sites cannot be as important and that reconnaissance at similarly well-preserved sites will be obviated by this particular project. And of course, it equates data with artifacts.

A research design is not a luxury, but neither is it necessary to fetishize research design as some great theoretical mystery. Any archaeologist with reasonable competence in a relevant culture area can come up with a decent research design for an endangered site. The truth is that we know so little in most cases that valid questions grow on trees. And it is not true that each piece of investigation must be justified by revolutionary ideas. Normal science is important, too. That still requires a research design, which is in itself an indispensable pedagogical tool. It is the research design and the analysis fitted together through a well-planned methodology, not the excavation methodology alone or the number of artifacts collected, that make archaeology a science and distinguish it from looting.

It is easy to make this clear by taking apart the deceptively simple question: What is there? First, define the term "what": pollen, radiocarbon dates, pedology, soil chemistry, ecofacts, fire-cracked rock, dirt floors, soil stains from decayed metal objects, and poorly preserved bone are just a few of the sources of data that will not be collected if these sources are not anticipated by the research design. In order to define "what," it is necessary to know the literature of the area under investigation and to know not only what sorts of data are possible, but also what sorts of data are particularly needed for understanding. Now define the verb "is": It is necessary to have an idea or—better yet—a testable proposition about the relationship between what was at the site and what is at the site. This brings up the question of chronology: Which period or periods are being investigated? A British colleague who was excavating a medieval structure for reconstruction argued that simple discovery required no research design, but the question implicit in his work was: Which occupation of a structure that was inhabited and modified over several hundred years would be reconstructed? In all archaeological sites, what is there is an accumulation of things that were not all there at any particular time. How and how much of this will be discovered, recorded, and presented to the public and to science are aspects of a research design that both scholars and laypeople need access to in order to evaluate the work. And finally, define "there": This requires a definition of the site; no small task, since site boundaries are often unknown and are invariably determined by the questions posed by the excavator. It also introduces issues of sample design, fraction, and size. Clearly, we are now deeply involved in the construction of a research design. The important point here is that the idea that it is possible to excavate without a research design is a pretense and amounts to excavating with a poorly conceived implicit research design likely to be fraught with unexamined assumptions that would shrivel in the light of day. It is, in fact, looting.

Who Are We Kidding?

Regarding the ineptitude of students, I think the case for this is dramatically overstated. Of course, students do not start out knowing what they came to learn, but after all, this is not rocket science. If we mix inches with centimeters, the project will not come crashing down around our ears. Is it really going to alter what we know about Greek city-states if a student maps a piece of tumble ten centimeters off? Is it really going to spoil the reconstruction of the building if the student map gets the north arrow backward? I have made some pretty awful blunders in the field myself since I became a professional, and as often as not it was green and inexperienced students who reminded me, "Uh, Dr. Pyburn, shouldn't we draw that before you pick it up?" I suspect if we made an accurate assessment we would find that field school students pay more attention to routine tasks than many twenty-year veterans. Students need to be trained and monitored carefully, they need to be put on tasks that increase in the degree of competence they demand as they display more proficiency, and they need to be reminded that what they are doing is contributing to something interesting and important. We also need to be honest about how imperfectly even the most seasoned professionals take measurements and keep records, so that we do not use "scientism" to impress the public and terrorize students, or set standards that are unnecessarily stringent and waste time. Precise measurements do not substitute for knowing when to measure what.

Here, I want to make a plea for the integration of method and theory in the field training of students, because I believe this addresses the major complaint about the inadequacy of academic training as preparation for nonacademic careers. The vast majority of employment opportunities in archaeology are now outside academia, in contract firms and in government agencies (Zeder 1997). As this situation has arisen over the past decade, few academic programs have been able to readjust from training future professors to training future government agents and entrepreneurs. But it is now clear that the few students who take up academic positions will themselves be training private-sector and government archaeologists.

There is general agreement that academic programs are not providing the needed skills, and there are plenty of suggestions about what new material needs to be taught. Some employers have argued that more pragmatic training is needed, such as hands-on equipment training and statistical extrapolation or even budget and research cost estimation. Others have argued for improved "people skills," such as public speaking and popular writing. The problem for academics is that besides amounting to too many courses for an undergraduate curriculum and requiring expertise beyond what their own training provided, there is little agreement about exactly which of the many possible skills need to be taught. Firms and agencies differ greatly in reconnaissance techniques, machines, budgeting, and management styles, so no specific set of additional skills will prepare students for all possible or even all likely employment. I think the answer is not in training people in more specific skills but in how to make the intellectual connection between stewardship and reconnaissance and specific skills.

The real problem for employers is not that new employees do not know how to use the company's particular transit, of which there are several types with innumerable computer applications, but that the employee does not know exactly what a transit can do, when it needs to be used, and why it might or might not be a better choice than a dumpy level, a plane table, a tape and compass, or a laser transit. The question is not which buttons to press, but what sort of map is needed at what resolution and at what cost. This is the knowledge that needs to be acquired in the classroom—or the field school. If an employee can make this determination, she can familiarize herself with the most appropriate equipment on the job. She can also decide the best course of action when the optimal equipment is not available. I do not mean to argue that students do not need experience in using mapping machines, but only that learning why and when are as important as learning exactly how, since the absolute specifics cannot be covered for all situations. Similarly, the specifics of double entry bookkeeping or the details of proposal writing for a specific agency need not be the goal of academic training. But the ability to translate an idea about the past into a concrete set of procedures that can be used to estimate cost is a skill that needs to be taught and that can fit into a field school experience.

Science is not technique. Although part of field training is teaching students to use instruments and take measurements, field school programs sometimes elevate measurement and mechanical recording past the point of significance. The idea is to err on the side of caution, but this has some negative results. First of all it wastes time. Practicing is good, but students can learn to use a transit or a tape measure with a plumb bob *before* they go into the field. In some cases, where field time is expensive and complex, it may be worthwhile to put some time into technical training before the actual field season starts. Second, I have seen students knock unphotographed artifacts out of place because they were concentrating on reading the millimeter lines on the tape. What this means is that the methodology, rather than the data, has become the focus. No, I am not equating data with artifacts; it is the relationship between the artifact and the tape measure that is creating the data. Knowledge of the nature of this relationship almost invariably excludes the need to record millimeters.

Students easily forget that the priority is the data, especially when the purpose of the measurements and record keeping is not clear to them. I know from personal experience that field directors often emphasize perfect measurements rather than attempt to teach students to evaluate the requirements of a particular test. But this attitude backfires, since students cannot be accurate if they do not really understand what they are measuring. Measuring the distance from a stone tool to a wall is done to make a particular cultural inference or to test an idea about site formation, not just because all distances must be measured. In fact, I propose that students need to learn that some measurements are necessary in some contexts, unnecessary in others, to drive home the point that science is not the same as methodology, though it cannot be divorced from it. This returns us to the pedagogical importance of the research design.

What Are They Paying For?

The majority of American field school students are inexperienced undergraduates who will not become professional archaeologists. In the field, these students often feel that they have a right to expect food and housing comparable to their home setting and a guarantee of research experience comparable to what they would get in a classroom. They often consider themselves, with some justification, to be paying customers.

Fiscal cutbacks at American universities encourage pandering to student desires and expectations, but this is a bad idea, both for the students and for the research. If we knew exactly what we would find, we could be sure each student got an equal share of experience, but if we knew that much we would not need to dig. I tell every tentative participant in my projects that the goals of stewardship and of the scientific research design come first and that this may mean they do not all get equally trained in all aspects of the work. I do not dig up burials so everybody can get a chance to dig a burial; I do not dig test pits in the settlement so each student can dig his or her own test pit. If I am digging burials and test pits for good scientific reasons (that relevant parties accept), then I will see that students get as much exposure and experience as is possible and appropriate. I find that students are usually very receptive to being told that field conditions are strenuous and unpredictable, and they are ready to participate in an adventure. In fact, this aspect of fieldwork is often the part they like the most, and I think it may also be the most important for the future of archaeology.

What I find lacking in my students when they begin working in archaeology is an ability to see that some projects are more important than their individual comfort and experience. But when they do see this, when they perceive that they are sacrificing something (comfort, familiar food, and/or daily phone calls home) to an important goal such as scientific discovery, preservation, or economic development, they actually bloom under adversity and come away with a new respect for both research and for people who live outside their cocoon of American wealth. They also develop a new sort of self-confidence that I associate with joining a group committed to a higher purpose.

Perhaps the greatest gift I give my students (at least those who can be convinced to accept it) is the understanding that the knowledge generated by research and discovery, scholarship, and intellectual life is not only a source of power and authority, but also a source of entertainment and pleasure. The idea that knowledge has intrinsic value is new to most generation Xers and their descendants; television and mass media are easier, cheaper, and faster diversions. Most college freshmen would ridicule the idea that sitting in the bug-infested jungle and arguing about the interpretation of a stratigraphic section or the cultural processes implied by an intrusive burial is fun, but experiencing this sort of intellectual play changes them forever. I do not buy the argument that wielding the scientific method in the pursuit of any sort of fact can be justified as a contribution to science. Knowledge is not neutral and cannot simply be justified for its own sake, but it can certainly be enjoyed for its own sake, and when it is created in the service of well-designed stewardship, it should be.

When we overdetermine the field experience so each Jane and John gets exactly the same experience protected from surprises and discomfort, we encourage them to feel entitled to do archaeology because they paid for it and we deprive them of triumphing over adversity and of the real experience of discovery that is at the heart of science. This is the experience that is almost always transformational for young people. This is why I run field schools. Modern archaeology needs a diverse, creative, and resilient constituency and a supportive public that know that neither money nor background entitles anyone to do archaeology. Our research is a privilege that we undertake with commitment, sensitivity, and awe.

Gender

One issue implicit in a field school but usually not discussed is gender. Gender roles and expectations color the student's experience, the perception of local groups who invariably are curiously watching the archaeologists, and the collection of data, which is often done through implicitly gendered tasks. Gender also affects the interpretation of data with consequences that must be made explicit, because when we train students, we define the future. In a very real sense, educators determine what questions the next generation of archaeologists will ask and who will ask them. Field directors need to consider the gender system employed by the people who live where the field school will be held, and they need to pay attention to their own stereotypes as well (see Rita P. Wright, chapter 17).

Local Customs

Field schools create social contexts that have repercussions for both the participants and local communities. These contexts also affect the collection and interpretation of data. Commitment to stewardship requires that archaeologists take into account how the behavior of their students and staff affects the community's attitude toward archaeology. If drinking in camp or wearing halter tops in town is going to inspire the local villagers to try to prevent archaeologists (and anyone who claims to be an archaeologist) from coming back, then it is probably important to talk to students about the priorities of fieldwork. Students are often shocked to be asked to curtail their personal freedom to be respectful of local customs; they need to learn that this is also a part of being a professional archaeologist.

Stereotyping Students

Joan M. Gero recounts (1996) a story about two students excavating features in a field school. Both features were relatively undistinguished and contained similar data. The female student uncovered her feature carefully and neatly and the project director looked at it and took a quick photo and went away. The male student pedestalled his feature so that it stuck up out of his excavation by almost a foot. The project director was delighted with this feature and took innumerable photos of it, lavishing praise on the student excavator. Clearly, the students' behavior played into the unconscious bias of the project director. Other less obvious situations of gender bias occur constantly in field situations: women somehow do more washing and labeling of artifacts and more lab work, and men do more mapping and surveying. Students fall easily into gender stereotypes, but if we want a more inclusive discipline with a broader constituency, we need to think carefully about letting these roles appear in our field schools. Thinking carefully about these situations, it is easy to see how such stereotyping affects what archaeologists find out about the past.

Studies of classroom interaction show how teachers in American public schools socialize students into gendered behavior without ever being conscious of their impact (Sadker and Sadker 1994). Students pick up cues of encouragement and discouragement from teachers who unintentionally foster the idea that women do not like some tasks that men usually like. Situations that are threatening, challenging, and new, as are most field contexts, and in which people do not know each other well, but are subject to absolute authority, are situations most likely to call forth stereotypic behaviors. As social scientists, it is incumbent on field school directors to not only be aware of these social processes, but also to attempt to mitigate them. My own tactic is simply to talk openly about the issues with students and point out that we are all susceptible to such behavior.

In an important way, our interpretations of archaeological data affect our students. If we have already decided which activity areas are female and male and if we already are convinced that the division of labor in the past we investigate was a mirror of our own, then we may need to rethink whether we really need to dig. Are we finding out anything new? Whatever the conclusion, it is time we stopped "digging for the good of mankind."

This returns me to one final point about the pedagogical importance of research design. Researchers who treat their excavations as simple recovery that involves no decision making and no hypotheses or assumptions about the past contribute to a preexisting vision of the past that they may not actually want to promote. For example, when project directors discover only the phase of occupation of importance to a funding agency in the present day, without regard for the recognition or stewardship of other phases of occupation, they contribute to a vision of the past as somehow timeless and unchanging. So if that occupation happens to be one in which warfare was common or women were oppressed, they add one more support for the premise that war and oppression are normal or natural or human. Such constructions need to be made explicit not only because they suggest that improved research designs are needed, but also because students and volunteers should know what vision of the past they are contributing to with their tuition and labor. Archaeology is not a technology or an industry with a single goal; it is a science that involves the selection of some questions, data, and research designs over others. As has been pointed out, archaeological data tell many stories about the past, but not all the stories are equally accurate or good. It is incumbent on professional archaeologists to make clear to the public and to themselves what it is that their research will try to find out and to be aware of the repercussions that may result.

Conclusion

I have proposed that the priority of stewardship creates an ethical context and a set of standards and considerations that apply to field schools. I have focused on the implications of the ethics of stewardship for teaching students, local communities, and descendent people through field schools. I have also considered some things that should not be taught. I have discussed ways in which research design, personal behavior, and archaeological interpretation have ethical repercussions for the future of our discipline and our success as stewards of the archaeological record. I chose gender to exemplify ethical aspects of identity in the field and in archaeological interpretation, since I can speak to those issues from personal experience. Nevertheless, I suspect that most of my observations about gender apply to other facets of identity, including race, class, and age distinctions.

Discussion Questions

1. What information and background should be provided to students *before* they arrive at the field school site?
2. Why is it important to explain the point of your research to students and the public?
3. Does it matter whether students are aware that there may be political repercussions of the investigations they help carry out?
4. What is the best way to teach students the relationship between method and theory?
5. What difference does it make to the research design that a site is endangered?

Note

During my first semester in graduate school at the University of Arizona, I took a course in archaeological method and theory from Michael B. Schiffer. He taught that it was necessary to use a problem-oriented research design so that research could be evaluated; that cultural resource management was scientific research just like any other archaeological research and must begin with a problem-oriented research design to justify its use of resources (time, money, and sites); that different sorts of maps were necessary for different reasons and what some of the different maps and reasons were; and that the connection between fieldwork and ideas about the past (which he sometimes called middle-range theory) was the most important part of what archaeologists do, and the hardest. He gave us a number of exercises that he and his previous students had invented to help us get the hang of making that connection. Much of the foregoing is a paraphrase of what I learned from that class. (The reader should bear in mind that I made an A-.) The rest of my suggestions are from things I have learned from field school students working with me in Belize during the past twenty years. My original draft was read and significantly improved by the editors of this volume and by Barb Roth.

Recommended Readings

Bender, Susan, and George Smith (editors)
    2000   *Teaching Archaeology in the 21st Century.* Society for American Archaeology, Washington, DC.

Making Archaeology Teaching Relevant in the XXI Century Project
    2002   at www.rihla.org/matrix/index.html (accessed December 2002).

Smardz, Karolyn, and Shelley J. Smith
    1997   *The Archaeology Education Handbook: Sharing the Past with Kids.* AltaMira, Walnut Creek, CA.

RITA P. WRIGHT

Chapter Seventeen

Gender Matters—A Question of Ethics

In the United States, gender equity issues are covered by federal and state laws, but in what ways do they, along with ethical and moral codes, play out in the domain of archaeology? How does our behavior in workplace settings—field, laboratory, classroom, or other—contribute to gender inequities? In what ways do archaeologists and their archaeological research suffer when workplace conditions fail to adhere to legal, ethical, and moral codes?

In this chapter, I address various gender matters specifically covered by federal laws and others that are not. They include discrimination involving various "money matters," such as hiring, salary, and advancement (Euben 2001); sexual harassment, such as overt but unwanted sexual advances; hostile environments, such as behaviors with sexual overtones that are persistent and "severe or pervasive" (Alger 1998:36) enough to inhibit an individual worker's ability to perform to full capacity; and chilly climate issues, such as invisible barriers brought about by conscious or unconscious discrimination, for example, by excluding women from important committees or informal working groups or failing to appoint them as supervisors of important research projects, in spite of their equal performance and productivity (Wylie 1995b; Nelson, Nelson, and Wylie 1994).

According to Virginia Valian (1998), these inequities frequently are the result of entrenched stereotypical beliefs that she refers to as "gender schemas." Gender schemas are "intuitive hypotheses about the behavior, traits and preferences of men and women, boys and girls" (11) that impact our ideas about appropriate roles and behaviors that affect our expectations of others. Valian's argument is based on statistical studies conducted in the laboratory and in the field and on her interpretation of the ways in which psychological processes interact with social and economic ones (1). In *Why So Slow?*, she argues that gender schemas are not unique to either sex. They begin to develop in childhood learning and are built on through life experiences. When men and women bring gender schemas to workplace settings, they affect their evaluations of the performance of others; when professional ideals conflict with perceptions of appropriate behaviors for women, they can profoundly retard a woman's career.

There are many instances in which gender schemas have been mapped onto archaeological workplaces, for example, when more valued tasks are assigned to men, and less valued ones to women. In archaeology, work in the dirt takes precedence over the laboratory, which tends to be considered less exciting or discovery oriented and more repetitive, like housekeeping (Gero 1994). Women are often assigned to laboratory duties, while men excavate because fieldwork is thought to be too strenuous for women or to protect them from workmen who use crude language. Female students have also been asked to do the cooking, grocery shopping, and laundry collection, while male students have rebuilt the sifters, conducted field surveys, or cleaned the tools. Although these examples might seem inconsequential or trivial, they add up to an accumulation of disadvantages that eventually result in disparities involving women's prestige and their perceived value to the field. As Valian points out, "It is unfair to neglect even minor instances of group-based bias, because they add up to major inequalities" (1998:3).

Aside from our notions of fairness, are these issues vital to archaeology and archaeologists as professionals? After all, great strides *have* been made in advancing the status of women, as more and more have entered the profession. Might we not expect that in the fullness of time or through some sort of progressive "evolution" women will gain parity with men? For the remainder of this chapter, I explore gender inequalities by providing a more in-depth analysis of various legal, ethical, and moral issues of relevance to this discussion.

What Are the Legal, Ethical, and Moral Codes?

There are laws designed to prevent gender discrimination and sexual harassment. Four involve hiring, salaries, and promotion: the Equal Pay Act, Title VII of the Civil Rights Act, Title IX of the Education Amendments, and Executive Order 11246. Specifics regulations are written into each law. Broadly, they require equal pay for equal work; prohibit discrimination in wages, employment, hiring, promotion, and dismissal based on race, color, religion, sex, and national origin; provide protection against sex discrimination for individuals working at educational institutions that receive federal funding; and mandate "affirmative action for minorities and women" (Euben 2002:82). Sexual harassment and so-called hostile environments are covered under Title VII of the Civil Rights Act of 1964, Equal Employment Opportunity Commission in Its Final Amendment to Guidelines on Discrimination because of Sex, Part 1604. Some of the statutes may apply only to academic institutions or other organizations that accept federal grants, whereas others apply equally to nonacademic and academic contexts.

Many professional organizations contain sections in their ethical codes that pertain to gender inequities and sexual harassment. For example, the ethical codes of the American Sociological Association and the American Psychological Association include strong sanctions against each of these practices. When it comes to the three professional organizations that archaeologists are most likely to join, the American Anthropological Association (AAA), the Society for American Archaeology (SAA), and the Archaeological Institute of America (AIA), the situation is mixed. Both the AAA and AIA include sanctions against sexual harassment and sections on discriminatory practices that could be construed to include wage, promotion, and hiring equity. The SAA does not include either gender equity or sexual harassment in its Principles of Ethics.

In the AIA Code of Professional Standards, "Responsibilities" include: "I. To the archaeological record"; "II. To the public"; and "III. To colleagues." Item four in section III states: "Professional archaeologists should not practice discrimination or harassment based on sex, religion, age, race, national origin, disability, or sexual orientation; project sponsors should establish the means to eliminate and/or investigate complaints of discrimination or harassment." A specific grievance procedure is outlined that includes the responsibility of the AIA to "ensure that the highest standards of professional and ethical conduct are followed in all archaeological research." For the full statement, consult the AIA website (see the appendix).

Two sections of the AAA code are relevant. On the question of research on human subjects, anthropologists are obliged to "respect the well-being of humans." This statement could be construed to include sexual harassment and conceivably other forms of equity, such as compensation of informants. A section on "responsibility to students and trainees" specifically addresses teaching and mentoring: "Teachers/mentors should conduct their programs in ways that preclude discrimination on the basis of sex, marital status, 'race', social class, political convictions, disability, religion, ethnic background, national origin, sexual orientation, age, or other criteria irrelevant to academic performance." Under section "IV. Teaching. Responsibility to students and trainees," it states: "Teachers/mentors should be aware of the exploitation and serious conflicts of interest which may result if they engage in sexual relations with students/trainees. They must avoid sexual liaisons with students/trainees for whose education and professional training they are in any way responsible." For the full code, see the AAA website (see the appendix).

Although in both the AIA and AAA codes sexual harassment and gender equity are addressed, there are some key differences. The AAA code stresses the power differential in the student/trainee relationship, and while it appears not to exclude sexual relations in consensual relationships, it does caution against "serious conflicts of interest" that may result in the student/trainee situation. The reference to discrimination may be construed to include equity practices with respect to money matters, but since it appears in the section on teaching and mentoring, it most likely would not include all workplace settings. The AIA language is clear in its intent to exclude sexual harassment and other forms of discrimination, apparently inclusive of money matters, and among colleagues not exclusively in teacher/mentor relations. It is much stronger in its requirement that those responsible for workplaces, for example, a project leader, assume the responsibility to "establish the means to eliminate and investigate complaints" to ensure that discriminatory practices and sexual harassment do not exist. Finally, specific procedures are included with which to implement deviations from the AIA code by taking responsibility for monitoring grievances and adjudicating them through its ombudsperson and Professional Responsibilities Committee. The AAA, on the other hand, does not accord any specific responsibility to an expedition leader and provides no specific procedures for implementation or involvement of the AAA code.

Considering the previous discussion, it is surprising that the SAA does not include sanctions against gender equity and sexual harassment that are found in the codes of other comparable professional societies. As it stands, the SAA narrowly defines our responsibilities as archaeologists to the material world and leaves out other important work in which we engage as professionals and colleagues—attention to the full scope of what we do as teachers, mentors, and leaders in other capacities and acknowledgment that our behavior in these contexts affects the success of the work being performed, as will be shown in the following examples. The absence of attention to gender matters is curious considering the conscious efforts archaeologists make to avoid other forms of discrimination. Finally, if we concede that a diversity of perspectives affects our understanding of the past, then a code of ethics that addresses gender equity and sexual harassment should be a positive step in that direction.

How Do Gender Inequities and Sexual Harassment Affect Archaeology and Archaeologists?

The most reliable sources of data with which to track gender inequities of relevance to the laws and ethical codes described are the long-term studies of academic salaries and hiring practices conducted by the American Association of University Professors (AAUP) and the AAA, some limited information from the 1994 SAA census, and other published data. Unfortunately, there is little available data with which to track employment in other sectors, such as museums, the National Park Service, or cultural resource management (CRM).[1]

With respect to salaries, we might expect that with the increasing numbers of women entering the academy they would have achieved parity. However, the AAUP data shows persistent, long-term differences between the salaries of men and women when differences are controlled for rank, institutional category, and public and private institution. For example, in a comparison of the periods between 1975 to 1988, and 1988 and 1998, there were "substantial" disparities in average salaries at all ranks.[2] The principal differences may be the result of the proportion of women compared to men employed at research universities, where salaries are higher than at master's- or bachelor's-granting institutions, and of the fewer numbers of women at the full professor rank.

The published data from the AAA are not broken down by subfield. In anthropology as a whole, 57 percent of the doctorates conferred in 1998 were to women (American Anthropological Association 1999). Following trends observed by the AAUP data, records of hiring practices indicate that women were employed in much lower proportions (38 percent) at doctorate-granting institutions. Fifty-nine percent of men earned salaries between $45,000 to $59,000, whereas 60 percent of females earned $35,000 to $44,999. These salary discrepancies most likely were the result of the same factors as the AAUP data, that is, women's lower employment in doctorate-granting institutions and possibly their lower numbers in the higher ranks. The 1994 SAA census documented gaps in a variety of money matters, such as pay and funding, between men and women archaeologists (Zeder 1997).

Another factor in salary disparities is in hiring practices and the pace with which women are promoted. Women may earn lower salaries because they advance more slowly as the result of bias in assignment of initial rank (Haignere 2002) or glass-ceiling factors that block their promotion (Valian 1998; Sonnert and Holton 1995a). For example, Donna R. Euben (2001) cites a case in which the AAUP chapter at Kent State University filed a complaint under Executive Order 11246 with the Office of Federal Contract Compliance. The case was based on data that showed substantial disparities in the 7.38-year difference in the time spent by men and women at the assistant professor rank. Of 464 men, the median time to promotion was 9.55 years; of 229 women, median time to promotion was 16.93 years. The longer time as assistant professors is estimated to have cost women $10,000 each.

Three data sources provide information relevant to promotion and hiring in anthropology and archaeology. The 1994 SAA census is based on responses from individual scholars. In that census, 24 percent of women in academic positions reported their rank as professors, 30 percent as associate, and 39 percent as assistant (Zeder 1997:100). The AAA data for 1995–1996 (1994–1995 was unavailable) for anthropology as a whole is based on responses from department chairs for individual departments. These data show that 26 percent of women were at the full professor rank, 39 percent at associate, and 53 percent at assistant professor rank. Finally, data analyzed by Pam Willoughby (1999) based on published information in *Lingua Franca* and the *AAA Guide to Departments of Anthropology* for hires of archaeologists for the years 1996–1999 show that of 266 tenure-track positions filled during that period, 14.3 percent went to archaeologists. Of the thirty-eight archaeologists hired into tenure-track positions, fourteen were women and twenty-four were men. During the same period, thirty-two archaeologists were tenured, nine women and twenty-three men; four others were hired with tenure, one woman and three men.

These data suggest that there were substantial disparities in percentages of women at the associate and assistant ranks in the subfield of archaeology as compared to anthropology as a whole and that in archaeology, the proportion of women hired into new positions and tenured was significantly lower than men.

Additionally important are data on part-time versus full-time employment. These data show that the majority of part-time positions are held by women. In anthropology as a whole, the AAA for 1997 data show 54 percent were women and 46 percent men. In the 1994 SAA census, 60 percent of women identified themselves in a category labeled "visiting professor." Data from a 1996 AIA census shows that 69 percent of women held temporary and part-time positions (Cullen 1998).

When we turn to sexual harassment, no statistical data are available, therefore I have relied on legal case studies, anecdotal accounts, and hypothetical examples. Although sexual harassment is by no means common, where it does occur, studies show that it is rooted in the psychological dynamics of the individual and the sexism present in our society. While what motivates the individual is poorly understood, societal factors reflect on concepts of gender stratification, power differentials, and the license that power provides (Zalk 1990:142). They come into play when teachers or mentors harbor misguided assumptions about appropriate sexual conduct. As Jill Kerr Conway, the president of Smith College between 1975 and 1985, explains, some faculty believe paternalistically "that pats on the behind or a little fondling should be accepted as a compliment, willfully unaware that it is annoying at best to be defined sexually by someone you want to take you seriously as a mind" (2001:44).

Women in such situations or others subjected to more overt sexual acts often feel as if they are held hostage because they fear reprisals that may come about as a result of rejecting unwanted advances. Although they may be outraged, they also may feel ashamed and even blame themselves, fearing that they provoked the unwanted sexual advances. There is a veil of silence about sexual harassment that keeps us from educating ourselves about what does and does not constitute sexual harassment and what paths we might follow if we or one of our colleagues or students finds herself in such a position. It is important to discuss sexual harassment openly while cautiously attending to fairness to all individuals involved—perpetrator and victim—and following appropriate procedures.

The implementation of sexual harassment legal codes can be challenging, as the following unsuccessful case made by a thirty-three-year-old graduate student in psychology against a male supervisor demonstrates. The student

> had an outside practicum at a counseling center, where her supervisor allegedly spent much of his time with her discussing his troubled personal relationships. He asked her out to dinner and for walks, wrote her romantic notes, and gave her poems and a book entitled *How to Make Love All the Time*. On one occasion, he placed his hand on her knee and started to slide it up her leg. She did not, however, have a sexual relationship with him, and she was able to complete the

practicum with a favorable final evaluation. A federal district court found that although the supervisor's conduct was "probably disconcerting and certainly inappropriate," it was not necessarily "conduct of a sexual nature" and did not rise to the level of sexual harassment. (Alger 1998:35)

The perplexing outcome of this case appears to be the result of complexities involved in defining sexual harassment and other associated factors. Circumstances that may have contributed to the judge's decision, according to Jonathan R. Alger, are that in the field of counseling discussion of one's emotions could be conceived as reasonable and while touching the student's leg would appear to fall out of the bounds of reasonableness, her age could be a factor. "If the student had been younger, or if the supervisor had touched her leg more than once" (37), the court's decision might have been different.

In archaeology, we all know of instances where women have been subjected to unwanted sexual advances, common enough in other fields, but particularly devastating in fieldwork situations or in the power differentials between students and teachers/mentors. Sexual harassment occurs in all varieties, including male to male, female to male, male to female, and female to female, and involves students and supervisors, bosses, maintenance workers in the buildings in which we work, and so forth.

Two hypothetical examples stress the ways in which sexual harassment affects individual archaeologists, their employment, research, and teaching. They are hypothetical scenarios that conform to the kinds of workplace settings in which archaeologists typically find themselves.

The first incident occurred between two colleagues, Jack and Jill, in connection with a successful field school that they conducted under the sponsorship of the different undergraduate institutions in which they taught. The field school provided its students with survey and excavation experience and the opportunity to conduct small research projects. Jill and Jack worked well together and routinely shared a late afternoon snack and beer at Jack's home after work, when they organized the next day's activities. On one unfortunate occasion, when Jack's wife was out of town, Jack made aggressive sexual advances that included sufficient bodily contact that Jill literally had to fight him off. After a lot of resistance, yelling, and name calling on the part of both Jack and Jill, she was able to break away and leave. Jill was outraged and immediately drove to the home of a friend, a psychologist, to talk over the incident. She searched her memory for any provocative acts that might have misled her colleague, going over the details of the encounter step by step. Fortunately, Jill's friend was able to point out to her that Jill seemed to be blaming herself for what had occurred, in spite of the fact that she was outraged. Her friend was able to show her just how wrong and how typical her reaction was among many women faced with the situation she described. Interestingly, when Jill returned to her office, there was a message from Jack, in which he explained that she appeared to be unaware of "the rules of the game." Apparently he was, because as a way of preserving the secret of his abortive advances, Jack offered her access to some important research materials. Jill never bothered to phone him back.

Although Jack was senior to Jill, like Jack she was a tenured professor. She never pressed any charges but decided to stay away from collaborating with Jack and having any further contact with him. But sometimes incidents of this sort are never forgotten. Years later at a large public gathering, Jack introduced Jill as one of the most stubborn individuals in archaeology, stating to others present that they should be cautious if they were thinking of collaborating with her. But by then Jill did know the "rules of the game" and realized that the perpetrator of this myth had a large reputation and no one present was likely believe him.

A second situation involved Nancy, a supervisor at a prestigious CRM firm whose coprincipals were Sam Knot and Susan Cann. Nancy reported an incident to Susan that had occurred the previous day during working hours, when Sam made unwanted advances, used troublesome language in a conversation, and hinted that if she objected to his invitation to have sex with him that she would be excluded from working on a major project for which she had been largely responsible for gaining a contract. Susan listened incredulously, since Sam had never been accused of these behaviors in the past, although she did remember that Sam had mentioned to her on several occasions that he found Nancy very attractive. What Nancy described sounded very real, though since it had occurred behind closed doors, it was going to be hard to prove. Susan asked Nancy to think about the possible actions that could be taken (ignore it, leave the firm, confront Sam, and/or follow company procedures that had been put in place though they had never been applied to a principal in the firm) and to very seriously evaluate the impact each course would have on her career—because it *was* going to impact her career whether she spoke up or shoved it under the table, as happened with Jack and Jill. She told Nancy that whatever she decided, she would guide her through the appropriate procedures. The following morning Susan received a call from Nancy, who had decided that Sam needed to be confronted; she and Susan set up an appointment to meet with him. Sam was outraged at the allegation, saying he was just "kidding around" and that Nancy should "lighten up." Both Nancy and Susan were incredulous on hearing Sam's response. Eventually, Nancy decided to file an official written complaint. This case is still pending, but in the meantime, Nancy has not been able to work on the project for which she won the contract and is thinking about leaving the firm. It should be noted that whether or not Nancy filed the complaint, Susan probably would have been obligated to investigate the matter in order to protect the firm. As a superior officer to whom the incident had been disclosed, the firm would have been on notice that harassment might be occurring and that it needed to take steps to stop that conduct.

These two situations differ in the power differentials and the ultimate decisions made by the individuals involved, but they share important characteristics. Although each woman came to a different solution, both took time to decide what action to take, found a trusted and knowledgeable person with whom to discuss the matter, decided on a course of action, and then gave judicious consideration to the consequences. The second incident falls most clearly into the federal legal codes and ethical principles of the AAA and AIA. The outcome of the first probably would not have been successful if filed as a legal complaint, if the example provided earlier in this chapter is any indication, since both were mature adults and both held tenure, that is, were roughly equal in status. The second incident would seem to fall within all the codes described in this chapter, although that need not predict the actual outcome.

Beyond these legal considerations, the losses to archaeology were significant in both instances. A successful field school came to an end because colleagues were no longer able to work together. If they had been forced to do so—if they had been employed in the same department—the teamwork, cooperation, and mutual respect required in resolving departmental matters and in fieldwork would have been absent in the aftermath of the sexual harassment. In the case of Nancy and Sam, delays and the potential success of the work resulted from Nancy's nonparticipation, since she was the most qualified person in the office. There also would be a significant loss to Sam and Susan. Sam's reputation and his effectiveness as a leader were diminished; he also lost the good will of his partner. Susan was faced with conflicting loyalties and a potential lawsuit against the firm. Devastated on a personal and professional level, Nancy was forced to consider changing jobs, thus Susan and Sam faced losing a valued employee.

Gender in Archaeology—Challenging Gender Schemas and Recoding Items in Memory

Although there clearly are workplaces where strong sanctions are in place against sexual harassment and hostile environments and in which well-advised leaders and colleagues are working toward gender equity—even have achieved it—much remedial work remains to be done toward these ends in archaeology. Organizations like the AAA and AIA have assumed some responsibility by including these factors in their ethical principles, recognizing that archaeologists engage in roles beyond stewardship and preservation of the material past, as teachers, professors, mentors, heads of laboratories and contract firms, curators and conservators, attorney and university administrators, and in many other professional capacities. A code of ethics should conceive of an archaeologist's professional life in broader and more inclusive terms than currently represented in the SAA code. Inclusion of this chapter in a book on archaeological ethics provides a window into the legal, ethical, and moral issues involved and the potential ways to modify or reconfigure current ethical standards. Archaeologists still need to take an active role in these debates

Some might protest that since federal laws and social sanctions address gender equity and sexual harassment, there is no need to have them covered in a professional code of ethics. Many professional organizations, however, have taken the lead in helping to rectify social and legal issues in the interest of raising the professional standards of their disciplines. The SAA has taken an active role in debates covered by governmental policies with respect to repatriation and antiquities laws. It would be consistent to turn to its own house and current membership by adding gender equity and sexual harassment concerns to its ethical principles.

Both the SAA and AAA have a Committee on the Status of Women that disseminates and collects data on the status of women; these committees need the full cooperation of their respective executive boards. The SAA committee should have access to concrete data, equal to that already supplied by the AAA, with which to track long-term trends in the status of women in the profession. The knowledge acquired through such studies assists women archaeologists in maneuvering successfully within the various workplaces they inhabit.

All institutions, whether in the public or private sectors, in academic or nonacademic settings, ought to have prescribed rules of conduct that are published and disseminated to employees. Archaeologists should lead their organizations toward establishing grievance procedures for equity in hiring, salary, and promotion and for formal and informal systems for reporting sexual harassment and submitting complaints. Some organizations have well-developed lines of communication that include committees or individuals responsible for implementing institutional policies.

More effective than remedial policies and procedures are preventive measures. First, men and women both need to understand what constitutes gender inequity and sexual harassment, be conversant with federal and local laws, and adhere to the ethical standards of their professional and institutional codes. Organizations, universities, and departments should establish objective criteria for the evaluation of employee performance, apply them consistently, and make them available to all employees (Euben 2001). With respect to sexual harassment, dialog can be established through seminar formats or publications that outline institutional policies and procedures so that men and women have a clearer understanding of what constitutes appropriate behavior. Although some women may still experience sexual harassment, they may be more able to avoid being victimized by it (Dziech and Weiner 1984). By the same token, individuals involved in sexual harassment may achieve a better understanding of the long-term rewards of changes in their behavior. In academic contexts, these rewards "include better communication with students, improved teaching effectiveness, and eventual realization of equal educational opportunity for all students" (Paludi 1990:19). In other workplace settings, supervisors, managers, or others in leadership positions can reap the same rewards in their interactions with colleagues.

Finally, a significant barrier to equality for women in archaeology may be its masculinist image.[3] This factor is relevant because when gender schemas become attached to professions, women may be perceived as "slightly unsuited . . . because [their] gender doesn't fit in" and their work is devalued as a result (Valian 1998:15). The Indiana Jones image of the quintessential archaeologist is clearly embedded in the public consciousness and to some degree within the discipline itself, as much as we may abhor his methodology! The recent introduction of the buxom Lara Croft is unlikely to constitute an improvement in reshaping the image. A major change needs to occur within the discipline itself. As a first step, we should implement the gender equity and sexual harassment policies discussed in this chapter insofar as we are able and carefully examine the histories we construct of the past and of our discipline, including the ways in which we regard the contributions of women.

Until recently, women have been all but invisible from the archaeological past. Viewed in that context, the absence of attention to gender equity in the present may reflect the same unstated assumptions that contributed to decades of archaeological research in which gender issues were not addressed. As archaeologists, we have been interested in the social relations of workplaces but failed to treat them as engendered places. Closer to the home front is our construction of histories of the discipline in which women archaeologists, though they have made important contributions, have almost totally been ignored. Several new biographies of Anna Shepard, Gertrude Bell, Dorothy Garrod, and other female archaeologists (Claassen 1994; Levine 1994; Romanowicz and Wright 1996) may partially rectify this. Troubling, however, with respect to the value we accord to women's work is Scott R. Hutson's (2002) recent study of gendered citation practices in *American Antiquity* and other journals. Citation rates are a strong measure of the value accorded to research. Hutson's study shows that the works of women were cited at a rate significantly below their rate of publication, irrespective of the gender of the citing author. This result runs counter to studies in other fields in which women were cited more frequently (Sonnert and Holton 1995b) than better-published men. It suggests that the gender schemas discussed in this chapter with respect to gender inequities and sexual harassment are present in more subtle forms that continue to inhibit a smooth trajectory toward gender parity.

Discussion Questions

1. What are the gender statistics for faculty (by rank) and students in your department?
2. What examples of chilly climates or gender schemas have you encountered in your archaeological experiences (classes, labs, fieldwork, and so on)? Did you or anyone else report or discuss them with anyone in a position of authority? Why or why not?
3. What role have female archaeologists played in the history of the discipline in your area of interest? How easy or hard is it to find out?

4. Explore the various legal and ethical codes that pertain to sexual harassment by searching the Internet for the full text. Check out websites for various professional website organizations not included in this discussion, for example, the Society for Historical Archaeology, the Society for Ethnohistory, or any other organization that you consider relevant. Where does each code stand with respect to consensual relationships? Where do you stand on this issue? What are the pros and cons?

5. Take the example given in this chapter concerning Nancy, Sam, and Susan at the CRM firm and change it into an academic situation. Nancy is either a graduate or undergraduate student and Sam and Susan are professors. Nancy and Sam (Professor Knot) are working together on a research project that she hopes to use for her honors thesis or dissertation project. What legal and ethical codes would apply? What are Susan's (Professor Cann's) responsibilities? Must she report the incident to her chair, and the chair report to the administration? How should Nancy proceed?

Notes

Many individuals contributed to this chapter and I wish to thank each of them. Graduate students and faculty in the anthropology department, especially Uzma Rizvi, at the University of Pennsylvania, provided me with many ideas for improving an initial draft that I presented at an archaeology colloquium. Muriel Poston of the AAUP's Committee on the Status of Women in the Academic Profession and members of the Committee W listserv assisted in supplying me with several references to ethical codes outside of the archaeological profession. Donna Euben, a counselor at the AAUP, read an earlier draft of this chapter and provided invaluable consultation on various points. Silvia Tomaskova, Julie Hollowell-Zimmer, and Karen D. Vitelli also provided insightful commentary relevant to archaeology. My thanks as well to the editors of this volume for their patience.

1. The SAA Committee on the Status of Women in Archaeology has been planning a full-scale study of CRM firms. Results of a pilot project based on a sample population of sixty-six individuals (thirty-seven men and twenty-nine women) show that 57 percent of women were in the top two highest salary categories (Hutira and Green 2000). Currently, this study is being extended to include 500 firms and as many as 1,650 individuals, but as an independent research project that is not sponsored by the SAA. Other studies of museums and governmental employment sectors may be developed in the future. Data available from the 1994 SAA census gave a different result in that salaries for women were lower than men employed in CRM sectors, perhaps reflecting the fact that larger numbers of men are chief executive officers.

2. These data and analyses are published by Ernst Benjamin (1998). Differences found at research universities and at the full professor rank are documented by Linda A. Bell (2001).

3. See Rita P. Wright and Mary Anne Levine (2000) for a discussion concerning the results of a questionnaire submitted by Warren R. DeBoer (1999) to his undergraduates, in which

seventy-six students (thirty-three female and forty-three male) were asked to draw an archae-ologist. Female students drew twice as many male archaeologists as female archaeologists.

Recommended Readings

Alger, Jonathan R.
 1998   Love, Lust and the Law: Sexual Harassment in the Academy. *Academe* 84(5):34–39.

Dziech, Billie Wright, and Linda Weiner
 1984   *The Lecherous Professor.* Beacon, Boston.

Euben, Donna R.
 2001   Show Me the Money: Salary Equity in the Academy. *Academe* 87(4):30–36.

Paludi, Michele A. (editor)
 1990   *Ivory Power: Sexual Harassment on Campus.* SUNY Press, Albany.

Valian, Virginia
 1998   *Why So Slow? The Advancement of Women.* MIT Press, Cambridge.

Chapter Eighteen

The Ethics of Research Knowledge

The editors of the present volume, inviting me to write this chapter, asked me to address "ethics in publication"—meaning the obligations of archaeologists to publish their work, associated issues of copyright, and so on. At my request, I broadened the subject to "ethics of research knowledge"; but within this, "ethics in publication" is a large issue, and within that I start with copyright. Publication, especially its copyright issues, is both a major area where ethics and attitudes toward research knowledge arise and a useful place to outline principles that apply more widely.

I take the view that ethics are about ideals and about the good behavior that sustains ideals. Exploring ethical issues in that frame, I then acknowledge that these ideals are expressed in a less-than-ideal real world.

Copyright as a Principle and in Law

Copyright, as the two words show from which this term was invented, concerns the right to copy and the right to prevent copying. Copyright gives the creator of a creative work exclusive rights to use it, and forbids others to copy it without the creator's consent. Invented to bring order to the world of book printing and publication, copyright now applies not only to books and writing of all kinds, but to drawings, graphics, photography, radio, film, and television and to all the digital media. Its principles are robust and straightforward; much copyright law and practice is more obscure and—as in other realms of life—U.S. law and practice have been idiosyncratic when set alongside common practice in other jurisdictions. Although they are more homogeneous now, different national legislations deal with copyright each in slightly different ways.

Copyright is awash with common misapprehensions such as: "Something becomes copyright when and only when you put the copyright sign, ©, the date, and your name on it." Not so; that affirms your copyright, and may help in legally defending it, but it does not create the copyright, which existed already. "Everything on the Internet is in the public domain unless someone specifically claims copyright to it." Not so; copyright exists in the usual way on the Web just as it does in print on paper, it's just that improper copying is so easy in the digital world that wrong and casual copying of others' copyright materials has become habitual there.

Copyright starts from the notion that *any* written, graphic, or other creative work is the rightful and exclusive property of its creator. The present chapter you are reading, for instance, was my copyright when I wrote it; that creation of a copyright text came about automatically by the act of my writing it—I did not have to do anything more to secure it. So is the letter with which I sent it to the volume editors (even if it was not a fine piece of writing!), and so would be the cartoon sketch of them or of me with which I decorated (or defaced) the envelope I sent it in, had I happened to do that.

To balance the private interests of the creator against those of the public good, copyright runs for a limited period only, generally for the whole lifetime of the creator plus a period of seventy years. At the end of that year, copyright ceases and the work moves into the "public domain," which means it belongs to no one; then anyone can use it and exploit it as he or she wishes. Gordon Childe died in 1956, so all his work is "in copyright" until the end of 2026; at the start of 2027, it will move into the public domain. Between 1956 and 2027, like any other thing of value he possessed, it belongs to his heirs. This is why books by living and recent authors are published only in the few editions licensed by the copyright creator, while the books by long-dead authors—Charles Dickens, William Shakespeare, and Mark Twain— exist in many editions issued by any publisher who cares to publish them.

Notice there is no copyright in *ideas* (which are protected instead, if at all, by patents), only in the particular words or pictures by which those ideas are *expressed.* The present chapter in its present wording is my copyright, but the idea of writing about this topic in this way with these kinds of emphases is not; as long as others do not copy this text word for word, they are free to write a close paraphrase of it— however parasitic it is on my work. (That new wording in turn will be their copyright by the creative act of so doing.) Similarly, a technical drawing or photograph (such as one used as an archaeological illustration) is protected only in the particular form it takes. You may not copy directly my copyright drawing without my consent, but you are free to make a similar drawing closely modeled on it (which, again, will be your copyright, not mine).

Copyright in Publishing Practice

Often, the creator actually wishes his or her work to be copied and used: the present chapter was created with that sole purpose, as are all writings intended for publication. So I have conveyed to AltaMira Press, the publisher of this book, the right to copy it as a chapter in this book in some formal and legal way. I may retain the copyright but "license" them so to use it. Or I may have effectively transferred the copyright to AltaMira so it is as if they own it. The agreement between us should provide a fair framework between us for all likely eventualities; it should prevent me from selling the right to print the self-same chapter to a rival publisher creating a rival copycat book—but it should leave me free to write as I wish about ethical matters; it should provide for AltaMira to be able to license varied editions as it can usefully publish them, or an electronic version, or other editions than its own such as a translation into German; and it should ensure I receive a fair proportion of any substantial income generated those ways. If I had been paid as an employee of AltaMira to write things for them, then as part of my employment they likely would have required me to cede copyright entirely to them in exchange for being paid my wages.

Now, if I were Stephen King and this text were his new novel, the commercial sums involved would be huge, and the exact terms agreed (or fought out) between me (and my agents and lawyers) and AltaMira would be critical. One misjudgment in negotiating and "bang!" goes my income from the German edition (or AltaMira's profit, depending on who misjudged what). This is the world of big-time novel writing, also now—to a certain extent—of nonfiction writing about popular science, where $X zillion are paid to star author Y for the new blockbuster; where 5 million copies sell for $30, and amount to $150 million.

The world of academic archaeology publishing, the much smaller world AltaMira that you and I inhabit, is of specialized publications printed in small editions. Five hundred copies (and some specialized monographs are printed in smaller editions than that) even at $50 (much of which goes in bookshop discounts and distribution costs) amount to $25,000, with bills incurred in editing, originating pictures, typesetting, printing, and binding just to manufacture the physical book, and likely not all the 500 printed will be sold.

Nevertheless, AltaMira can and does make a living—and it is essential it does; if it and its kin do not survive and flourish, where is this academic archaeologist going to publish her stuff?

Good Practice in Copyright Specifics

Although I use copyright in this chapter to explore more generally how knowledge is and is not owned, readers may find it helpful if I state here, in the briefest form possible, the specifics of good copyright practice.

There is (as mentioned earlier) no copyright in ideas, only in the words and images by which those ideas are expressed. So you are always free to repeat other people's ideas and knowledge, provided only you do not use their exact words and pictures. (But the standard academic convention of referencing applies, as a courtesy rather than a legal or necessary consequence of copyright.) A principle of "fair dealing" means you can freely use short quotations in your printed text without specific permission. For lengthy reuse, you may go beyond what fair dealing allows, and you will need to have the copyright owner's permission to use it. (That owner has the right to refuse you, and will usually charge for granting permission.)

The same applies to images. If you redraw, revise, or adapt an image, you do not need copyright permission (but again the academic convention of referencing applies, so state "after X" to show where the original idea came from). If you want to reuse the exact image, then you must seek the copyright owner's consent and expect to pay for it.

At the same time, be aware of your own rights as a creative worker, and do not feel any pressure to be deflected from them. Remember, for instance, that a science writer in a newspaper or magazine reporting new research (yours, if you are lucky) does useful and honorable work (work that is the writer's or the writer's employer's copyright) when he or she tells the world what you have done—without him- or herself doing any research whatever.

Private Interest and Public Good

In these ways, authors and publishers collaborate so that publishers publish authors' copyright work in ways that suit both parties. It is also the case that the publishers' and the authors' interests are not actually the same.

AltaMira needs to maximize its income, and therefore—for instance—seeks to ensure that people *buy* copies of the book rather than photocopy the one from the library, which loses AltaMira a sale. As an author, I am less dependent on the money. Most academic journals make no payment at all to contributors who write the papers they publish—so the author cedes permission for his or her copyright work to be used in exchange for no direct benefit at all. Some journals, especially in the sciences, make a page charge that the contributor (or his or her university) pays, so the contributor actually loses money by publishing there. I have to carry the costs myself of any illustrations to papers that have to be drawn for it or that need copyright permission fees to be paid (since my university will not). If AltaMira pays me for the present chapter, it will be a small sum—the fact that I do not remember if or what AltaMira pays for it as I sit down to write it shows that is not a main concern of mine. (I dimly remember some request that I give it to the Society for American Archaeology's Native American Scholarship Fund anyway, so there it goes. Fair enough, they need it more than I do; fair enough, it wasn't many dollars anyway; but I do have a lunch to pay for tomorrow.) Publishers of academic books pay their authors modest sums. Publishers of academic monographs and very specialized books often pay their authors nothing at all. Writing journal papers leaves an author actually out of pocket. Sometimes, writing many other kinds of academic publications may earn me some small sums, but not sums commensurate with the hours a skilled professional has spent on them. (Although a successful textbook on a central theme, a well-illustrated and long-lasting book on Stonehenge, or a snappy book on the prehistory of sex may begin to generate serious money, if never up at the Stephen King level.)

Why do I write journal articles then, and chapters like the present one? Not for the money, but for the recognition, for the acknowledgment, for the chance to influence, for the chance of reaching a larger audience (though still a small one, since academic archaeology remains a small world). Also, and before those, because I do believe the knowledge I have is of value, so I would like it to be spread. I try to do good research, and my dream is to do *really* good research, and for that research to be *noticed* and recognized—to the point that it influences other archaeologists and anthropologists and, in a little way, even goes outside that closed world to influence how a wider public sees the past, and the things in a past world that I study. It makes no immediate difference at all to an academic researcher whether the ideas that—say—the senior senator falls across and that influence the draft for the new Antiquities Act that reshapes the landscape of American archaeology are read in the chapter of a book as AltaMira publishes it, in a pirate edition, a photocopy, or a photocopy of a photocopy. What matters to the researcher is only that his or her authorship is known and remembered. However many people jump on the bandwagon (thank you, to all of you who do!) though, it's only fair that they remember to tell the senator whose idea it was in the first place; I think they should, and perhaps some of them will. At the same time, in the debate and argument over my idea, I know it has been advanced and improved (and also spoiled, in my personal view), so it moves from being my personal property to having been created more by a collective.

There are five separate reasons beyond my own self-interest why I do not do well to hold my work, and whatever ideas and merits it has, close to my chest as my personal private property, which is what the idea and the law of copyright rather expects (until, that is, seventy years after my death).

First, my work is funded directly and indirectly in large part by public money, or by private gifts intended to advance a public good. Like many archaeologists, I am employed by a university whose income comes from public funds, from student fees, and from grants of public and private money (though I also pay some research costs out of my own pocket). Supported that way, I have no right to pretend I am self-contained as a private individual in my research.

Second, although I contribute what I can by way of new ideas and observations, and although the words I write awkwardly to express anything novel are by the copyright principle my personal property, most of what I deal with is a *collective* knowledge. It is built and shaped from all the previous workers and from what they have contributed to the literature, from ideas circulating around the conferences, from talks and seminar papers I have heard, from questions and comments after class or public lectures, and from gossip and shop talk with colleagues in the coffee room. The cute idea "of mine" that catches the senator's fancy is sure to derive in part from someone else before me. The snappy phrase I dropped into a rather technical and labored research paper earlier this evening, hoping it would enliven it, may have come not from my free imagination but from an article on the *Scientific American* Web page, which I chanced across earlier in the week when looking for something else. For the increasing number of us who work closely with indigenous communities of origin and feel privileged by their consenting to our doing work in the land that is theirs, it is automatic now to acknowledge their overriding interest in the knowledge, rather than it being somehow the exclusive possession of the research scientist and his or her academic community.

Third, archaeologists study for the most part ancient people, human beings who lived and died and had their being on this earth, and without whose lives and deaths we would have nothing to study. It is wrong to treat their bodily and material remains as objects to be exploited for our private profit as individuals.

Fourth, I do most of my work collaboratively with colleagues and publish it in jointly authored publications with them. (That creative work is copyrighted in the usual way, the copyright belonging jointly to the authors.) Working harmoniously with colleagues follows from a whole-hearted commitment to team approach, not from each possessing his or her own.

The fifth reason I express in personal terms, though I believe many colleagues share it. When a novice researcher, I was inclined—as I half-remember—to cling to what few things I had discovered; there weren't many of them, and each had taken so much time and effort in the creating. What if I lost it to someone else? With practice and experience (and much generosity toward me by older colleagues), I have come to realize there are masses of worthwhile things I *could* do, some doubtless more worthwhile than others. There are only a limited number of things I *will* ever do. So there are a few subjects and places where I want and plan to continue working (mostly, I hope in a team rather than on my own), and in respect to those I really would prefer some ignorant newcomer didn't mess them up by crashing into them. There are many, however, where it would be great if some energetic and capable person had similar interests, especially if he or she brought skills different from my own, and especially if he or she worked perhaps partly with me and partly on his or her own, and where two or three or a team of us could do so much more than I could do alone (and enjoy it more by working together). Beyond that, there's that approach X that could be adapted for Scandinavia and there's that area Y in Australia where so much needs doing, and there's that overlooked technique Z that should work so well in southern African conditions: I would love to do all of those things, but I never will, so if I give away what little germ of an idea I have, someone else may—and good luck to them. In a haphazard and unfair world, I may sometimes be remembered or acknowledged or even credited for sowing the seed, or—more often—not noticed at all, as chance falls. It doesn't matter, and over time you get credited—I have been credited—for some things and not for others, and often people are generous to you and sometimes they are not, and you spend time reading colleagues' drafts and trying to help improve them, and they help you the same way, and lend you a marvelous slide from Alaska when you are really stuck for it (and then they are not as mad with you as they should be when you lose it); and the world is a better and happier place for people being generous and giving than it is if each of us pursues his or her own narrow, calculated, and immediate self-interest.

These last paragraphs are written as if a private self-interest and a public good were opposed, and those indeed were the two opposed interests I began with in sketching the idea of copyright. But in practice, they are not opposed at all in the world we live in. My university, like so many, rewards me with promotion and material benefits if I publish enough high-quality research. My career advances in proportion to how much I share my copyright work.

In short, and to summarize these large issues I have explored from a base in the narrow formalities of copyright, there are large benefits for the individual and the community if archaeological knowledge is seen as, primarily, a public good.

Private Interest and Public Good: Archaeology in the Real World

These ideals, if they mean anything, need to be expressed in a real world that has other values. It is committed to the idea of private property, and to the virtue of competition among individuals. Students are continually being assessed in competition with each other. (A very few of them may cheat.) If they survive that process, then they practice archaeology in a competitive marketplace of contract archaeologists or in the continuing competitive world of the academy. (A very few of them may cheat.) If they do archaeology as avocationals, mercifully released from those competitive pressures, then that is because they spend their working lives doing other things, there often within a competitive framework. In the business world, we know that "copycat" corporations often do better than those that are genuinely original in what they do and incur more risks in so doing.

Occasionally, outright theft or deceit does take place. From time to time, it is said, a colleague who has access to another's work in confidence—as a reviewer of a paper submitted for publication or of a grant application—might find something good and original in it, and then publishes it as if his or her own. This is plagiarism. It is wrong and unforgivable, and it is the worse if the thief is senior and the stolen from is junior, as may be the case. One also hears of professors who regard their students' work as their own and feel they can appropriate student work for their own advancement.

To protect the interest of researchers and authors, some granting agencies and publishers or journal editors ask their reviewers to destroy the materials they have read. I think, when the work is of interest and merit, many referees do not; and even if they do, it is impossible for them, when they come across and read with care good ideas and reports of good work done or planned, then just to empty it from their mind. It actually remains there.

There is no effective protection against expert thieves. The only advice is: When you are on to something new and remarkable, don't give it away! Get on with presenting it as a paper at a national or specialized meeting, or submitting it for publication. If you talk to all and sundry about it, but don't publish it properly, then sooner or later it will be published under some other name; or—more likely—the idea will be picked up and come into general circulation, rather than be acknowledged as your contribution.

In general, do think if someone else might also legitimately feel he or she had a part in it. This is where generous acknowledgments come in; if in doubt, acknowledge more colleagues rather than fewer, naming them if you can identify actual individuals or in less personal ways when you cannot remember just what you learnt from whom (e.g., see the acknowledgments to this chapter). Sometimes, no one knows with whom an idea or an approach originated. In a recent publication of my own, I mentioned an idea (concerning how best to manage Stonehenge) which I think—without knowing for certain—arose in conversation between me and two colleagues, an idea expressed in a particular phrase that I think—without knowing for certain—one of those other colleagues created. So I asked him if it was okay for me to use it. Generously and genially—for most colleagues are generous and genial in these matters—he said that was fine; so I have used it, and in a note to the publication I named the two colleagues and the one whom I think is rightly to be credited with the specific phrase of which I have become fond.

Some colleagues are uncollegial and possessive by instinct and attitude. One comes to mind who has much experience and knowledge in a region where I also work and with whom it is hard to keep good relations: If you publish a study consistent with what he thinks (and has published—so it is entirely proper for you to use and depend on it), then he is outraged that you have "stolen" his personal possession; if you publish a study that takes a different view, then he is affronted at your asserting he is wrong. I try to keep smiling and also to keep a certain distance, rather than acknowledging there is cause for dispute between us.

At the same time, there is no need to be frightened away by that kind of possessiveness. Many archaeologists, especially if they have worked for many years on a particular topic or aspect to the regional record, begin to believe they have staked out that territory as their own. They haven't, and they have no right to act as if they possess it.

A persistent difficulty concerns the records from a particular site or excavation. This is the particular property initially of the researcher but—by the usual principles, and the more so since excavation is a destructive process in which an enduring record of what was found has to substitute in perpetuity for what was actually found—is knowledge for the public good, which should end up in the public domain. Accordingly, good practice requires that the finds and the field records should be placed in a secure repository with public access, once the original researcher has finished with them. What is harder to judge is how long it is reasonable for the original researcher to have exclusive access—a couple of years? Ten years? However long he or she wants? If you think too long has passed, and especially if it is many years since the materials were collected, then it is reasonable for you to ask directly for access.

Most research is specialized, and perhaps increasingly so. A large part of my own current research addresses rock art, and I have a large community of colleagues who share concerns with the common issues that affect rock art work everywhere. But when it comes to the specifics of particular panels at particular sites in particular regions where I have worked, then the colleagues with close knowledge are immediately reduced to not many, even to just a single colleague with whom I worked at that site in a field pairing. Even before one goes down to those field specifics, that large community of colleagues with the "same" research interests is rapidly reduced when one thinks instead who are the colleagues who share a particular interest with me or particular research attitudes. Accordingly, in my view, the great risk for the researcher is isolation and loneliness, and the most important thing for the researcher to hold to is teamwork and collegiality.

Conclusion

I see research knowledge as a common property, to be shared by the interested community, rather than privately possessed by individuals within that community. This is the correct ideal, because private possession alienates and removes access to that knowledge from the broad constituency that should reasonably benefit from it. I have mostly written here in relation to the benefit that a generous attitude brings for the individual, which rather assumes—as copyright law does—that knowledge starts with and in the individual, who may or may not share it with a wider group. This is the conventional attitude of Western societies today. Other societies of other traditions have different attitudes to knowledge, in which it is not a commodity that can be privately owned; instead, knowledge is by its nature held in common, and the role of the individual is to hold it for the common group for a certain period. The archaeological materials we deal with are the artifacts and objects, and sometimes the very bodies themselves, of people who were on this earth before us. Like us, they lived and had their being and died. As archaeologists, we interfere with their material objects and their surviving material reality as we choose, perhaps with some sense of what counts as good behavior, but without their permission. If any good is to come of that, that benefit is of a nature to belong to a broad community rather than to the individual or for the individual's benefit.

Archaeologists are not the only communities involved in what should fittingly happen to archaeological things. The special considerations that arise when indigenous communities, or other communities of origin are involved, are—thank goodness—routinely understood by archaeologists and are covered elsewhere in this book. (Copyright, when it has an impact on those communities, can have odd and damaging effects, because it is based on the fundamental of individual ownership of knowledge, which in turn is based on the idea that creativity resides in the individual.) In this chapter, I therefore have concentrated on knowledge within the archaeological community, where the same or similar issues arise, but which are less often given attention.

Discussion Questions

1. As a staff member on a field project, you happen to be supervising the portion of the excavation that produces the most interesting information of the season. As the individual who did the actual related excavating, what "rights" do you have to photograph, to present in public lectures, or to publish anything about the information and finds?
2. If an archaeological site is on private land, does the knowledge from and about it rightly belong to the landowner?
3. Archaeologists often dig up the possessions and sometimes even the physical remains of long-dead individuals whom we cannot identify as named individuals. Do you think this fact means knowledge about them naturally belongs in the public domain, as a common good?
4. Convention and usual good practice mean that an excavator has pretty well exclusive access to the site records for the time it takes to complete the fieldwork, do the laboratory studies, write, and publish. Suppose a site takes three years to excavate, another three years for laboratory work, and another three years to write and publish: nine years altogether. Many sites take much longer in practice! When is it reasonable for another researcher to be entitled to access for his or her own studies of the same material? Before the nine years are up? After ten or eleven years, to allow for a bit of slippage? Longer? How long?
5. Copyright protects a specific drawing, but allows anyone to make a new drawing that is practically the same—and gives the copyist copyright on his or her copy. In what ways does this seem fair? In what ways unfair?
6. As a graduate student, in class one day you came up with a great idea that became a focus of discussion for the course. You felt you had made a pos-

itive contribution and were certain it played a role in the grade you eventually received in the course. A few years later you read an article by the professor who taught the class with what was clearly a version of the idea you came up with that day, but with no acknowledgment of your contribution. What should you do?

7. Some articles—in general books, school textbooks, magazines, and newspapers—are not referenced, and sometimes don't say at all where their ideas originally came from. This chapter is unreferenced. Is it ethical to write without references or other specific acknowledgment of who the author is indebted to? Do you think my rather vague acknowledgments are good enough?

Note

I thank the editors of the present volume for their advice and guidance; the team that developed its predecessor, the Society for American Archaeology ethics handbook of some years ago; those who developed it at a workshop at the University of Nevada, Reno; and Don Fowler, David Gill, Emily Salter, and others who have discussed these issues with me and from whom I have learned much.

Recommended Readings

Archaeological Records of Europe: Network Access
    2002   at minerva.york.ac.uk/arena/ (accessed April 2002).

Fowler, P. J.
    2002   Fyfield and Overton Project, 1959–1998, at
        ads.ahds.ac.uk/catalogue/projArch/fyfod/index.cfm (accessed April 2002).

Templeton, Brad
    2002   A Brief Intro to Copyright, at www.templetons.com/brad/copyright.html
        (accessed 15 July 2002).
    2002   10 Big Myths about Copyright Explained, at
        www.templetons.com/brad/copymyths.html (accessed 15 July 2002).

U.S. Copyright Office, Library of Congress
    2002   at www.loc.gov/copyright/ (accessed June 2002).

HESTER A. DAVIS

Chapter Nineteen

Creating and Implementing a Code and Standards

[T]he discipline [of archaeology] has defined a normative behavior set and/or ethical standards for its practitioners. Correct behavioral modes (i.e., how to go about doing archeology) peculiar to the discipline are necessary so that sanctioned participation can be distinguished from nonsanctioned activity. In short, definition of the discipline is a prerequisite to its existence. This sharpening of the focus, along with the drawing of lines between acceptable and unacceptable professional behavior, has lessened the chaos by giving the discipline a sense of place as well as a sense of purpose. —Rhea J. Rogers (1990:10)

Creating a Code and Standards

On January 26, 1976, a group of distinguished archaeologists gathered in Fayetteville, Arkansas. They were the appointed members of the Society for American Archaeology (SAA) Interim Committee on Professional Standards, and they met for the following four days to deliberate their charge, which was

- To explore, in the light of the new understanding resulting from the debate and referendum (regarding setting up a Register of Professional Archeologists) the several options available to the archaeologists of the country for promoting professional standards (see Society for American Archaeology 1975:520–22])
- To assess the needs of the profession at the time and to determine whether the register as proposed was adequate to satisfy those needs
- To develop a modern statement of professional standards with special attention to the problem of coordination with the criteria and standards being developed by various government agencies

- To make recommendations for an appropriate course of action
- To submit a report to the Executive Committee and to the cooperating societies (see the following list of society representatives) as soon as possible and certainly before the annual meeting in St. Louis in May 1976.

The members of the Interim Committee at this meeting were Edward B. Jelks, SAA chair, Charles Cleland (representing the Society for Historical Archaeology [SHA]), Jane Buikstra (representing the American Association of Physical Anthropologists), James Hester (representing the American Society for Conservation Archaeology, no longer in existence), Jesse Jennings (SAA), Tom King (National Park Service), William Lipe (SAA), William McDonald (representing the Archaeological Institute of America [AIA]), and Charles R. McGimsey III (former SAA president). Stuart Struever, the president of the SAA, attended for a portion of the meeting in an ex officio capacity, and when he had to leave, I served in his place.

The committee discussed all options that had been brought to its attention and concluded that "the option to do absolutely nothing was not one mandated to the group" (Jelks 1976:2), in light of the 78 percent vote in support of establishment of some form of register for professional archaeologists. The meeting was spent in drafting, discussing, and revising a code of ethics and "standards of professionalism for research, for institutions, and for individuals" (2–3). Once there was a satisfactory draft of these statements, the committee again reviewed the options and "determined that, while the Registry as proposed (which would have been under the umbrella of the SAA) would accomplish certain limited goals, a more viable and effective option which would incorporate the best portions of all of the options considered would be the establishment of an active society of concerned professional archeologists" (3).

The committee members felt that a well-designed code and a set of agreed-on standards were at the very core of the practice of archaeology. Furthermore, given that archaeological resources are scarce, fragile, and rapidly disappearing, largely through factors beyond the control of archaeologists, they determined that it was incumbent on archaeologists to take the lead in developing this core of documents then, rather than waiting passively for others (e.g., the federal government) to impose them on the profession through enacted laws or by regulation.

After reaching these conclusions, and discussing how an "active society of concerned professionals" might be organized and created, the SAA Interim Committee officially ended its meeting. However, between the end of January and the annual meeting of the SAA in St. Louis in early May, the committee, under Jelks's leadership, continued to discuss the option of the "establishment of an active society." Jelks, McGimsey, and Cleland met with a member of a law firm in Chicago, who helped them draft bylaws and disciplinary procedures. At some time, now lost in the mists of memory, a decision was made to form the Society of Professional Archeologists (SOPA), incorporate it in the State of Illinois, and bring this as an accomplished fact to the SAA meeting (legend has it that the decision was made by some members of the Interim Committee meeting, appropriately, on the top of Monks Mound at the Cahokia site). It was felt that the SAA Executive Committee might well accept the recommendations of the committee, but then not act with the immediacy that the committee felt the times required.

The Code and Standards

The code and standards developed by SOPA have been adopted (with minor word changes, such as, it is now the Code of Conduct rather than the Code of Ethics) by the Register of Professional Archaeologists (RPA). These statements about proper behavior for an archaeologist and minimum accepted standards for research did not just pop out of the heads of these worthy archaeologists in Fayetteville; they were based on earlier ethics statements by the SAA and other organizations. The first draft of the Code of Ethics, however, in a "thou shall" and "thou shall not" format, did come overnight full-blown from the head of Tom King during the Fayetteville meeting. In this first draft, the idea that archaeologists had an ethical responsibility toward the public, toward their colleagues, employees, and students, and toward employers and clients resulted from the concentrated discussions of the committee.

The code has been tweaked and amended since 1976 in light of experience, tightening up the statements and adding a number of both "thou shalls" and "thou shall nots." The first amendment, made within about two years, was 2.2e, "An archaeologist shall not submit a false or misleading application for registration by the SOPA" (now the RPA). It had not occurred to the committee that someone might do this until it happened and was brought to the attention of the grievance coordinator. The code and standards can and should be flexible enough to allow for changes as archaeology—and archaeologists—change.

The standards were not difficult to set down on paper—they were and are, after all, standard practice and had been taught to graduate students for decades. Over the years since 1976, the wording has been made more precise so that violations are more precise and clear, but the basic concepts of what is appropriate research performance are still the same as drafted in 1976. They are designed to apply to any registered archaeologist whether he or she is working in Texas or Greece, and whether the research is on a lithic scatter in Montana, a Roman site in France, or a collection curated at the Smithsonian. They are, in point of fact, practices that could have been articulated by any archaeologist for many years prior to their actually being set down in writing. Having them in writing, however, gives them a certain power to influence. Asking an archaeologist to agree in writing to abide by standards and a code of conduct, as is required when applying for registration, is far different from two archaeologists arguing over a drink about whether or why they should, for example, share their data with that #$&*%$ archaeologist at the U of X (see Register of Professional Archaeologists 1998:standards II 2d, 2e).

Most national archaeological societies and a good many state archaeological societies (which have large amateur memberships) have some kind of code of ethics.

The AIA and RPA, however, are the only U.S. archaeological organizations in which violations by a professional member (in the case of the AIA) or by a registered archaeologist can be investigated and sanctions laid on the violator. (A professional member of the AIA who is also a registered archaeologist could, conceivably, be investigated by both organizations.) In other words, the RPA Code and Standards are not generalized statements of good and bad, moral and immoral actions, nor are they presented as "principles" as articulated by the SAA. The RPA adopted the mechanism developed and used by SOPA for twenty years, whereby if any one or more of the "thou shalls" or "thou shall nots," or any section of the standards, allegedly has not been followed by an archaeologist who agreed in writing to abide by them, the alleged transgression will be investigated. This is a form of social control of the behavior of archaeologists by one's peers.

The RPA Disciplinary Procedures

The RPA Disciplinary Procedures (also referred to as the RPA Grievance Procedures) that currently guide the investigation of any transgression by registered archaeologists were designed specifically to provide protection for the rights of anyone being investigated, confidentiality of the investigation until the case is heard before the Standards Board, and due process in all proceedings. It is a quasi-legal procedure; more informal in some respects, but based on accepted legal principles, particularly that a person is considered innocent until proven guilty.

The RPA grievance coordinator (GC) is the point of contact for all actions dealing with possible violations of the code and standards (which are treated in the same way as far as investigations are concerned). Anyone—another registered archaeologist, one not registered, an amateur, or whoever—can contact the GC if it is suspected or known that a violation of the code or standards by a registered archaeologist has taken place. Registered archaeologists have agreed in writing to abide by the code and standards; archaeologists not listed in the register have not publicly agreed and so cannot be subject to any investigation. These latter may be long-time practicing archaeologists, and/or senior members of the profession, but if they transgress and are not listed in the register, any alleged misconduct cannot be investigated by the RPA.

Implementing the Code and Standards

A copy of the RPA Disciplinary Procedures can be obtained from the GC. They are straightforward as to the steps that an investigation of an alleged violation takes, so rather than repeat them in detail here, perhaps an example of how the process might work would be most useful.

What should you do if you have heard or know firsthand that an archaeologist is doing something you think is unethical? First, look at the current RPA Directory (available on the RPA Web page, see the appendix, or in hard copy from any registered archaeologist) and make sure the person is listed. Then, look at the code and standards (on the Web page or in the RPA Directory) and see if you can pinpoint the specific section that the registered archaeologist may have violated. This is not as easy as it might seem because each instance will be a little different and because the wording in the code allows for flexibility. Take, for example, item I.1.2b in the Code of Conduct: "An Archaeologist shall not: give a professional opinion, make a public report, or give legal testimony involving archaeological matters without being as thoroughly informed as might reasonably be expected."

The flexibility in the final phrase means that you must know of something that the archaeologist knew or should have known and didn't mention. But is that enough evidence to be a violation? Even if you are not sure the situation fits one of the sections of the code or standards, you can contact the GC (preferably by phone) and tell him or her the circumstances. The GC will probably say: "I really need to see what evidence you have before I can determine if there may have been a violation. Send me something in writing, with an indication of which sections you think have been violated."

Now you have to decide whether to put your "evidence" down in writing. This is sometimes an extremely hard decision. Perhaps, the person is or was your professor, is or was your supervisor, or is or was a friend in graduate school. Can you really bring yourself to rat on an archaeologist who is a colleague, or one who might be able to affect your career in the future? If what you have heard seems only a tiny transgression that probably won't happen again, should you report it? Or is it an obvious, blatant violation? Does a tiny transgression deserve an investigation if the rumored misconduct doesn't really hurt the resources or the reputation of another archaeologist? If you don't bring this to the attention of the GC, might the archaeologist continue in this unethical behavior?

If you decide that what you know seems to reflect unethical or substandard behavior, and you think it should be investigated, then you should put the evidence in writing, in as much detail as possible, and send it to the GC. The GC will decide whether he or she thinks the evidence is compelling enough to pursue a thorough investigation. If not, he or she will tell you and the case will be closed. If the GC thinks there is sufficient evidence, he or she will tell you that a Grievance Committee is being created to investigate and at that point your role in the case is over, unless you are questioned about evidence during the investigation or are called to testify if the case goes to the Standards Board. In any case, you have done your ethical duty by reporting what you think is unethical behavior (see Register of Professional Archaeologists (RPA) 1998:section II 2.1g), and the RPA takes over the responsibility of pursuing the allegations further.

The GC will notify the registered archaeologist of the allegations but will *not* normally give that archaeologist your name, only that someone has alleged unethical behavior or substandard research. The GC will then appoint two registered archaeologists to a Grievance Committee, with the GC serving as a third member of the committee. The committee takes the information you have provided and pursues the circumstances of the alleged violations through interviews with the accused registered archaeologist and others as appropriate, examines other written documents, or possibly arranges personal visits, until it feels it has enough information to make a decision. There are three alternative decisions the committee can make: 1) it may find that the allegations have no substance and that no violation or misconduct has occurred and the case should be closed. Both you and the accused will be so notified. 2) It may feel that the alleged violations did occur, but they are not "serious" enough to convene the Standards Board for a formal hearing. In this case, it may recommend *admonishment* or *censure*. Admonishment means that some small level of misconduct has occurred; the registered archaeologist is notified of the findings of the Grievance Committee and is asked to formally accept admonishment. If admonishment is accepted, the case is then closed and no public announcement of the investigation or the decision is made. If censure is recommended, the GC notifies the registered archaeologist and if he or she accepts this punishment, the findings of the committee are published in the RPA Directory. 3) If the registered archaeologist does *not* accept admonishment or censure, or if the Grievance Committee feels that a serious violation seems to have occurred, the case will be referred to the Standards Board (the Standards Board is made up of three elected registered archaeologists and three alternates, one or more of whom can serve at a hearing in case of a conflict of interest by one regular Standards Board member).

Again, the Disciplinary Procedures are clear about the nature of the hearing on any case before the Standards Board. You might be called as a witness—not as the instigator but as someone with information about the circumstances. The hearing may last a day or more, and may or may not involve lawyers on both sides. After the hearing concludes, the Standards Board also has alternative decisions to make. It can dismiss the case for lack of evidence; it can recommend *suspension* from the register for no more than two years, or it can recommend *expulsion.* An expelled archaeologist can apply again for registration after three years.

Does This System Work?

The procedures have been in place in SOPA and now the RPA for twenty-five years, but how have they really worked? In the twenty years of SOPA's existence, there have been some cases that went all the way to the Standards Board; some in which the Grievance Committee made recommendations for admonishment or censure;

and many, many instances of investigations that did not go beyond either the Grievance Committee or the GC for lack of good evidence of misconduct. The same is true of the first years of the RPA's existence. As has been outlined, all investigations that end in dismissal of the allegations or in admonition are not made public, so most of the profession is not aware that an investigation of any kind has taken place. Rumors of misconduct or unethical behavior may abound, and as far as most people know, nothing is being done. This perceived lack of action is perhaps unfortunate, but it is necessary to protect the reputation of an accused archaeologist. The alleged misconduct is usually not a violation of law (although some behavior considered unethical, such as plagiarism, might also be illegal and subject to suit), but it is a violation of self-imposed ethics and standards, and the violations are investigated by peers. Unless the accused archaeologist wants to dispel the rumors by making public the fact that the investigation took place and he or she was cleared, nothing about the case will be revealed by the RPA.

Investigations that end in censure, suspension, or expulsion are made public and the RPA assumes that this information will make a difference in the behavior not only of the individual archaeologist, but will also be the proverbial "wake up call" for all registered archaeologists to pay attention to the code and standards.

Generally, ethical violations are not black-and-white actions; they are often various tints of gray and occur in various degrees of severity. For example: Section 2.1a of the RPA Code of Conduct says: "An archaeologist shall give appropriate credit for work done by others." What does "appropriate" mean? Is listing the contribution in the acknowledgments enough credit? Should it be joint or junior authorship in a publication? How much work on a project is enough to receive "credit"? Each case reported to the GC where someone thinks credit has not been "appropriately" given is investigated. The accused is allowed to explain his or her actions and decisions with regard to "credit," and others familiar with the situation are asked for an opinion. Is the person making the allegations the one who feels he or she didn't receive appropriate credit or did someone else bring this to the GC? Is this a personal vendetta or a relationship gone bad, or did the individual who is alleged not to have received appropriate (not *adequate,* mind you, but *appropriate*) credit actually contribute all that much to the project or the report? The procedures allow for consideration of all these shadings implicit in the code and standards and many recommendations have been made by the GC that have allowed all parties to be satisfied rather than having the situation simmer and relationships sour or having to go through a formal hearing.

On the other hand, until such time as the register is viewed by a large majority of professional archaeologists as a means of committing oneself to ethical behavior and minimum standards of research, the idea of registration and commitment is not working to its full potential. But the fact that (as of 2002) the four largest professional membership organizations to which archaeologists belong (SAA, SHA, AIA, and American Anthropological Association) are sponsors of the register indicates that they feel it should and will work; perhaps even that it has worked in the past.

Until such time as the registry is viewed *by others* as a means of identifying who is a professional archaeologist, being censured, suspended, or expelled from the RPA will not necessarily mean the end to one's career. There may well be an organization, business, agency, or university that will hire you anyway based on your resume. But times are changing, and with competition being what it is, being registered (which is a voluntary act, remember) is a process that many other professions and the public understand. They know it means minimum educational requirements, minimum experience requirements, review by peers, and commitment to a code and/or standards. Even parents may know that if the university field school that they are paying for you to attend is accredited by the RPA and that the field instructor is on the register, then you are probably getting a good introduction to field archaeology, and not just being used as labor for some professor's research project for which he or she received no requested National Science Foundation funds.

Does the commitment to ethical conduct and standards of research make a registered archaeologist a better archaeologist than one who is not registered? Probably. Just as laws against murder do deter some people from killing, they don't deter everyone. Just as the commandment "thou shall not kill" deters some, it does not deter all. It is certainly possible that an archaeologist may deliberately not apply for registration because he or she is a professional archaeologist, by golly, and is insulted by the idea that he or she needs to have a colleague review his or her career and then be registered to "prove" that. Surely, a doctorate from Harvard should "prove" you are a reputable archaeologist! Well, no, not necessarily. A master's or a doctorate really only means you have successfully gone through certain hoops in the past. It does not guarantee that you will conduct yourself according to an ethical code or principles, or conduct your research according to accepted standards in the future. Some may not apply because they are too busy, don't want to take the time to gather together the documentation required, don't want to risk being "caught" doing something unethical or substandard, or don't think they have any reason to be registered because they are tenured faculty. They know, of course, that the code and standards cannot be invoked if the archaeologist suspected of unethical behavior is not a registered archaeologist.

Some think that the whole idea of registration and signing on to the code and standards is worthless because, they say, there are individuals listed as registered archaeologists who are known to have been sloppy in their work, mean to their students and/or employees, and in general have the reputation for all kinds of nefarious activities. Or, they say, "How can so-and-so be a member? She doesn't even have a master's, and I know of a project report she wrote that was rejected by the Corps of Engineers so it must have been really bad." There are three things that must be taken into account here. First, when SOPA was created, all archaeologists who had been working as "professional archaeologists" for the previous three years could become members without meeting the educational requirements (they did, however, have to meet the experience requirements). Second, all SOPA members automatically could become registered archaeologists when the RPA was formed just by indicating they wanted to, without having to resubmit documentation to the RPA's registrar. Third, an archaeologist may have committed some unethical act prior to signing the agreement to abide by the code and standards, but he or she cannot be investigated for that transgression, only for unethical behavior after signing the agreement.

One likes to presume that the more archaeologists who become registered, the better the code and standards will work because everyone will know that unethical behavior and substandard research will not be tolerated.

Or will it?

The most important consideration is that the code and standards will *not* work if individuals do not report violations when they occur. If a violation is not reported, the individual will remain unscathed, uninvestigated, free to continue in the violations, and free to give the whole profession a bad name. Think about it.

Discussion Questions

1. What is the difference between a registered archaeologist and one who is not registered and how is the difference significant to the profession of archaeology? Have the archaeology professors at your institution registered? You might politely inquire why each did or did not choose to register.
2. Are the RPA Disciplinary Procedures fair? Are they strong enough? Too complicated? Should more information be available to the profession and/or the public about investigations of alleged misconduct? Why or why not?
3. You are assisting at a field school directed by your major advisor, who is a registered archaeologist. Nevertheless, and much to your surprise, you find many of her procedures and instructions to be damaging to the archaeological resource, as well as to staff and volunteers. You know you should talk to the GC, but would you? Would you respond differently if she were not from your university or not your advisor? What other options do you have?
4. Are there any sanctions not currently a part of the Disciplinary Procedures that you think the RPA should consider? Compare the RPA Grievance Procedures with those of the AIA (see the appendix).
5. Your excavation recovered a fair number of charred seeds—not in wonderful condition, not in huge quantities, but still, you wanted to have them properly studied and published. You were successful with the grant proposal to fund a paleobotanist's visit to the site and storeroom and subsequent research. Several years later, as the rest of the specialist reports on

your site are ready to go to press, the paleobotanist, who had been promising a written report, informs you that the material really isn't very interesting and he no longer chooses to be part of your project. What can you do?

Recommended Readings

Jelks, Edward B.
   1990   Professional Ethics in Archeology. In *Predicaments, Pragmatics, and Professionalism: Ethical Conduct in Archeology,* edited by J. Ned Woodall, 19–26. Special Publication no. 1, Society of Professional Archeologists, Oklahoma City.
   1995   Professionalism and the Society of Professional Archeologists. In *Ethics in American Archaeology: Challenges for the 1990s,* edited by Mark. J. Lynott and Alison Wylie, 14–16. Society for American Archaeology, Washington, DC.

McGimsey, Charles R., III
   1995   Standards, Ethics, and Archaeology: A Brief History. In *Ethics in American Archaeology: Challenges for the 1990s,* edited by Mark J. Lynott and Alison Wylie, 11–13. Society for American Archaeology, Washington, DC.

Register of Professional Archaeologists
   1998   Code of Conduct and Standards of Research Performance, at www.rpanet.org/ (accessed March 2002).

Rogers, Rhea J.
   1990   The Genesis of an Archeological Ethic. In *Predicaments, Pragmatics, and Professionalism: Ethical Conduct in Archeology,* edited by J. Ned Woodall, 9–18. Special Publication no. 1, Society of Professional Archeologists, Oklahoma City.

Wildesen, Leslie E.
   1984   The Search for an Ethic in Archaeology: An Historical Perspective. In *Ethics and Values in Archaeology,* edited by E. L. Green, 3–12. The Free Press, New York.

Websites for Professional Codes of Ethics and Standards

American Anthropological Association (AAA)
1998 Code of Ethics of the American Anthropological Association, at www.
aaanet.org/committees/ethics/ethcode.htm (accessed December 28, 2002)

American Association of Museums (AAM)
1991 Code of Ethics for Museums, at www.aam-us.org/aamcoe.htm (accessed December 28, 2002).

American Cultural Resources Association (ACRA)
1996 Code of Ethics and Professional Conduct of the American Cultural Resources Association, at www.acra-crm.org/Ethics.html (accessed December 28, 2002).

American Institute for the Conservation of Historic and Artistic Work (AIC)
1994 AIC Code of Ethics and Guidelines for Practice, at aic.stanford.edu/pubs/ethics.html (accessed December 28, 2002).

Archaeological Institute of America (AIA)
1994 Code of Professional Standards, at www.archaeological.org/pdfs/AIA_Code_of_Professional_StandardsA55.pdf (accessed December 28, 2002).

Australian Association of Consulting Archaeologists, Inc. (AACAI)
1980 Code of Ethics, at www.archaeology.usyd.edu.au/aacai/ethics/index.html (accessed December 28, 2002).

Canadian Archaeological Association (CAA)
1999 Statement of Principles for Ethical Conduct Pertaining to Aboriginal Peoples, at www.canadianarchaeology.com/ethicseng.html (accessed December 28, 2002).

European Association of Archaeologists (EAA)
1997 EAA Code of Practice, at www.e-a-a.org/Codeprac.htm (accessed December 28, 2002).

Institute of Field Archaeologists (IFA)
1985 Code of Conduct, at www.archaeologists.net/code.html (accessed December 28, 2002).

International Council of Museums (ICOM)
1986 ICOM Code of Ethics for Museums, at www.icom.org/ethics.html (accessed December 28, 2002).

Register of Professional Archaeologists (RPA)
1998 Code of Conduct and Standards of Research Performance, at www.rpanet.org/conduct.htm (accessed December 28, 2002).

Society for American Archaeology (SAA)
1996 Principles of Archaeological Ethics, at www.saa.org/Aboutsaa/Ethics/prethic.html (accessed December 28, 2002).

Society for Historical Archaeology (SHA)
1993 Standards and Guidelines for the Curation of Archaeological Collections, at www.sha.org/curation.htm (accessed December 28, 2002).

World Archaeological Congress (WAC)
1989 Vermillion Accord on Human Remains, at www.wac.uct.ac.za/archive/content/vermillion.accord.html (accessed December 28, 2002).
1990 First Code of Ethics, at www.wac.uct.ac.za/archive/content/ethics.html (accessed December 28, 2002).

Bibliography

Adcock, G. J., E. S. Dennis, S. Easteal, G. A. Huttley, L. S. Jermin, W. J. Peacock, and A. G. Thorne

    2001   Mitochondrial DNA Sequences in Ancient Australians: Implications for Modern Human Origins. *Proceedings of the National Academy of Sciences of the USA* 98:537–42.

Advisory Council on Historic Preservation

    n.d.   Protecting Historic Properties: A Citizen's Guide to Section 106 Review. Pamphlet. Washington, DC.

Alexander, B.

    1990   Archaeology and Looting Make a Volatile Mix. *Science* 250:1074–75.

Alger, Jonathan R.

    1998   Love, Lust and the Law: Sexual Harassment in the Academy. *Academe* 84(5):34–39.

Ali, Ihsan, and Robin Coningham

    2001   Recording and Preserving Gandhara's Cultural Heritage. In *Trade in Illicit Antiquities: The Destruction of the World's Archaeological Heritage,* edited by Neil Brodie, Jennifer Doole, and Colin Renfrew, 25–31. McDonald Institute Monographs. McDonald Institute, Cambridge.

Alva, Walter

    2001   The Destruction, Looting and Traffic of the Archaeological Heritage of Peru. In *Trade in Illicit Antiquities: The Destruction of the World's Archaeological Heritage,* edited by Neil Brodie, Jennifer Doole, and Colin Renfrew, 89–96. McDonald Institute Monographs. McDonald Institute, Cambridge.

American Anthropological Association

    1999   *1998 Biennial Survey of Departments of Anthropology in the United States,* compiled by Patsy Evans and Thomas Jablonsky. American Anthropological Association, Arlington, VA.

Anderson, Duane
    1996   Reburial: Is It Reasonable? In *Archaeological Ethics,* edited by Karen D.
        Vitelli, 200–8. AltaMira, Walnut Creek, CA.

Australian Archaeological Association
    1994   Code of Ethics. *Australian Archaeology* 39:129.

Babbitt, Bruce
    2000   Letter to Louis Caldera, Secretary of the Army. U.S. Department of the
        Interior, Washington, DC, September 21.

Bahn, Paul G. (editor)
    1996   *The Cambridge Illustrated History of Archaeology.* Cambridge University
        Press, Cambridge.

Baker, Joe (editor)
    2000   The Pennsylvania Cultural Resource Management Symposium. *Journal of the
        Middle Atlantic Archaeological Conference* 16.

Banks, M. Kimball, Myra Giesen, and Nancy Pearson
    2000   Traditional Cultural Properties vs. Traditional Cultural Resource Management.
        CRM 23(1):33–36.

Bell, Linda A.
    2001   Annual Report on the Economic Status of the Profession 2000–2001:
        Uncertain Times. American Association of University Professors, at
        www.aaup.org/research/salary/2001sept.htm (accessed December 2002).

Bender, Susan (editor)
    2000   A Proposal to Guide Curricular Reform for the Twenty-First Century. In
        Teaching Archaeology in the 21st Century, edited by Susan Bender and
        George Smith, 31–48. Society for American Archaeology, Washington, DC.

Benjamin, Ernst
    1998   Disparities in the Salaries and Appointments of Academic Men and Women:
        An Update of a 1988 Report of Committee W on the Status of Women in the
        Academic Profession. American Association of University Professors, at
        www.aaup.org/issues/WomeninHE/wrepup.htm (accessed December 2002).

Binford, Lewis
    1962   Archaeology as Anthropology. *American Antiquity* 28(2):217–25.

Bok, Sisela
    1979   *Lying: Moral Choice in Public and Private Life.* Vintage, New York.

Bowdler, S.
    1992   Unquiet Slumbers: The Return of the Kow Swamp Burials. *Antiquity*
        66:103–6.

Bowler, J. M.
    1998   Willandra Lakes Revisited: Environmental Framework for Human
        Occupation. *Archaeol, Oceania* 33:120–155.

Bowler, J. M., R. Jones, H. Allen, and A. G. Thorne
1970   Pleistocene Human Remains from Australia: A Living Site and Human
       Cremation From Lake Mungo, Western New South Wales. *World Archaeology*
       2:39–60.

Bowler, J. M., and A. G. Thorne
1976   Human Remains from Lake Mungo: Discovery and Excavation of Lake
       Mungo III. In *The Origin of the Australians*, R. L. Kirk and A. G. Thorne,
       eds. Canberra: Australian Institute of Aboriginal Studies. 127–138.

Brah, A.
1996   *Cartographies of Diaspora: Contesting Identities.* Routledge, London.

Bray, Warwick
2000   Malagana and the Goldworking Tradition of Southwest Columbia. In
       Precolumbian Gold: Technology, Style and Iconography, edited by C.
       McEwan, 94–111. British Museum Press, London.

Brent, Michel
1996   A View inside the Illicit Trade in African Antiquities. In *Plundering Africa's
       Past*, edited by Peter R. Schmidt and Roderick J. McIntosh, 63–78. Indiana
       University Press, Bloomington.

Brew, J. O.
1961   Emergency Archaeology: Salvage in Advance of Technological Progress.
       Proceedings of the American Philosophical Society 105(1):1–10.

Brodie, Neil, Jennifer Doole, and Colin Renfrew (editors).
2001   *Trade in Illicit Antiquities: The Destruction of the World's Archaeological
       Heritage.* McDonald Institute Monographs. McDonald Institute, Cambridge.

Brodie, Neil, Jennifer Doole, and Peter Watson
2000   *Stealing History: The Illicit Trade in Cultural Material.* ICOM UK, the
       Museums Association and the McDonald Institute for Archaeological
       Research, Cambridge.

Brommer, F.
1979   *The Sculptures of the Parthenon: Metopes, Frieze, Pediments, Cult-Statue.*
       Thames and Hudson, London.

Bruseth, James E., James E. Corbin, Cecile E. Carter, and Bonnie McKee
1994   Involving the Caddo Tribe during Archaeological Field School in Texas: A
       Cross Cultural Sharing. *SAA Bulletin* 12(1):9–10.

Bureau of Land Management
2002   Project Archaeology, Heritage Education Program. U.S. Bureau of Land
       Management, Anasazi Heritage Center, at www.co.blm.gov/ahc/projarc.htm
       (accessed 29 May 2002).

Cameron, Catherine (editor)
1996   Special Issue on the Loss of Cultural Heritage—An International Perspective.
       Nonrenewable Resources 6(2).

Canouts, V., and F. MacManamon
   2001   Protecting the Past for the Future: Federal Archaeology in the U.S. In *Trade in Illicit Antiquities: The Destruction of the World's Archaeological Heritage,* edited by Neil Brodie, Jennifer Doole, and Colin Renfrew, 97–110. McDonald Institute Monographs. McDonald Institute, Cambridge.

Carrell, Toni L.
   1990   Ethics Versus Commercial Exploitation: What's It Worth to the Future? *In Predicaments, Pragmatics, and Professionalism: Conduct of Archeological Inquiry,* edited by J. Ned Woodall, 61–72. Society of Professional Archeologists, Special Publication no. 1, Oklahoma City.

Champe, J. L., D. S. Byers, C. Evans, A. K. Guthe, H. W. Hamilton, E. B. Jelks, C. W. Meighan, S. Olafson, G. S. Quimby, W. Smith, and F. Wendorf
   1961   Four Statements for Archaeology. *American Antiquity* 27:137–39.

Chippindale, Christopher, and David W. J. Gill
   2000   Material Consequences of Contemporary Classical Collecting. *American Journal of Archaeology* 104 (3):463–511.
   2001   On-line Auctions: A New Venue for the Antiquities Market. *Culture without Context* 9:4–13.

Chippindale, Christopher, David W. J. Gill, Emily Salter, and Christian Hamilton
   2001   Collecting the Classical World: First Steps in a Quantitative History. *International Journal of Cultural Property* 10(1):1–31.

Chueca, J. G.
   2001   Fakes in Peru's Gold Museum. Art Newspaper.com, 10 December, at www.theartnewspaper.com/news/article.asp?idart=8392 (accessed 14 December 2001).

Claassen, Cheryl
   1994   *Women in Archaeology.* University of Pennsylvania Press, Philadelphia.

Clark, George A.
   1996   Letter to the Editor. *SAA Bulletin* 14(5):3.

Clifford, James
   1997   *Routes: Travel and Translation in the Late Twentieth Century.* Harvard University Press, Cambridge, MA.

Coe, Michael
   1993   From Huaquero to Connoisseur: The Early Market in Pre-Columbian Art. In *Collecting the Pre-Columbian Past,* edited by E. H. Boone, 271–90. Dumbarton Oaks Research Library and Collection, Washington, DC.

Colorado Historical Society
   2002   Program for Avocational Archaeological Certification (PAAC) Volunteer List. List available from Kevin Black, PAAC Coordinator, Office of the State Archaeologist, Colorado Historical Society, Denver.

Confederated Tribes of the Umatilla Indian Reservation
    2001   Ancient One Determined to Be Culturally Affiliated with Five Tribes. Press release. September 25, at www.umatilla.nsn.us/kennman6.html (accessed December 2002).

Conway, Jill Kerr
    2001   *A Woman's Education.* Knopf, New York.

Cornwell, G. H., and E. W. Stoddard (editors)
    2001   *Global Multiculturalism: Comparative Perspectives on Ethnicity, Race, and Nation.* Rowman & Littlefield, Lanham, MD.

Craig, E. (editor)
    1998   *Encyclopedia of Philosophy.* Routledge, New York.

Cullen, Tracy
    1998   Archaeology in 1996: AIA Survey Update. *AIA Newsletter* 13(2):3.

Culture, Media and Sport Committee
    2000   *Cultural Property: Return and Illicit Trade.* 3 vols. House of Commons, London.

Davidson, Ian
    1991   Notes for a Code of Ethics for Australian Archaeologists Working with Aboriginal and Torres Strait Islander Heritage. *Australian Archaeology* 32:61–64.

DeBoer, Warren R.
    1999   Metaphors We Dig By. *Anthropology News* 40(7):7–8.

De Cunzo, Lu Ann, and John. H. Jameson Jr.
    2000   "Unlocking the Past." SHA Public Outreach Project. Paper presented at the 33rd Conference on Historical and Underwater Archaeology, Quebec.

Deloria, Vine, Jr.
    1969   *Custer Died for Your Sins: An American Indian Manifesto.* Macmillan, New York.

Dongoske, K. E., M. Aldenderfer, and K. Doehner (editors)
    2000   *Working Together: Native Americans and Archaeologists.* Society for American Archaeology, Washington, DC.

Donnan, Christopher B.
    1991   Archaeology and Looting: Preserving the Record. *Science* 251:498.

Dorfman, John
    1998   Getting Their Hands Dirty? Archaeologists and the Looting Trade. *Lingua Franca* 1 and 2 (May), at www.linguafranca.com/9805/dorfman.html (accessed 5 February 2002).

Doumas, Christos G.
    2000   *Early Cycladic Culture: The N. P. Goulandris Collection.* N. P. Goulandris Foundation, Museum of Cycladic Art, Athens.

Dupree, Nancy H.
 1996 Museum under Siege. *Archaeology* 49(2):42–51.

Dyson, Stephen L.
 1998 *Ancient Marbles to American Shores: Classical Archaeology in the United States.* University of Pennsylvania Press, Philadelphia.

Dziech, Billie Wright, and Linda Weiner
 1984 *The Lecherous Professor.* Beacon, Boston.

Early, Ann
 1999 Profiteers and Public Archaeology: Antiquities Trafficking in Arkansas. In *The Ethics of Collecting Cultural Property: Whose Culture? Whose Property?* 2nd ed. Edited by Phyllis Mauch Messenger, 39–50. University of New Mexico Press, Albuquerque.

Echo-Hawk, R. C.
 2000 Exploring Ancient Worlds. In *Working Together: Native Americans and Archaeologists,* edited by K. E. Dongoske, M. Aldenderfer, and K. Doehner, 3–7. Society for American Archaeology, Washington, DC.

Edgar, Blake
 2000 Whose Past Is It, Anyway? Review of *Skull Wars* (2000) by David Hurst Thomas, *Scientific American* (July):106–7.

Edwards, P. (editor)
 1967 *Encyclopedia of Philosophy.* Macmillan, New York.

Elia, Ricardo J.
 1992 The Ethics of Collaboration: Archaeologists and the Whydah Project. *Historical Archaeology* 24(4):105–17.
 1993 ICOMOS Adopts Archaeological Heritage Charter: Text and Commentary. *Journal of Field Archaeology* 20:97–103.
 1997 Looting, Collecting and the Destruction of Archaeological Resources. *Nonrenewable Resources* 6(2):85–98.
 2001 Analysis of the Looting, Selling, and Collecting of Apulian Red-Figure Vases: A Quantitative Approach. In *Trade in Illicit Antiquities: The Destruction of the World's Archaeological Heritage,* edited by Neil Brodie, Jennifer Doole, and Colin Renfrew, 145–54. McDonald Institute Monographs. McDonald Institute, Cambridge.

Elkins, Aaron J.
 1999 *Loot.* Avon, New York.

Errington, E., and J. Cribb (editors)
 1992 *The Crossroads of Asia: Transformation in Image and Symbol in the Art of Ancient Afghanistan and Pakistan.* Ancient India and Iran Trust, Cambridge.

Euben, Donna R.
 2001 Show Me the Money: Salary Equity in the Academy. *Academe* 87(4):30–36.
 2002 U.S. Laws on Gender-Based Wage Discrimination. In *Paychecks: A Guide to Conducting Salary-Equity Studies for Higher Education Faculty,* edited by

Lois Haignere, 81–82. American Association of University Professors, Washington, DC.

Eyo, Ekpo
1994   Repatriation of Cultural Heritage: The African Experience. In *Museums and the Making of "Ourselves": The Role of Objects in National Identity,* edited by F. Kaplan, 330–50. Leicester University Press, London.

Fagan, Brian
1975   *The Rape of the Nile.* Scribner's, New York.

Farnsworth, Kenneth B., and Stuart Struever
1977   Ideas on Archaeological Curation and Its Role in Regional Centers. In *Regional Centers in Archaeology: Prospects and Problems,* edited by William H. Marquardt, 13–15. Missouri Archaeological Society, Research Series no. 14, Columbia.

Ferguson, T. J.
1984   Archaeological Ethics and Values in a Tribal Cultural Resource Management Program at the Pueblo of Zuni. In *Ethics and Values in Archaeology,* edited by Ernestine L. Green, 224–35. The Free Press, London.
1996   Native Americans and the Practice of Archaeology. *Annual Review of Anthropology* 25:63–79.

Figgins, J. D.
1934   Folsom and Yuma Artifacts. *Proceedings of the Colorado Museum of Natural History* 13(2).
1935   Folsom and Yuma Artifacts, Part II. *Proceedings of the Colorado Museum of Natural History* 14(2).

Fitton, J. Lesley.
1995   *The Discovery of the Greek Bronze Age.* British Museum Press, London.

Fletcher, Joseph
1966   *Situation Ethics, the New Morality.* Westminster, Philadelphia.

Ford, Richard I.
1980   A Three-Part System for Storage of Archaeological Collections. *Curator* (23)1:55–62.
1984   Ethics and the Museum Archaeologist. In *Ethics and Values in Archaeology,* edited by Ernestine L. Green, 135–42. The Free Press, London.

Fowler, Don
1987   Uses of the Past: Archaeology in the Service of the State. *American Antiquity* 52(2):229–48.

Gero, Joan M.
1994   Excavation Bias and the Woman-at-Home Ideology. In *Equity Issues for Women in Archeology,* edited by Margaret Nelson, Sarah Nelson, and Alison Wylie, 37–42. Archeological Papers of the American Anthropological Association no. 5, Washington, DC.

1996   Archaeological Practice and Gendered Encounters with Field Data. In *Gender and Archaeology*, edited by Rita Wright, 251–80. University of Pennsylvania Press, Philadelphia.

Gilgan, Elizabeth
2001   Looting and the Market for Maya Objects: A Belizean Perspective. In *Trade in Illicit Antiquities: The Destruction of the World's Archaeological Heritage*, edited by Neil Brodie, Jennifer Doole, and Colin Renfrew, 73–87. McDonald Institute Monographs. McDonald Institute, Cambridge.

Gill, David W. J., and Christopher Chippindale
1993   Material and Intellectual Consequences of Esteem for Cycladic Figures. *American Journal of Archaeology* 97:601–59.
In press The Trade in Looted Antiquities and the Return of Cultural Property: A British Parliamentary Inquiry. *International Journal of Cultural Property* 11.

Goldstein, Lynne
1992   The Potential for Future Relationships between Archaeologists and Native Americans. In *Quandaries and Quests: Visions of Archaeology's Future*, edited by LuAnn Wandsnider, 59–71. Center for Archaeological Investigations, Occasional Paper no. 20. Southern Illinois University, Carbondale.

Golson, J.
1996   What Went Wrong with WAC3 and an Attempt to Understand Why. *Australian Archaeology* 41:48–54.

Green, William F., and John F. Doershuk
1998   Cultural Resource Management and American Archaeology. *Journal of Archaeological Research* 6(2):121–67.

Greenfield, Jeanette
1989   *The Return of Cultural Treasures*. Cambridge University Press, Cambridge.

Grün, Rainer, N. A. Spooner, A. Thorne, G. Mortimer, J. J. Simpson, M. T. McCulloch, L. Taylor, and D. Curnoe
2000   Age of the Lake Mungo III Skeleton, Reply to Bowler and Magee and to Gillespie and Roberts. *Journal of Human Evolution* 38:733–741.

Hackenberger, S.
2000   Cultural Affiliation Study of the Kennewick Human Remains: Review of Bio-Archaeological Information. Report by National Park Service, at www.cr.nps.gov/aad/Kennewick/hackenberger.htm (accessed April 2002).

Hadjisavvas, Sophocles
2001   The Destruction of the Archaeological Heritage of Cyprus. In *Trade in Illicit Antiquities: The Destruction of the World's Archaeological Heritage*, edited by Neil Brodie, Jennifer Doole, and Colin Renfrew, 133–39. McDonald Institute Monographs. McDonald Institute, Cambridge.

Haignere, Lois (editor)
2002   *Paychecks: A Guide to Conducting Salary-Equity Studies for Higher Education Faculty*. American Association of University Professors, Washington, DC.

Halsey, J. R.
  1991   "State Secrets": The Protection and Management of Archaeological Site Information in Michigan. In *Ethics and Professional Anthropology,* edited by C. Fluehr-Lobban, 117–29. University of Pennsylvania Press, Philadelphia.

Hamilton, Christopher E.
  1990   Shipwreck and Cultural Resource Management: Archaeology in Different Compliance Situations. In *Predicaments, Pragmatics, and Professionalism: Conduct of Archeological Inquiry,* edited by J. Ned Woodall, 73–82. Society of Professional Archeologists, Special Publication no. 1, Oklahoma City.

Hardesty, Donald L., and Barbara J. Little
  2000   *Assessing Site Significance.* AltaMira, Walnut Creek, CA.

Harrington, Spencer P. M.
  1991   The Looting of Arkansas. *Archaeology* 44(3):22–31.
  1996   The Looting of Arkansas: How One State Copes with the Erosion of Its Heritage. In *Archaeological Ethics,* edited by Karen D. Vitelli, 90–105. AltaMira, Walnut Creek, CA.

Hassan, F.
  1995   The World Archaeological Congress in India: Politicizing the Past. *Antiquity* 69(266):874–77.

Heath, Dwight B.
  1974   Economic Aspects of Commercial Archeology in Costa Rica. *American Antiquity* 38(3):259–65.

Herrmann, Frank
  1980   *Sotheby's: Portrait of an Auction House.* Chatto and Windus, London.

Hester, James
  1977   Specialized and Generalized Models of Regional Centers. In *Regional Centers in Archaeology: Prospects and Problems,* edited by William H. Marquardt, 4–10. Missouri Archaeological Society, Research Series no. 14, Columbia.

Hillerman, Tony
  1989   *Talking God.* Harper and Row, New York.

Hingston, Ann Guthrie
  1989   US Implementation of the UNESCO Cultural Property Convention. In *The Ethics of Collecting Cultural Property: Whose Culture? Whose Property?* Edited by Phyllis Mauch Messenger, 129–47. University of New Mexico Press, Albuquerque.

Hippocrates
  1993   Oath and Law of Hippocrates. Internet Wiretap Edition, at ftp.std.com/obi/Hippocrates/Hippocratic.Oath (accessed March 2002).

272   Bibliography

Howland, Richard Hubbard (editor)
   2000   *The Destiny of the Parthenon Marbles: Proceedings from a Seminar
            Sponsored by the Society for the Preservation of the Greek Heritage and
            Held at the Corcoran Gallery of Art Washington, DC, February 13, 1999.*
            Society for the Preservation of the Greek Heritage, Washington, DC.

Hutira, Johna, and Margerie Green
   2000   Women in CRM: A Pilot Study. *COSWA Corner:*8.

Hutson, Scott R.
   2002   Gendered Citation Practices in *American Antiquity* and Other Archaeology
           Journals. *American Antiquity* 67(2):331–42.

Hutt, Sherry, Elwood W. Jones, and Martin E. McAllister
   1992   *Archeological Resource Protection.* Preservation Press, Washington, DC.

Jameson, John H., Jr.
   1994   The Importance of Public Outreach Programs in Archaeology. *SAA Bulletin*
           12:4.
   2000   Public Interpretation, Education and Outreach: The Growing Predominance
           in American Archaeology. In *Cultural Resource Management in
           Contemporary Society,* edited by Francis P. MacManamon and Alf Hatton,
           288–99. One World Archaeology no. 33. Routledge, London.
   2001   Art and Imagery as Public Interpretation and Education Tools in
           Archaeology. Paper presented at the 66th Annual Meeting of the Society for
           American Archaeology, New Orleans, LA.
   In press Public Archaeology in America. In *Public Archaeology,* edited by Nick
           Merriman and Tim Schadla-Hall. Routledge, London.

Jameson, John H., Jr. (editor)
   1997   *Presenting Archaeology to the Public: Digging for Truths.* AltaMira, Walnut
           Creek, CA.
   1999   Archaeology and the National Park Idea: Challenges for Management and
           Interpretation. *The George Wright Forum* 16(4):8–15.

Jameson, John H., Jr., and John E. Ehrenhard
   1997   Foreword. In *Presenting Archaeology to the Public: Digging for Truths,*
           edited by John H. Jameson Jr., 9. AltaMira, Walnut Creek, CA.

Jameson, John H., Jr., John E. Ehrenhard, and Christine A. Finn (editors)
   In press *Ancient Muses: Archaeology and the Arts.* University of Alabama Press,
           Tuscaloosa.

Jamieson, D.
   1991   Method and Moral Theory. In *A Companion to Ethics,* edited by Peter
           Singer, 476–87. Blackwell, Oxford.

Janke, Terri
   1999   *Our Culture, Our Future: Proposals for the Recognition of Indigenous
           Cultural and Intellectual Property.* Monograph prepared for Australian
           Institute of Aboriginal Studies and the Aboriginal and Torres Strait Islander
           Commission, Canberra.

Jelderks, John
    2002   Opinion and Order, Civil no. 96-1481-JE, in the U.S. District Court for the District of Oregon, at www.Tri-CityHerald.com/kennewick (accessed March 2002).

Jelks, Edward B.
    1976   A Report on the Establishment of a Code of Ethics and a Statement of Standards for Professional Archeologists and on the Founding of the Society of Professional Archeologists. Report submitted to the Executive Committees of the Society for American Archaeology, the Society for Historic Archeology, the Archaeological Institute of America, and the American Society for Conservation Archeology by the (SAA) Interim Committee on Professional Standards. Mimeographed.

Jenkins, Ian
    1992   *Archaeologists and Aesthetes in the Sculpture Galleries of the British Museum, 1800–1939.* British Museum Press, London.

Jones, C.
    2002   Bones of Contention. *The Bulletin* (Australia) (April)9:37–39.

Karoma, N. J.
    1996   The Deterioration and Destruction of Archaeological and Historical Sites in Tanzania. In *Plundering Africa's Past,* edited by Peter R. Schmidt and Roderick J. McIntosh, 191–200. Indiana University Press, Bloomington.

Kehoe, Alice Beck
    1998   *The Land of Prehistory.* Routledge, New York.

King, Mary Elizabeth
    1980   Curators: Ethics and Obligations. *Curator* 23(1):10–18.

King, Thomas F.
    1985   The Whiddah and the Ethics of Cooperating with Pothunters: A View. *SOPA Newsletter* 9(3–4):1–3.
    1998   *Cultural Resource Laws and Practice.* AltaMira, Walnut Creek, CA.

King, Thomas F., Patricia Parker Hickman, and Gary Berg
    1977   *Anthropology in Historic Preservation.* Academic Press, New York.

Kintigh, Keith W.
    1996   SAA Principles of Archaeological Ethics. *SAA Bulletin* 14(3): 5, 17.

Kleiner, Fred S.
    1990   On the Publication of Recent Acquisitions of Antiquities. *American Journal of Archaeology* 94:525–27.

Knecht, Rick
    1994   Archaeology and Alutiiq Cultural Identity on Kodiak Island. *SAA Bulletin* 12(5):8–10.

LaBelle, Jason M.
    In press   The Slim Arrow Site: The Long-Forgotten Yuma Type-Site in Eastern Colorado. *Current Research in the Pleistocene.*

LaBelle, Jason M., V. T. Holliday, and D. J. Meltzer
   In press Early Holocene Paleoindian Deposits at Nall Playa, Oklahoma Panhandle,
             U.S.A. *Geoarchaeology.*

Langford, Ros
   1983   Our Heritage—Your Playground. *Australian Archaeology* 16:1–6.

Lapham, Increase A.
   1855   *The Antiquities of Wisconsin.* Smithsonian Contributions to Knowledge, 7.

Lee, Ronald R.
   2000   The Antiquities Act of 1906. *Journal of the Southwest* 42:2:198–269.

Leed, E. J.
   1991   *The Mind of the Traveler: From Gilgamesh to Global Tourism.* Basic, New
             York.

Lees, William B.
   1985   Should the Sheep Lie Down with the Wolves? A Reply to King. *SOPA News*
             9(6):2–4.

Levine, Mary Ann
   1994   Presenting the Past: A Review of Research on Women in Archeology. In
             Equity Issues for Women in Archeology, edited by Margaret Nelson, Sarah
             Nelson, and Alison Wylie, 23–37. Archeological Papers of the American
             Anthropological Association no. 5, Washington, DC.

Lewis, D., and D. Rose
   1985   Some Ethical Issues in Archaeology: A Methodology of Consultation in
             Northern Australia. *Australian Aboriginal Studies* 1:37–44.

Lipe, William D.
   1974   A Conservation Model for American Archaeology. *The Kiva* 39:213–45.
   1996   In Defense of Digging: Archaeological Preservation as a Means, Not an
             End. *CRM Magazine* 19(7):23–27.

Little, Curtis J.
   1904   Chickasawba Mound, Mississippi Valley. *Records of the Past* 3(4):118–22.

Lynott, Mark J.
   1997   Ethical Principles and Archaeological Practice: Development of an Ethics
             Policy. *American Antiquity* 62(4):589–99.

Lynott, Mark J., and Alison Wylie
   1995a   Overview: The Work of the SAA Ethics in Archaeology Committee. In
             Ethics in American Archaeology: Challenges for the 1990s, edited by Mark
             J. Lynott and Alison Wylie, 28–32. Special Report, Society for American
             Archaeology, Washington, DC.

Lynott, Mark J., and Alison Wylie (editors)
   1995b   *Ethics in American Archaeology: Challenges for the 1990s.* Special Report,
             Society for American Archaeology, Washington, DC.

2000   *Ethics in American Archaeology.* 2nd ed. Society for American Archaeology, Washington, DC.

Mapunda, B.
2001   Destruction of Archaeological Heritage in Tanzania: The Cost of Ignorance. In *Trade in Illicit Antiquities: The Destruction of the World's Archaeological Heritage,* edited by Neil Brodie, Jennifer Doole, and Colin Renfrew, 47–56. McDonald Institute Monographs. McDonald Institute, Cambridge.

Marchand, Suzanne L.
1996   *Down from Olympus: Archaeology and Philhellenism in Germany, 1750–1970.* Princeton University Press, Princeton, NJ.

Marquardt, William H. (editor)
1977   *Regional Centers in Archaeology: Prospects and Problems.* Missouri Archaeological Society, Research Series no. 14, Columbia.

Marsden, Barry M.
1974   *The Early Barrow Diggers.* Noyes Press, Park Ridge, NJ.

Marthari, Marisa
2001   Altering Information from the Past: Illegal Excavations in Greece and the Case of the Early Bronze Age Cyclades. In *Trade in Illicit Antiquities: The Destruction of the World's Archaeological Heritage,* edited by Neil Brodie, Jennifer Doole, and Colin Renfrew, 161–72. McDonald Institute Monographs. McDonald Institute, Cambridge.

Mason, Ronald J.
1997   Letter to the Editor. *SAA Bulletin* 15(1):3.

Matsuda, David
1998   The Ethics of Archaeology, Subsistence Digging, and Artifact "Looting" in Latin America: Point, Muted Counterpoint. *International Journal of Cultural Property* 7(1):87–97.

McBryde, Isabel
1986   *Who Owns the Past?* Oxford University Press, Melbourne.

McGimsey, Charles R., III
1995   Standards, Ethics, and Archaeology: A Brief History. In *Ethics in American Archaeology: Challenges for the 1990s,* edited by Mark J. Lynott and Alison Wylie. Special Report, Society for American Archaeology, Washington, DC.
1996   The Archaeological Field School in the 1990s: Collaboration in Research and Training. *SAA Bulletin* 14(5):18–20.

McGirk, Tim
1996   A Year of Looting Dangerously. *Independent on Sunday* (London), *Sunday Review,* 20 March:4–8.

McGuire, Randall
    2000   Comment on a Critical Archaeology Revisited. *Current Anthropology*
           41(5):766–67.

McIntosh, Roderick J.
    1996   Just Say Shame: Excising the Rot of Cultural Genocide. In *Plundering
           Africa's Past,* edited by Peter R. Schmidt and Roderick J. McIntosh, 45–62.
           Indiana University Press, Bloomington.

McManamon, Francis P.
    2000   Memorandum: Results of Radiocarbon Dating the Kennewick Human
           Skeletal Remains. National Park Service, Washington, DC, January 13, at
           www.cr.nps.gov/aad/kennewick/c14memo.htm (accessed December 2002).

Meier, Barry
    1998   The Case of the Contested Coins: A Modern-Day Battle over Ancient Objects.
           New York Times, 24 September:C1.
    1999   Turkish Government, 1,700; A U.S. Investor, 1. *New York Times,* 5 March:C4.

Meltzer, D. J.
    1994   The Discovery of Deep Time: A History of Views on the Peopling of the
           Americas. In *Method and Theory for Investigating the Peopling of the
           Americas,* edited by R. Bonnichsen and D. G. Steele, 7–26. Center for the
           Study of the First Americans, Corvallis, OR.

Meltzer, D. J., L. C. Todd, and V. T. Holliday
    2002   The Folsom (Paleoindian) Type Site: Past Investigations, Current Studies.
           American Antiquity 67(1):5–36.

Messenger, Phyllis Mauch (editor)
    1999   *The Ethics of Collecting Cultural Property: Whose Culture? Whose Property?*
           2nd ed. University of New Mexico Press, Albuquerque.

Meyer, Karl M.
    1977   *The Plundered Past.* Atheneum, New York.

Miller, Robert
    1984   Healthcare on Field Projects. *Journal of Field Archaeology* 11(4):438–40.

Mills, Barbara J.
    1996   The Archaeological Field School in the 1990s: Collaboration in Research and
           Training. *SAA Bulletin* 14(5):18–20.

Moody-Adams, Michelle
    1997   *Fieldwork in Familiar Places.* Harvard University Press, Cambridge, MA.

Mulvaney, D. J.
    1991   Past Regained, Future Lost: The Kow Swamp Pleistocene Burials. *Antiquity*
           65(246):12–21.

Native American Graves Protection and Repatriation Act
    1990   at www.cast.uark.edu/other/nps/nagpra/nagpra.dat/lgm003.html (accessed
           April 2002).

National Park Service
  1996   Essential Competencies: For National Park Service Employees. National Park
         Service, Washington, DC, at www.nps.gov/training/npsonly/npsescom.htm
         (accessed March 2002).
  2001   Effective Interpretation of Archaeological Resources: The Archeology-
         Interpretation Shared Competency Course of Study. National Park Service,
         Washington, DC, at www.nps.gov/training/crsestudy/Final.doc (accessed
         March 2002).
  2002   Kennewick Man, at www.cr.nps.gov/aad/Kennewick/index.htm (accessed
         April 2002).

Nelson, Margaret, Sarah Nelson, and Alison Wylie
  1994   *Equity Issues for Women in Archeology.* Archeological Papers of the American
         Anthropological Association no. 5, Washington, DC.

Nicholas, George P., and Thomas D. Andrews (editors)
  1997   *At a Crossroads: Archaeology and First Peoples in Canada.* Archaeology
         Press, Department of Archaeology, Simon Fraser University, Burnaby, BC.

Novick, Andrea Lee
  1980   The Management of Archaeological Documentation. *Curator* 23(1):35.

O'Keefe, Patrick J.
  1997   *Trade in Antiquities: Reducing Destruction and Theft.* Archetype, UN
         Educational, Scientific, and Cultural Organization, London.

Ortiz, George
  1994   *In Pursuit of the Absolute: Art of the Ancient World from the George Ortiz
         Collection.* Benteli-Werd, Berne.
  1998   The Cross-Border Movement of Art: Can It and Should It Be Stemmed? *Art,
         Antiquity and Law* 3(1):53–60.
  2001   Chance Finds, at www.unidroit.com/ChanceFinds.htm (accessed 13 December
         2001).

Özgen, Engin
  2001   Some Remarks on the Destruction of Turkey's Archaeological Heritage.
         In *Trade in Illicit Antiquities: The Destruction of the World's
         Archaeological Heritage,* edited by Neil Brodie, Jennifer Doole, and Colin
         Renfrew, 119–20. McDonald Institute Monographs. McDonald Institute,
         Cambridge.

Paludi, Michele A. (editor)
  1990   *Ivory Power: Sexual Harassment on Campus.* SUNY Press, Albany.

Pardoe, Colin
  1991   Farewell to the Murray Black Australian Aboriginal Skeletal Collection.
         World Archaeology Bulletin 5:119–21.

Pendergast, David M.
  1991   And the Loot Goes On: Winning Some Battles, but Not the War. *Journal of
         Field Archaeology* 18:89–95.

Peregoy, Robert M.
    1992   The Legal Basis, Legislative History, and Implementation of Nebraska's
            Landmark Reburial Legislation. *Arizona State Law Journal* 24(1):329–90.

Piggott, Stuart
    1989   *Ancient Britons and the Antiquarian Imagination.* Thames and Hudson, New
            York.

Pluciennik, Mark (editor)
    2001   *The Responsibilities of Archaeologists: Archaeology and Ethics.* BAR
            International Series 981, Lampeter Workshop in Archaeology no. 4.
            Archaeopress, Oxford.

Poirier, David A., and Kenneth L. Feder (editors)
    2001   *Dangerous Places: Health, Safety, and Archaeology.* Bergin and Garvey,
            Westport, CT.

Putnam, Frederick W.
    1890   The Serpent Mound of Ohio. *Century Magazine* 39:698–703.

Pyburn, K. Anne, and Mary Ann Levine
    2000   COSWA Corner. *SAA Newsletter* 18(2):8, 10.

Pyburn, K. Anne, and Richard W. Wilk
    1995   Responsible Archaeology Is Applied Anthropology. In *Ethics in American
            Archaeology: Challenges for the 1990s,* edited by Mark J. Lynott and Alison
            Wylie, 71–76. Special Report, Society for American Archaeology,
            Washington, DC.

Rachels, J.
    1998   *The Elements of Moral Philosophy.* 2nd ed. McGraw-Hill, New York.

Rayne, A. M.
    1997   *Colorado Absolute Date Synthesis.* Technical Series no. 9, Archaeometric
            Lab, Department of Anthropology, Colorado State University, Ft. Collins.

Reeves, Nicholas
    2000   *Ancient Egypt: The Great Discoveries.* Thames and Hudson, New York.

Register of Professional Archaeologists
    1998   Code of Conduct and Standards of Research Performance, at
            www.rpanet.org/(accessed March 2002).
    2002   at www.rpanet.org/about.htm (accessed April 2002).

Renaud, E. B.
    1931   Prehistoric Flaked Points from Colorado and Neighboring Districts.
            Proceedings of the Colorado Museum of Natural History 10(2).
    1934   *The First Thousand Folsom-Yuma Artifacts.* Archaeological Series, First
            Paper, Department of Anthropology, University of Denver, Denver.
    1947   *Archaeology of the High Western Plains: Seventeen Years of Archaeological
            Research.* Miscellaneous Paper, Department of Anthropology, University of
            Denver, Denver.

Renfrew, Colin
    2000   *Loot, Legitimacy and Ownership: The Ethical Crisis in Archaeology.* Duckworth, London.

Reno, Ronald L., Stephen R. Bloyd, and Donald L. Hardesty
    2001   Chemical Soup: Archaeological Hazards at Western Ore Processing Sites. In *Dangerous Places: Health, Safety, and Archaeology,* edited by David A. Poirier and Kenneth L. Feder, 205–19. Bergin and Garvey, Westport, CT.

Resnik, D. B.
    1998   *The Ethics of Science: An Introduction.* Routledge, New York.

Riding In, James
    1992   Without Ethics and Morality: A Historical Overview of Imperial Archaeology and American Indians. *Arizona State Law Journal* 24(1):11–34.

Roberts, Michael E.
    1995   The Failed Promise of Public Archaeology. Paper presented at the 60th Annual Meeting of the Society for American Archaeology, Minneapolis, MN.

Rogers, Rhea J.
    1990   The Genesis of an Archeological Ethic. In *Predicaments, Pragmatics, and Professionalism: Ethical Conduct in Archeology,* edited by J. Ned Woodall, 9–18. Special Publication no. 1, Society of Professional Archeologists, Oklahoma City.

Romanowicz, Janet V., and Rita P. Wright
    1996   Gendered Perspectives in the Classroom. In *Gender and Archaeology,* edited by Rita P. Wright, 199–223. University of Pennsylvania Press, Philadelphia.

Sadker, Myra, and David Sadker
    1994   *Failing at Fairness: How American Schools Cheat Girls.* Scribner's, New York.

Samford, Patricia
    1994   Searching for West African Cultural Meanings in the Archaeological Record. *Newsletter of the African-American Archaeology Network 12,* edited by Thomas R. Wheaton, New South Associates, at www.newsouthassoc.com/winter1994.html (accessed December 2002).

Scally, R. J.
    1995   *The End of Hidden Ireland: Rebellion, Famine, and Emigration.* Oxford University Press, New York.

Schiffer, Michael B.
    1976   *Behavioral Archaeology.* Academic Press, New York.

Schmidt, Peter R., and Roderick J. McIntosh (editors)
    1996   *Plundering Africa's Past.* Indiana University Press, Bloomington.

Seebach, J. D.
    2000   *Drought or Development? Papers of Paleoindian Site Discovery and Distribution in Western North America.* Poster presented at the 65th Annual Meeting of the Society for American Archaeology, Philadelphia.

Shanks, Hershel
    1999   Biting the Hand That Feeds You: Taking Ingratitude to New Heights.
            Biblical Archaeology Review 25(6):6, 64, at www.bib-arch.org/barnd99/
            firstperson.html (accessed March 2002).

Sherlock, David
    1988   A Roman Combination Eating Implement. *Antiquaries Journal* 68:310–11.

Sherratt, Susan
    2000   *Catalogue of Cycladic Antiquities in the Ashmolean Museum: The Captive
            Spirit.* 2 vols. Oxford University Press, Oxford.

Silverberg, Robert
    1967   *Men against Time.* Macmillan, New York.

Silverman, Sydel
    1992   Introduction. In *Preserving the Anthropological Record,* edited by Sydel
            Silverman and Nancy J. Parezo, 1–10. Wenner-Gren Foundation for
            Anthropological Research, New York.

Singer, Peter (editor)
    1991   *A Companion to Ethics.* Blackwell, Oxford.

Smith, Claire, and Heather Burke
    In press Joining the Dots . . . Managing the Land and Seascapes of Indigenous
            Australia. In *Northern Ethnographic Landscapes: Perspectives from the Cir-
            cumpolar Nations,* edited by I. Krupnik and R. Mason. Smithsonian Institu-
            tion Press, Washington, DC.

Smith, George S., and John E. Ehrenhard
    1991   *Protecting the Past.* CRC Press, Boca Raton, FL.

Smith, Grant H.
    1943   The History of the Comstock Lode, 1850–1920. *University of Nevada
            Bulletin* 27(3). 1966 revision by Nevada Bureau of Mines and Geology,
            University of Nevada, Reno.

Smith, Linda Tuhiwai
    1999   *Decolonizing Methodologies: Research and Indigenous Peoples.* 2nd ed.
            Zed, London.

Society for American Archaeology
    1975   Minutes of the SAA meeting in Dallas, May 10. *American Antiquity*
            40(4):520–22.
    1992   Editorial Policy. *American Antiquity* 57:749–70.
    1995   By-Laws. In *Membership Directory,* 17–25. Society for American
            Archaeology, Washington, DC.

Society of Professional Archaeologists
    1991   Code of Ethics. In *Guide to the Society of Professional Archaeologists,* 7–8.
            Society of Professional Archaeologists, College Station, TX.
    1997   *Directory of Certified Professional Archeologists.* 22nd ed. Baton Rouge, LA.

Sonnert, G., and G. Holton
1995a *Gender Differences in Science Careers: The Project Access Study.* Rutgers University Press, New Brunswick, NJ.
1995b *Who Succeeds in Science? The Gender Dimension.* Rutgers University Press, New Brunswick, NJ.

South, Stanley
1997 Generalized versus Literal Interpretation. In *Presenting Archaeology to the Public: Digging for Truths,* edited by John H. Jameson Jr., 54–62. AltaMira, Walnut Creek, CA.

Spiegler, Howard N., and Lawrence M. Kaye
2001 American Litigation to Recover Cultural Property: Obstacles, Options, and a Proposal. In *Trade in Illicit Antiquities: The Destruction of the World's Archaeological Heritage,* edited by Neil Brodie, Jennifer Doole, and Colin Renfrew, 121–32. McDonald Institute Monographs. McDonald Institute, Cambridge.

Squier, E. G., and E. H. Davis
1848 *Ancient Monuments of the Mississippi Valley.* Smithsonian Contributions to Knowledge no. 1, Washington, DC.

Staley, David P.
1993 St. Lawrence Island's Subsistence Diggers: A New Perspective on Human Effects on Archaeological Sites. *Journal of Field Archaeology* 20:347–55.

Stead, I. M.
1998 *The Salisbury Treasure.* Tempus, Stroud.

Sullivan, Sharon
1999 Repatriation. *Conservation, The Getty Conservation Institute Newsletter* 14(3), at www.getty.edu/conservation/resources/newsletter/14_3/ (accessed 14 April 2002).

Swidler, Nina, Kurt E. Dongoske, Roger Anyon, and Alan. S. Downer (editors)
1997 *Native Americans and Archaeologists: Stepping Stones to Common Ground.* AltaMira, Walnut Creek, CA.

Thomas, Cyrus
1894 *Report on the Mound Explorations of the Bureau of Ethnology.* Twelfth Annual Report of the Bureau of American Ethnology for the Years 1890–91, Washington, DC.

Thomas, David Hurst
2000 *Skull Wars: Kennewick Man, Archaeology, and the Battle for Native American Identity.* Basic, New York.

Thompson, Raymond H.
2000 Edgar Lee Hewett and the Political Process. *Journal of the Southwest* 42(2):271–318.

Thorne, A. G.
1976 *Origins of the Australians.* Australian Institute of Aboriginal Studies, Canberra.

Tompkins, J. F. (editor)
    1983   *Wealth of the Ancient World: The Nelson Bunker Hunt and William Herbert Hunt Collections.* Kimbell Art Museum, Fort Worth, Texas.

Toner, Mike
    1999   Past in Peril: Lost Treasures of Peru. *Atlanta Journal-Constitution,* 7 November, at stacks.ajc.com/ (accessed March 2002).

Trigger, Bruce
    1980   Archaeology and the Image of the American Indian. *American Antiquity* 45(4):662–76.

Tubb, Kathryn W. (editor)
    1995   *Antiquities: Trade or Betrayed? Legal, Ethical and Conservation Issues.* Archetype, London.

Ubelaker, Douglas, and Lauryn Guttenplan Grant
    1989   Human Skeletal Remains: Preservation or Reburial? *Yearbook of Physical Anthropology* 32:249–87.

U.S. Forest Service
    2000   Welcome to Passport in Time! At www.passportintime.com/ (accessed 29 May 2002).

U.S. Government Printing Office
    1987   *Hearing before the Subcommittee on Public Lands, National Parks and Forests of the Committee on Energy and Natural Resources.* U.S. Senate, 100th Cong., 1st sess. on S. 858, September 19, 1987.

Valian, Virginia
    1998   *Why So Slow? The Advancement of Women.* MIT Press, Cambridge.

Vassilika, Eleni
    1998   *Greek and Roman Art.* Fitzwilliam Museum Handbook. Cambridge University Press, Cambridge.

Vitelli, Karen D.
    1984   International Traffic in Antiquities: Archaeological Ethics and the Archaeologist's Responsibility. In *Ethics and Values in Archaeology,* edited by Ernestene L. Green, 143–55. The Free Press, London.
    1996a   Paleolithic Obsidian from Franchthi Cave: A Case Study in Context. In *Archaeological Ethics,* edited by Karen D. Vitelli, 17–28. AltaMira, Walnut Creek, CA.
    2000   "Looting" and Theft of Cultural Property: Are We Making Progress? *Conservation, The Getty Conservation Institute Newsletter* 15(1):21–24.

Vitelli, Karen D. (editor)
    1996b   *Archaeological Ethics.* AltaMira, Walnut Creek, CA.

von Bothmer, Dietrich
    1987   *Greek Vase Painting.* Metropolitan Museum of Art, New York.

von Bothmer, Dietrich (editor)
1990   *Glories of the Past: Ancient Art from the Shelby White and Leon Levy Collection.* Metropolitan Museum of Art, New York.

von Nordenskiöld, Gustaf
1893   *The Cliff Dwellers of the Mesa Verde, Southwestern Colorado: Their Pottery and Implements.* Translated by D. L. Morgan and P. A. Norstedt. Soner, Stockholm.

Warnow-Blewett, Joan
1992   Discipline History Centers in the Sciences. In *Preserving the Anthropological Record,* edited by Sydel Silverman and Nancy J. Parezo, 17–30. Wenner-Gren Foundation for Anthropological Research, New York.

Watkins, Joe
2000   *Indigenous Archaeology: American Indian Values and Scientific Practice.* AltaMira, Walnut Creek, CA.

Watson, Peter
1997   *Sotheby's: The Inside Story.* Bloomsbury, London.

Westfall, T.
2002   *Mostly Sand and Gravel: Artifact Adventures on the High Plains.* Writer's Showcase, San Jose, CA.

Wilcox, U. Vincent
1980   Collections Management with the Computer. *Curator* 23(1):43–52.

Willey, Gordon R., and Jeremy A. Sabloff
1980   *A History of American Archaeology.* 2nd ed. W. H. Freeman, San Francisco.

Willoughby, Pam
1999   Hiring Practices in Archaeology. *SAA Bulletin* 17(5):11–12.

Winter, Joseph C.
1980   Indian Heritage Preservation and Archaeologists. *American Antiquity* 45(1):121–31.

Woodall, J. Ned (editor)
1990   *Predicaments, Pragmatics and Professionalism: Ethical Conduct in Archaeology.* Special Publication no. 1, Society of Professional Archaeologists, Oklahoma City.

Wylie, Alison
1995a   Archaeology and the Antiquities Market: The Use of "Looted" Data. In *Ethics in American Archaeology: Challenges for the 1990s,* edited by Mark J. Lynott and Alison Wylie, 17–21. Special Report, Society for American Archaeology, Washington, DC.
1995b   The Contexts of Activism on "Climate" Issues. In *Breaking Anonymity: The Chilly Climate for Women Faculty,* edited by the Chilly Collective, 29–60. Wilfrid Laurier University Press, Waterloo, ON.

1996   Ethical Dilemmas in Archaeological Practice: Looting, Repatriation, Stewardship, and the (Trans)formation of Disciplinary Identity. *Perspectives on Science* 4(2):154–94.

1999   Science, Conservation, and Stewardship: Evolving Codes of Conduct in Archaeology. *Science and Engineering Ethics* 5(3):319–36.

Yeager, C. G.
2000   *Arrowheads and Stone Artifacts: A Practical Guide for the Amateur Archaeologist.* 2nd ed. Pruett, Boulder, CO.

Zalk, Sue Rosenberg
1990   Man in the Academy: A Psychological Profile of Harassment. In *Ivory Power: Sexual Harassment on Campus,* edited by M. A. Paludi, 142–76. SUNY Press, Albany.

Zeder, Melinda A.
1997   *The American Archaeologist: A Profile.* AltaMira, Walnut Creek, CA.

Ziedler, James A.
1982   Pot Hunting and Vandalism: An Ecuadorian Example. In *Rescue Archeology,* edited by R. L. Wilson and G. Loyola, 49–58. Papers from the First New World Conference on Rescue Archeology. Preservation Press, Washington, DC.

Zimmerman, Larry J.
1989   Made Radical by My Own: An Archaeologist Learns to Understand Reburial. In *Conflict in the Archaeology of Living Traditions,* edited by R. Layton, 60–67. Unwin Hyman, London.

1995   We Do Not Need Your Past: Archaeological Chronology and "Indian Time" on the Plains. In *Beyond Subsistence: Plains Archaeology and the Post-Processual Critique,* edited by P. Duke and M. Wilson, 28–45. University of Alabama Press, Tuscaloosa.

1996   Sharing Control of the Past. In *Archaeological Ethics,* edited by Karen D. Vitelli, 214–20. AltaMira, Walnut Creek, CA.

2000   Usurping Native American Voice. In *The Future of the Past: Native Americans, Archaeologists, and Repatriation,* edited by T. Bray, 169–84. Garland, New York.

Zimmerman, Larry J., and Leonard R. Bruguier
1994   Indigenous Peoples and the World Archaeological Congress Code of Ethics. *Public Archaeology Review* 2(1):5–8.

Index

Onondaga wampum belts, 130
oral history, 154
Ortiz, George, 37, 41
outreach, viii, 10, 24, 95, 107, 108, 124, 153–61
   passim, 163, 166. *See also* participatory
   education; public education
ownership of the past, xiii, 18, 22–23, 47, 241; by
   collectors, 115; by everyone, 132, 137; by no
   one, 129; the shipwrecked past, 61, 64; by
   whom, 158, 159, 177, 187, 191
Oxford University Research Lab, 39

Paleo-Indian, 93, 117–19, 120, 121, 122, 123, 126n3
parole, 78
participatory education, 51–52, 53. *See also*
   public education
partnerships, 144, 154, 156, 160, 166
Passport in Time, 156
patents, 240
Peabody Museum, 18
Pearce, Susan, 78, 79
permits/permission, 19, 45, 57, 75; federal, 138;
   to publish, 242
Persian Empire, 31
Peru, 37, 172–73
Phases I–III, 86, 89, 91
philosophical ethics, 7
philosophical traditions, 7
plagiarism, 245, 257
Pliny the Elder, 31
plowzone sites, 92–93
Poeurn, Chuck, 51
pothunters, vii, viii, 50, 115, 134, 137. *See also*
   looters; tomb robbers; *tombaroli*
pre-Columbian: gold, 34, 37, 38; people, 180
preservation: ethic, xvi; process, 91; of resources,
   90; of sites, 18, 25, 50. *See also* conservation;
   historic preservation
professional v. amateur, 117, 118
professional behavior, 39, 119, 160, 251
professional standards, 109, 188, 191, 251, 252,
   253
professionalism, 20, 31
professionalization, 117, 178
Program for Avocational Archaeological
   Certification (PAAC), Colorado, 122
provenance, 39, 40, 75–76
provenience, 10, 51, 52, 75–76, 105
pseudoarchaeology, 164, 168
public archaeology, 154. *See also* outreach; public
   education

public domain, 240, 247
public education, 10, 24, 50–51, 115, 119, 153–62
   passim, 213; CRM and, 90, 94, 95; Irish
   history and, 147–49; media and, 163–76
   passim; surface hunters and, 115, 122–23,
   124. *See also* outreach; participatory
   education
public good, xv, 242, 243, 245
public health, ethnography of, 206
public money, 25, 243. *See also* funding
publication, 58, 239–49 passim; amateur findings
   of, 122; collections of, 75, 106; disciplinary
   findings of, 257; electronic (Web and CD-
   ROMS), 167–68; indigenous approval of,
   192; lack of, by salvors, 59; looted data of, 9,
   10, 39–40; as outreach, 155; policies of
   archaeological journals, 14n5, 24, 39, 76;
   standards for, 64; unprovenanced material of,
   39–40, 75–76. *See also* gray literature
publishing, vii, viii, xv; looting and, 53; practices,
   3, 5; principle of fair dealing in, 242; reports
   of research, 19, 20; site locations, 9, 67

reality TV, 165
reburial, 21, 135, 179, 187, 188. *See also*
   repatriation
recompression chamber, 67
record preservation, 24. *See also* field records,
   ownership of
reflective equilibrium, 13, 15n12
Register of Professional Archaeologists (RPA),
   21, 91, 188, 192, 202, 251–59 passim;
   creation of, 25; Directory, 255, 256; expulsion
   or suspension from, 203, 256, 258; Standards
   Board, 254, 255, 256. *See also* Society of
   Professional Archaeologists (SOPA)
Registered Archaeologist, 255–56, 257, 258, 259
relic collector. *See* collectors
religious and moral absolutism, 12
Reno. *See* Nevada, University of
repatriation, 23, 134, 135, 136, 179, 185, 234; of
   human remains, 130; as looting, 45; reburial
   and, 21; of Tyrant Slayers, 31. *See also* reburial
repositories, 75, 80; of building assessment,
   103–4; for collections, 74, 102; guidelines for,
   109; of infrastructure assessment, 107–8; of
   system assessment, 104–7. *See also* museums
rescuing artifacts and sites, 214
research: design, 75, 215, 216, 218, 219, 221–23;
   goals, 9; money, ethics of accepting, 165;
   strategy, 89

About the Contributors

ALEX W. BARKER is curator of North American archaeology and chair of the Milwaukee Public Museum Anthropology Department. He previously served in various capacities at the Dallas Museum of Natural History, including curator of archaeology, chief curator, and interim director. Barker received his doctorate in 1999 from the University of Michigan and the Society for American Archaeology (SAA) Dissertation Award in 2000. He serves on the National Program Committee of the American Association of Museums, the SAA Curation Committee, and the Curation Standards Committee of the Wisconsin Archaeological Survey, as well as chairing the SAA Committee on Ethics.

GEORGE F. BASS, founder of the Institute of Nautical Archaeology based at Texas A&M University where he is an emeritus distinguished professor, has conducted shipwreck excavations and underwater surveys off the Turkish coast since 1960. He has been awarded the Archaeological Institute of America's (AIA) Gold Medal for Distinguished Archaeological Achievement, an Explorers Club Lowell Thomas Award, a National Geographic Society La Gorce Gold Medal and the Centennial Award, the J. C. Harrington Medal from the Society for Historical Archaeology (SHA), and honorary doctorates by Bogaziçi University in Istanbul and the University of Liverpool.

CHRISTOPHER A. BERGMAN, a member of the Register of Professional Archaeologists (RPA), is director of the Cultural Resources Group for BHE Environmental, Inc., an environmental consulting firm based in Cincinnati, Ohio. He received his doctorate in prehistoric archaeology at the Institute of Archaeology, University of London. Since his return to the United States in 1989, Dr. Bergman has been involved in the cultural resource management (CRM) profession. In both 1998 and 1999, his work on behalf of Williams Gas Pipelines-Transco, under the auspices of the

Federal Energy Regulatory Commission, was highlighted by the secretary of the interior in his annual report to the U.S. Congress.

NEIL BRODIE is coordinator of the Illicit Antiquities Research Centre at the McDonald Institute for Archaeological Research, University of Cambridge. He was previously a research fellow of the Fitch Laboratory at the British School at Athens and has worked on several archaeological projects in Greece and Cyprus.

HEATHER BURKE has over thirteen years of experience as a consultant archaeologist, working in New South Wales, Queensland, South Australia, and the Northern Territory. She has worked extensively on historical and indigenous archaeological projects and has a particular interest in the interpretation and presentation of heritage sites. She holds a doctorate in historical archaeology from the University of New England in New South Wales and published *Meaning and Ideology in Historical Archaeology* (1999). She teaches archaeology at Flinders University in South Australia.

CHRISTOPHER CHIPPINDALE is a reader in archaeology and a curator in the Cambridge University Museum of Archaeology and Anthropology. He worked in print production before he turned to archaeology by editing the journal *Antiquity* from 1987 to 1997. Working from the Australian National University in outback northern Australia brings him in touch with issues concerning indigenous communities of origin. Studying the commercial market in antiquities, and its consequences, reminds him of ethical issues in Western society.

HESTER A. DAVIS received a bachelor's in history from Rollins College, a master's in social and technical assistance from Haverford College, and an master's in anthropology from the University of North Carolina, Chapel Hill. She retired in 1999 after serving from 1959 to 1967 as preparator and assistant director of the University of Arkansas Museum and from 1967 to 1999 as state archaeologist with the Arkansas Archeological Survey. She has served as president and grievance coordinator of the Society of Professional Archeologists (SOPA), on the SAA and AIA Executive Boards, as chair of the SAA Committee on Public Archaeology, as president of American Society of Conservation Archaeology, and is currently (2002) the RPA interim grievance coordinator. She received doctorates from Rollins College and Lyon College. She is currently preparing a manuscript on the history of CRM.

JOHN F. DOERSHUK, a member of the RPA, has been a consulting archaeologist since 1995 with the Office of the State Archaeologist at the University of Iowa. He was previously (1990–1995) with a private-sector consulting firm, 3D/Environmental of Cincinnati, Ohio, where he was an archaeological principal investigator and for two years manager of the firm's Cultural Resources Program. Dr. Doershuk has conducted CRM archaeology in nineteen states for a diverse clientele including private firms, various federal agencies, and state, county, and local governments. His research interests include CRM archaeology, site structure and spatial analyses, Archaic period hunter-gatherers, and late prehistoric societies in the Midwest and the Great Plains.

BRIAN FAGAN is professor of anthropology at the University of California, Santa Barbara, and the author of many general books on archaeology.

DAVID GILL is senior lecturer in ancient history at the University of Wales, Swansea, and subdean of the Faculty of Arts and Social Studies. He has been involved with the Methana field survey in Greece and is currently preparing a manuscript on the British excavation of the Greek city of Euesperides in Cyrenaica for publication. A former Rome scholar at the British School at Rome, he was a curator in the Department of Antiquities in the Fitzwilliam Museum, University of Cambridge, before moving to Swansea. He is coauthor with Michael Vickers of *Artful Crafts: Greek Silverware and Pottery* (1994) and has published widely on the archaeology of the Greek world.

DONALD L. HARDESTY is professor of anthropology at the University of Nevada, Reno. He received his doctorate in anthropology from the University of Oregon and did undergraduate work at the University of Kentucky. His research interests include historical archaeology, mining history, the archaeology of overland emigration, and environmental studies. Hardesty has done archaeological fieldwork for nearly forty years in Mexico, Guatemala, the southeastern United States, and the U.S. West. He is a former president of the SHA, the Mining History Association, and the RPA.

JULIE HOLLOWELL-ZIMMER is a doctoral candidate in the Archaeology and Social Context Program of Indiana University's Department of Anthropology with a master's in alternative education. Her research interests combine indigenous art and archaeology with issues of cultural and intellectual property rights. Her dissertation is a multisited ethnography of the interests and claims involved in a legal market for archaeological goods from Alaska's Bering Strait. She has worked since 1998 with a National Science Foundation–funded excavation in the village of Wales, Alaska. She is a member of the SAA Committee on Ethics.

JOHN H. JAMESON, JR. is a senior archaeologist with the National Park Service's (NPS) Southeast Archaeological Center in Tallahassee, Florida. His twenty-plus years of federal service have included archaeological fieldwork and CRM in the United States and overseas. Jameson's work with the NPS has focused on public interpretation and education. He is originator and coordinator of the center's Public Interpretation Initiative, a public outreach program that has involved numerous government-sponsored symposia, training workshops, seminars, interpretive art projects, and publications. He also created and maintains the center's website, one of the most popular Internet sites dedicated to archaeology.

JASON M. LABELLE is a doctoral candidate in the Department of Anthropology at Southern Methodist University. His dissertation research on Paleo-Indian lithic technology and settlement systems utilizes over100 Paleo-Indian sites from across the western Great Plains, the majority of which were previously unreported sites collected by amateur archaeologists during the Dust Bowl. Fieldwork has led him across the Great Plains, working in Colorado, Nebraska, New Mexico, Oklahoma, Texas, and Wyoming. Additional research interests include modern and prehistoric adaptations to arid/semiarid environments, the history of archaeology, and developing public outreach programs in archaeology.

MARK LYNOTT is manager of the Midwest Archeological Center, NPS, Lincoln, Nebraska. He studied anthropology and archaeology at Western Michigan University (bachelor's) and Southern Methodist University (master's and doctorate). During the last thirty years, he has conducted research in the Great Lakes, Ohio River Valley, the Ozarks, and the southern Great Plains. As cochair of the Ethics in Archaeology Task Force, he helped develop the current ethics policy for the SAA. Dr. Lynott has been a member of SOPA and the RPA since 1976 and served as president of SOPA from 1989 to 1991.

EUGENE A. MARINO is an archaeologist with the Mandatory Center of Expertise for the Curation and Management of Archaeological Collections, U.S. Army Engineer District, St. Louis. His principal interests include federal archaeology and collections management. He has written numerous technical reports and several articles pertaining to archaeological curation issues within the federal government and has presented lectures on federal legislation and collections management issues to various groups and organizations across the country.

CHARLES E. ORSER JR. is distinguished professor of anthropology at Illinois State University and adjunct professor of archaeology at the National University of Ireland at Galway. He received his doctorate in 1980 and has spent his career using archaeology to investigate the lives of men and women usually left out of official history. His initial research focused on Native Americans impacted by the European fur trade. He then spent more than a decade studying African American slaves in the American South, and codirected the first excavations at Palmares, the large, seventeenth-century runaway slave kingdom in northeast Brazil. He began to work in Ireland in 1993, and has conducted excavations at three townlands in north County Roscommon. He is the author of *The Material Basis of the Postbellum Tenant Plantation* (1988), *A Historical Archaeology of the Modern World* (1996), *Historical Archaeology* (1995; with Brian Fagan), and *Race and the Archaeology Identity* (2001) and founding editor of the *International Journal of Historical Archaeology* and editor of the *Encyclopedia of Historical Archaeology*.

K. ANNE PYBURN serves on the ethics committee of the American Anthropological Association (AAA), directs the MATRIX Project, and cochairs the SAA Task Force for Curriculum Development. She attempts to practice what she preaches in Belize at the site of Chau Hiix, where she researches an ancient Maya town and convenes a field school on alternate years at the invitation of the government of Belize and the residents of Crooked Tree Village. She attempts to preach what she practices at Indiana University, where she is an associate professor. She writes about ethics, gender, and the ancient Maya.

MARK ROSE received his doctorate from the Program in Classical Archaeology at Indiana University in 1994, specializing in Aegean prehistory. He is executive editor of *Archaeology* magazine and editor of the magazine's website.

THERESA A. SINGLETON is associate professor of anthropology at Syracuse University. She has written numerous articles and edited two books on the archaeology of African Americans: *The Archaeology of Slavery and Plantation Life* (1985), and *I, Too, Am America: Archaeological Studies of African-American Life* (1999). She is currently undertaking an archaeological study of slavery in Cuba, in which she focusses on coffee plantations.

CLAIRE SMITH is a senior lecturer in archaeology at Flinders University, Adelaide, Australia. Smith's main field experience is in indigenous archaeology. She has conducted fieldwork in the Barunga-Wugularr region of southern Arnhem Land since 1990. She recently returned to Australia after spending twelve months in the United States on a prestigious Fulbright postdoctoral. Her publications include the coedited volume *Indigenous Cultures in an Interconnected World* (2000) and the authored book *Country, Kin and Culture: Survival of an Aboriginal Community* (in press). Smith is deputy academic secretary of the Fifth World Archaeological Congress, to be held in Washington, DC, in June 2003.

MICHAEL. K. TRIMBLE is director of Mandatory Center of Expertise for the Curation and Management of Archaeological Collections, U.S. Army Engineer District, St. Louis. He has authored and coauthored numerous papers pertaining to federal archaeology and collections management and is currently on the SAA and SHA Curation Committees. His principal interests are collections management, design of collection centers, and use of archaeological collections by the public. He has served as a member of the Save America's Treasures Committee for the White House for the past three years and has lectured across the United States to Native American, private, and federal agencies on a range of collections management topics.

KAREN D. VITELLI began following and reporting on the illicit market in antiquities for the *Journal of Field Archaeology* in 1976. She's been thinking about the impact of that market on archaeological practice and understanding ever since. The process led her to ponder and engage other aspects of archaeological ethics, which she pursues in her classrooms, as professor of anthropology at Indiana University, Bloomington; as vice president for Professional Responsibilities of the AIA (1992–1994); as member (1992 to present) and chair (1999–2002) of the SAA Committee on Ethics, and, since 1992, as director of the Franchthi Cave, Greece, Publication and Conservation Project. She also edited *Archaeological Ethics* (1996).

JOE WATKINS is one-half Choctaw Indian. His early childhood experiences with his Choctaw grandmother influenced his desire to learn more about American Indian precontact history. As an American Indian and an archaeologist, his research interests include the ethical practice of anthropology and the study of anthropology's relationships with aboriginal populations. He has served as chair of the AAA Committee on Ethics (2000–2002) and as a member of the SAA Ethics Committee (1998–2003). He is also the author of *Indigenous Archaeology: American Indian Values and Scientific Practice* (2000).

RITA P. WRIGHT is an archaeologist in the Department of Anthropology at New York University. Her current research is in Indus Valley, Pakistan, where she directs the Beas River Survey Project. She is the former chair of SAA Committee on the Status of Women.

ALISON WYLIE is professor of philosophy and teaches in the Program for Social Thought and Analysis at Washington University in St. Louis. She is a philosopher of social science who writes chiefly on questions raised by archaeological practice: questions about the status of evidence, ideals of objectivity, and the role of values in science. Her forthcoming book *Thinking from Things* (2002) presents a cross-section of this work; her essays on archaeological ethics appear in *Perspectives on Science* (1996), *Science Engineering Ethics* (1999), and in the coedited collection *Ethics in American Archaeology* (2000).

LARRY J. ZIMMERMAN is head of the Archaeology Department at the Minnesota Historical Society. He has been adjunct professor in the Department of Anthropology at the University of Iowa and was Distinguished Regents Professor of Anthropology at the University of South Dakota. He has published more than 300 articles, CRM reports, and reviews and is the author, editor, and coeditor of 15 books. He has served as editor of *Plains Anthropologist* and the *World Archaeological Bulletin* and as associate editor of *American Antiquity*. Working closely with American Indians, he researches interests in cultural property issues as well as the archaeology of the Great Plains and Midwest.